MY MAGIC CARPET RIDE

Garry Birtles

First published 2010
ISBN 978-0-9558807-4-2

All photographs courtesy of the Nottingham Evening Post
Book design by Tony Rose
Printed by MPG Biddles Limited, Kings Lynn, Norfolk PE30 4LS

Reid Publishing, 53 Church Gate, Loughborough, Leicestershire LE11 1UE
reidpublishing@fsmail.net   www.reidpublishing.co.uk

For my mum and dad Norma
and Ray, my sister Tina and my
four children, James, Natalie,
Nina and Elyshia

Introduction

by Garry Birtles

FORGING a successful career in any sphere, whether it be industry, politics or sport, requires a list of ingredients which all need to be combined correctly to help you rise to the top of your chosen profession. Good fortune, ability, encouragement, parental support, the correct environment and expert guidance all have to mix in the right amounts, at the right time for anyone to achieve any kind of success.

In the form of Brian Clough and Peter Taylor, in the expert guidance category I was extremely fortunate to have the best two in the business and while they played a key role in elevating me from a carpet fitter to the pinnacle of European club football, there were many more, less illustrious and high-profile figures, but equally important who helped bring together my 16-year professional career playing the game I loved.

Any young kid who spends time in his bedroom staring at posters of their football heroes, dreaming of becoming the subject of a poster himself one day, needs encouragement and I was hugely fortunate to have it in spades. From teachers at Alderman White School, such as Mr Hackett and Mr Whittaker, and coaches like Ernie Roberts and Gerald Mellors, who helped nurture my raw ability at Attenborough Colts.

Those fantastic blokes, who gave up so much of their own free time to run kids' football in and out of school hours, are on a par with John Raynor, my former Clifton All Whites chairman, who actually phoned Brian Clough direct to urge him to have a look at me before I took up the offer of signing for another club, lower down the league ladder. It was a ballsy move and one for which I will be eternally grateful.

Coaches and managers are all very well, but supportive parents and siblings are vital. My mother Norma and father Ray were a constant source of backing. My old man lost count of the number of miles he did in the car and his taxi service must have visited every ground in Nottinghamshire and I can only apologise to my sister Tina for the number of times I dragged him away on a Saturday when she had designs on spending time with her father. Sorry Sis. Having said that, my parents supported Tina fully in her love of horses, taking her to gymkhanas all over the county. So I suppose we were doubly fortunate.

When things come to someone so quickly, as they did to me in the first two full seasons I played at the City Ground, it would have been easy for the whole thing to leave me with a head bigger than old "Big Ead" himself. The fact that I was always able to get my cranium through the head of the door of my second home, The Cadland pub in Chilwell, is largely down to the inhabitants inside who provided a constant grounding to my life.

Dick, Lennie, Mick Sweet, Martin Northfield, Brett Carnelley, his brother Lol, Mad Ralph, and Benchy, Cas, Kev Collins, Mick Howard , Kelvey, Tracey Jarvis and Leon were part of a crew that I could always rely upon to take the piss out of me if ever I showed any vague designs on becoming a big time Charlie. They were my bodyguards when some idiot wanted to take a pot shot at fame in the bars and clubs of Nottingham and they were the first to ensure I got roaring drunk when my troubles at Old Trafford hung like a black cloud over my head.

The same goes for the crowd at Long Eaton Rovers: Dave Hailwood, Ian "Sammy" Sinclair and Vic Plumb. I still have to apologise to Geoff Elliott for getting the Gaffer to open his business in the Lace Market and instead of cutting the ribbon, the Gaffer cut his very expensive tie clean in half. We are still friends to this day and I will never forget the friendship and the help of good pals Nikki and Keith who were so supportive during the days of real hardship and signing on the dole. If I have missed out anyone, I can only apologise.

Through football I made some wonderful friends too. Gary Mills accompanied me on most of my journey with Forest and Willie Young was there when I needed somewhere to lay my head.

Nigel Clough has remained a true friend from our early days at the City Ground and Alan Buckley and Arthur Mann were a constant source of happiness in my final days playing for Grimsby Town.

I'd also like to thank Ian Edwards for putting my story down in print. I have known Ian for almost 20 years since his days as the Forest reporter for the Nottingham Evening Post. His reputation as a writer and journalist grew when he joined the Daily Mirror and he remains one of the leading experts on football in the national media.

No one is perfect and I have made mistakes along the way which will have upset and hurt people in my life. For that I would like to apologise profusely. Football certainly played a part in showing me a glamorous world which took me away from my first wife Sandra and left her with the difficult task of raising our three children, Natalie, James and Nina. Many of her friends advised her not to let me have access but she was having none of it and I was allowed to help bring them up every step of the way without restriction. We remain friends today and not a Christmas passes by when we don't meet up.

The fact that all three have grown up into such rounded and wonderful people is a testament to Sandra's outstanding qualities as a mother. When I married a second time, to Samantha, I thought the days of fatherhood were behind me until the birth of a third daughter Elyshia and all four of my children get along famously. Football gave me some fantastic times, some incredible memories, but I would swap it all for the kids in a heartbeat.

The question I am often asked is: Do you wish you were playing today with all the money in the game? My answer always is: 'A few more quid would be nice but I wouldn't change my time in the game for the money they pay now'.

I was being well paid back in the 1980s and I was being paid for my passion. You can only play when it's your time and I feel very privileged to have played with and against such fantastic groups of players, nearly all of them great blokes.

When your career is over, the things you miss the most are the camaraderie and the banter. The pre and mid-season tours and of course the end of season ones as well. Players now do not seem to have that bond and sometimes the vulgarity of wealth is nauseating to say the least.

There are certain ways to behave and there are many good pros around who do things the right way. Good luck to them, enjoy the financial trappings of success but more importantly enjoy your career. It is soon over. Remember why you played the game in the first place. Embrace it and never forget your roots and where you came from.

Foreword

by Nigel Clough

THEY say in life that you should never meet your heroes because it only turns out to be a disappointment; Garry Birtles definitely disproves the rule in my case.

I not only got to meet Garry, but also play alongside him and ultimately become his friend.

The thing with Gaz is that he won't appreciate me praising him in this foreword; he doesn't like sycophants and is more comfortable with banter at his expense rather than compliments.

In an industry where many egos do not match achievements, Gaz is the polar opposite.

He is a man who won the European Cup and played for Manchester United and England, but still refers to himself as a carpet fitter.

That attitude and honesty has defined his career and life; it is why he is so thoroughly respected by his peers and loved by his friends.

Gaz was one of my favourite players growing up. Along with John Robertson, he was someone I admired and enjoyed watching.

My abiding memory of him as a player is from the 1980 European Cup Final, where Nottingham Forest beat Hamburg 1-0 in Madrid's magnificent Bernabeu stadium.

Much of the pre-match hype was about Kevin Keegan and how we would be able to stop him playing; Forest were massive underdogs, especially as Trevor Francis missed the game with a torn Achilles tendon.

Gaz played as a lone striker that evening, with the team playing a 4-5-1 formation. Although common place today it certainly wasn't at the time, particularly with English clubs.

Gaz worked phenomenally hard and gave definition to the phrase 'defending from the front'. Although John Robertson took the headlines for scoring the winning goal, it was Garry's performance that left a lasting impression on me.

After playing at Manchester United, he returned to Forest in the mid 1980s and by this time I was a young pro looking to make my way in the game.

It was a great experience playing alongside him for Nottingham Forest, when he returned for his second spell at the club.

I learned a great deal from the way he conducted himself and way he understood and read the game.

His character off the pitch was the same as on it. He was a working man who expected to graft for his pay cheque and he always did. And not forgetting a fair amount of talent as well.

In the 'Baby Bentley' age where success and reward are not often fairly married, Garry's story should serve as an example to all young players looking to make it today.

He started at Long Eaton United but ended up winning the biggest prize in club football, as well as playing for Manchester United and representing his country.

In football, as with life, you collect a lot of acquaintances, but a far smaller number of people you can describe as true friends.

Gaz is and remains a close friend and I look forward to reading his story in this book.

Contents

1. **Driven to despair**   **1**
The highway to hell

2. **Hot Bovril**   **13**
Table manners in trial and terror

3. **In the court of King Clough**   **30**
The old Palais act

4. **That was the week that was**   **43**
Liverpool and Jap sub sunk

5. **Champions of Europe**   **61**
The road from Mansfield to Munich

6. **Theatre of bad dreams**   **82**
Golden Shot meets Blankety Blank

7. **Birtles scores!**   **101**
Iran hostages relieved

8. **The prodigal returns**   **119**
Back in the old routine

9. **Red letter day**   **139**
Black and white revival

10 **Reunited with the game I love**   **160**
...and the manager too

1

DRIVEN TO DESPAIR
The highway to hell

"Living easy, living free
Season ticket on a one-way ride
Asking nothing, leave me be
Taking everything in my stride
Don't need reason, don't need rhyme
Ain't nothing I would rather do
Going down, party time
My friends are gonna be there too
I'm on the highway to hell..........

I WAS never much of a George Benson type. So I grabbed the volume knob between thumb and index finger and kept turning until I felt resistance. ACDC at nose-bleed level in the confined space of the Jag normally helped. I could almost feel the door panel on my right nudging against my right calf as it vibrated to the voice-full-of-gravel lyrics of Bon Scott.

I was singing along, well shouting would be more accurate, adding to the high decibel levels that were mercifully drowning the irritating swish-swosh of windscreen wipers fighting in tandem to brush away the pissing down rain and clear a line of sight. They were on high-speed, such was the ferocity of the rain that March evening that remains with me as if it only happened yesterday.

Angus Young's fingers must have been bleeding from those guitar riffs, but the jagged noise of one of my favourite bands could not shake the mess in my head. Most people would struggle to think straight in competition with that. Usually, the overwhelming power of sound would force any attempt at rational thought, any kind of thought, to be abandoned. The process futile, but ACDC with the full power of their stacks of Marshall Amplifiers in the boot would not have stopped me.

MY MAGIC CARPET RIDE

I'd had some soulless and goalless drives to the sanctuary of Nottingham. I'd clocked so many miles back and forth to Manchester I could probably find my way blindfold from either Old Trafford or the United training ground at The Cliff, to my front door in Chilwell. I had been doing the journey seven months, almost every day.

I was as used to the drudgery of those B roads, through Ashbourne, Leek and Macclesfield as I was with my own face in the mirror and as for whatever weather the Peak District could throw in my direction, whether it was into or out of Manchester, nothing was a surprise. I had experienced four seasons in one drive on numerous occasions.

The boredom of the road could not soothe me, the violence of the music was incapable too. All I could hear was a familiar voice, crystal clear in my head. It was not mocking. It was devoid of sympathy and it was not angry, just the same as usual.

"Oh Gaz, that's crap. That's bloody crap."

It was oscillating around my skull like the number 42 ball spins before it gets sucked up and spewed out of Guinevere on a Saturday night.

For some reason, I could hear Cloughie's voice in my head. He was never afraid of letting you know what he felt. I had heard it hundreds of times. Everyone thought they could imitate his strange lilt and Mike Yarwood came close, but I knew the real thing when it reached my ears and he was inside my head, feeding my neurosis.

Had I shot it? Shot it was one of his favourite phrases. He trotted it out like most people say hello. It was his way of saying that you were finished. That you could not hack it anymore. He used it about himself throughout his career. But he never meant it of himself.

Normally, the mere imagination of Clough's voice and his finger-wagging rebukes would make me smile. It would evoke those warm memories of amazing days on the banks of the River Trent. I would have an image of Cloughie stalking the training ground in that yellow rugby top. It was yellow in the early days, normally accompanied with white shorts and a squash racquet. It was only in the later days he changed to green.

They were the same days I could never in my wildest, most outrageous dreams, have ever imagined when I was a local kid, growing up as fast as the team at the City Ground was decaying in the old Second Division, before the arrival of the Messiah down the A52 from Derby. Almost without fail Cloughie jumping into my psyche would lighten the mood. I have often laughed out loud just thinking of something he might say or do, but not tonight.

I had suffered some low points in a series of bottom-dredging incidents since my £1.25m move from Nottingham Forest to Old Trafford. None had descended to this nadir. When you go almost a whole calendar year, as a striker without a league goal, let's just say you are bound to have the odd moment of self-doubt, especially when it seems that the whole world is taking the piss out of you. Don't get me wrong, I can have a laugh at myself with the best of them, but this joke was not funny anymore.

There seemed to be no escape. No matter what I tried to focus on to lighten the mood, I kept getting dragged back under, enveloped by black waters of self doubt. I had never plumbed these depths. This was a new nadir. Snakes wotsits spring to mind. I had never felt so fed up and depressed about the whole game.

Why the hell did Billy Wright have to have such a fucking good game for Everton that night?

Why should I be bothered? We had won 1-0 and we were finishing the season strongly at United. Things seemed like they were clicking into place for the team I had joined the previous September. The following season could not come fast enough.

I should be delighted we'd won another game, especially as I had helped earn myself another win bonus and with £1,000 a point on offer for every one we managed over 45 there was money to be made. That always eases the pain. Nothing like cold hard cash to smooth a furrowed brow, right? Wrong. Wrong with a capital W. I could barely care less that we had won.

I had not scored, for the umpteenth game running that season. Seven months and counting and Manchester United's flagship signing that season had not managed a solitary fucking goal and Billy Wright had just made sure that my embarrassing sequence stretched out for one more match to give the critics even more ammunition.

Wright never put a foot wrong. He never made one false move. I have played against some irritating central defenders in my career and, on several occasions, there have been more than a few who have had the better of me. Until the next time anyway.

But that night at Goodison, Wright had made me look like a novice. Like I was still playing for Long Eaton United and that non-league was my real level.

MY MAGIC CARPET RIDE

When you dream of the ideal debut, you to try to quell your stomach that has suddenly become a 1200 spin-speed Bosch washing machine.

My dream was to see the net bursting on my first appearance in United red at Old Trafford. Effortless efficiency and goals to win the adulation of the Stretford End and the crowning of a new hero in the Theatre of Dreams. Walter Mitty could not have come up with a better debut than the one I imagined.

So why is it all turning pear-shaped? Why had Wright just made my life an even bigger misery? Every high ball, I jumped, his forehead smashed into the ball first and every now and then to add injury to insult I copped a stray elbow.

Every ball that was tossed in the general direction of both of us, like kids used to do with sweets to encourage a scrum, he got his size 9s there ahead of me. He was first and in a two-horse race, I was last and there is nothing for losers in this game.

I glanced across to the passenger seat, just in case he had got in my car first too, before flicking my gaze back to the road and the headlights, those hypnotising headlights, advancing at you in the rain, causing the droplets of water on your windscreen to refract and blur your vision slightly. Concentrate. Concentrate. Watch the road and Cloughie will leave you in peace.

"He's shot it. He's shot it. He's shot it."

That was the problem. I kept shooting and I couldn't score a goal for United if my bloody life depended on it. I would have sold my granny to get one. Cloughie used to say he would quite happily put it in with his backside or his dick - they all count. I would have taken tripping up, over my bootlaces and somehow knocking one in with my nose. I would take anything to get this primate the size of Godzilla off my back.

I just wanted to get home. Get back to Beeston and to the consoling taste of a pint and the group of long-standing mates, who would temporarily remove me from this miserable place. At least until Monday morning when I went back to the Cliff for training.

I knew there was a cut-through around here to avoid going through a village and the slowest part of the journey, where you always get caught up by great big juggernauts. So I decided to follow a line of cars, just on complete hunch. Anything that would get me home quicker, the better. Let's see if I can find it. I needed that pint.

"He's shot it. He's shot it. He's shot it."

DRIVEN TO DESPAIR

I had heard Cloughie and his old mate Peter Taylor bring the curtain down on one or two players' careers in that chillingly matter-of-fact manner. There was no great debate, just one would pass judgment. There would be a sage nod of the head from the other and, in unison, they would triumphantly trot out those condemnatory three words.

My head was full of Cloughie, my inability to hit a cow's arse with a banjo and what the newspapers were going to make of my latest inability to trouble the scorers. When you have been described as "statuesque" in national newspapers and your game and reputation had been constructed on sheer willingness to run marathons in 90 minutes, things are not good.

My head was swimming with all kinds of negatives. Had I made a mistake leaving Forest? Was Cloughie right to sell me because I had been a flash in the pan? Should I have stayed fitting carpets for a living? At least I would have been spared all this angst and gut-wrenching self analysis. There would not have been that pressure on me to get the gripper down straight.

The usual excuse when things go wrong for strikers at any level is that he has lost his confidence. It is an elusive thing confidence. A precious commodity that all players and all people desire. When you are full of it, nothing can go wrong. Goals do fly in off your arse when you just happen to pop up in the right place at the right time.

Some external force makes you go there. Your instincts take you into that part of the penalty area. It is almost as if you have seen the build-up to the play hours before, when no one else on the pitch has and you are just rubbing your hands, waiting for that moment of certainty when the ball drops to you.

That is a given talent. You can't teach that. Ian Rush had it. Gary Lineker had it. They were born with that sixth sense and were heading for the penalty area from the moment they could first string two steps together.

When you have that confidence you could scale Everest. Ask Madonna, or any other A-lister that takes your fancy, out for dinner with not even a millisecond's doubt that she will say yes and offer to foot the bill. Nothing is out of reach. Everything is possible.

When it's gone you imagine you would never score a sale selling the Big Issue and the custard pie you would get from Madge is big enough to get into the Guinness Book of Records. You never see anyone steal it. There is no thief in the night. One day you have it. The next day it is like it never existed.

Ask Diego Forlan. You remember him, the Uruguayan striker Fergie signed. He was saddled with the same levels of expectancy, even if the United fans cruelly reckoned he looked like Mrs Doubtfire. Mrs Cantfirestraight more like!

When he was going through all that, I shared his pain. The poor bugger was so bad at United, many years after I had set the low-mark for strikers, they even nicknamed him Diego Birtles! Fans never forget when you are having a crap time of it, in the same way they remember every single goal you score when the good times are rolling.

I don't care what any other player will tell you. Defenders, midfielders, wingers. Forget them. It's worse for strikers. Bryan Robson could mis-place a pass, Roy Keane might take the wrong option and Norman Whiteside could fail to go with a runner from midfield, but those errors are never highlighted.

The only poor sods that get stuck in the dock and charged with grave errors are strikers and goalkeepers. Forlan had it, before he went back to Seville and started scoring goals again when he rediscovered that Midas touch all centre forwards dream of. Massimo Taibi, the Italian goalkeeper signed by Sir Alex Ferguson, had it too for letting the ball through his legs on that fateful day that meant he would never make it at Old Trafford.

There is always evidence for the prosecution to level against people who occupy those crucial positions. Everytime I missed a sitter there was a crimesheet building against me. You haven't killed anyone, but you feel like a criminal.

That's why I always admired Andy Cole when he was at United. Everyone reckoned to start with that he needed five chances to score one goal. Every time I missed I wanted the ground to open up and swallow me. Each chance that Cole fritted away, just seemed to make him even more determined to get on the end of the next one. It seemed as if he had masochistic streak to put himself through the torture and intense scrutiny.

I had lost that edge at United. You have to have the confidence to go back. The desire and self-belief that it will turn. Now I was questioning whether I had lost that strength of character. It did not feel like it at the time, but maybe it had gone and sub-consciously I was scared to miss. Once you are scared to miss, you are in trouble.

What made it worse was I was trying too hard. I kept telling myself to relax and all the time I could feel my muscles tensing up. I was too uptight.

DRIVEN TO DESPAIR

You know when Ronnie O'Sullivan does not cue smoothly and snatches at his action, or when on the odd occasion Phil Taylor can't let the darts go in the right way. That was the space I was in.

And that affects your decision making process. I was trying too hard. I was desperately trying to make an impact and the harder I tried the worse it became. I started shooting when I should be passing and passing when I should be shooting. Every choice I seemed to make was wrong. It was horrendous.

My play outside the box, for which I had always been given a huge amount of credit, was still as sharp as ever. I was bringing other people into the game, just like I did at Forest and setting up goals for others to get the glory.

But I could not survive on that and I knew it. Everyone kept looking at my stats, it was approaching a year without a goal for United. That is £1.25m for absolutely nothing in terms of the goals I was brought in to deliver.

I was signed to score goals. I was bought in by Dave Sexton as the man to help with the transformation of a great club that was trying to put a stop to Liverpool's dominance of the domestic scene at that time.

From the moment I lifted that United scarf above my head, I could feel the eyes of thousands of expectant United fans burning into me. Passing over their complete faith that I was going to stop that red machine up the East Lancs road.

Anyone who has won two European Cups and arrives with that kind of transfer fee hanging around his neck has to be the answer. You know how supporters think. You know the logic they employ and it was hard to argue with them.

I came with some kind of guarantee of goals and I was not doing what it said on the CV. The rumblings had started fairly early on in my United career. There were people from day one who were not overly impressed with my arrival and the rumblings were getting louder and louder. How could I complain? I had no justification for that. I had to keep taking it and keep trying to answer them back in the only way I knew.

At the start the gripes and criticism had not affected me. I brushed them off like dandruff from the shoulders of a dark suit. It was a minor irritant that I would overcome and that was not an attitude born out of arrogance. Footballers at the very highest level, sportsmen and women at the pinnacle of what they do, get to that point because they have a certain conceit about themselves. They have to possess those traits, otherwise they fall by the wayside. But I was not an arrogant man then and I never had been, no matter what I had achieved in my short career up to that point.

My crime was simple and that was the reason I could not understand why things had turned out so differently. A footballer, or any sports person, who has tasted success of any kind just expects that more will follow with the same certainty that night follows day. That is the way their brain works. They never focus on negatives, just tell themselves "you have done it once and you can do it again."

I merely expected, with no great weight of reasoning, that because I had been such a whirlwind success at Forest that there would be a knock-on-effect and that the cycle would repeat itself, just in a different time and place.

When I was at Forest I had played with good players and fitted in. Pulled my weight and made my contribution. My logic was that I was now at Manchester United, a bigger club, with more resources and equally good players so it was obvious to me more of the same would follow. I should not be having these problems. I should not be riddled by self-doubt.

What made it worse was no one wanted to score more than me. Just like opening batsmen want a Test hundred every time they go out to bat. They are never happy with 30s and 40s. I had the same kind of mindset, only in a pair of football boots and a football kit. I wanted to score hat-tricks, football's equivalent of a hundred at Lord's, in the first Test match of a summer series. That was what drove me from the moment I first discovered I had a knack of scoring goals.

My black mood was getting darker by the minute and it was not helped by the fact that I am a perfectionist. Some players always walk away and forget about the game within moments of leaving the dressing room. Win, lose or draw, they are already looking forward to the next game. There is no self-analysis with them and there were no DVDs in those days to have to sit through and have your performance dissected by the coaching staff.

So once the deodorant had been applied, aftershave slapped on they were out the door and ready for a night out. Plotting their way around the usual haunts and deciding on the last port of call later that evening. Not me. Don't get me wrong, I was not teetotal and I never stayed in moping. I loved a night out as much as the next bloke and would have been at the head of the advance party, but I could not just shove everything to the back of my mind like clearing the chairs in the school hall to make way for a sixth-form disco. I always beat myself up. I was always looking for ways of doing things better. I was always my own biggest critic and I am a shocking loser.

Just ask my old squash partners at Chilwell Olympia. I used to play there every Thursday afternoon without fail, when I was at Forest. Incredible I know and you can't even go out for a stroll for a carton of milk 48 hours before a game these days without asking permission of the fitness trainer and the manager. Imagine Wayne Rooney popping off to have a few games with his mates two days before they play Arsenal in the Premier League. Fergie would do his nut.

The Gaffer loved squash though and it was never a problem in those days. Not playing that is, but it was a problem for my racquet if I lost. To add a little bit of interest there was always a side bet on the game. It was a fiver a game. So hardly the kind of pots Phil Ivey and his mates play for at the World Series of Poker. It was only to add a bit of interest. To spice things up.

I was a pretty good squash player. I thought about taking it up before football and I must have been half decent because the Gaffer had me play with him at Trent Bridge squash club on a regular basis. But I lost count of the number of racquets I smashed up in anger on the back wall just because I had lost a poxy game of squash to a mate!

But that was the way I had been bought up. The Gaffer always drilled it into us at Forest that if you are 3-0 up, go 4-0 up and 5-0 up. Never let up, never let the bastards off the hook. Never take the foot off the pedal. That is a weakness. Destroy them, grind them into the dirt and they will have an inferiority complex about you the next time you play them and you will have won before you get on the pitch. Your opponents know they are in for another battering before a ball has been kicked.

No stop signs, speed limit
Nobody's gonna slow me down
Like a wheel, gonna spin it
Nobody's gonna mess me round
Hey Satan, payed my dues
Playing in a rocking band
Hey Momma, look at me
I'm on my way to the promised land
I'm on the highway to hell........

I was not familiar with the road and everything gets blurred when there are no street lights and headlights mixing with the sheen of water on pitch black B roads and the bend just came up on me far too quickly for me to do anything about it. I bet Billy Wright would have reacted fast enough. He would have doubled the clutch, decelerated, knocked it down a gear and smoothed his way around the sharp right-hander, accelerating as he came out of it with a big smile on his face.

Not me. I was not concentrating on a road that I was not familiar with. I lost control of the Jag and just could not drag it back under control in time. Fighting the steering wheel, I careered across the other side of the road into the darkness and braced myself for the impact.

One of the last things I remember seeing was a metal five-bar gate and I was flying towards it, skidding across the sodden tarmac and could not get any traction on my tyres. The brakes seemed to take an age to get a grip. I was clinging on to the steering wheel for dear life when I finally regained control of the car and it stopped snaking and slammed to a halt facing the wrong way, half way through the vacant space the open gate had left.

I have had some adrenalin rushes. I have scored goals at Wembley. I have played in European Cup finals and wore the Three Lions, all of which make your heart pump as if it is going to burst out of your chest. Imagine that alien flying out of John Hurt and you will be somewhere close.

Scoring a goal - even though my last one was some time ago - gives you that rush. Don't worry, you never forget the feeling, even if you lose the knack of mastering the most crucial art of the game. There is nothing better and there is nothing more terrifying than thinking you are going to meet your maker on an unfamiliar road, years before your time, because of a game of football.

If a lorry had come round that bend at the same time as I went sliding, my inability to score goals and trying to find a solution to my problem would have been the last of my concerns. Literally.

Lorry drivers used that route, to avoid the torturous M62. Anyone who has ever travelled across country from Nottingham to Manchester will appreciate that and I could so easily have been pizza in the middle of Ashbourne. Even now, just recounting the incident makes me shudder. Shudder at the mess a ruddy big lorry would have made of me and the only worries would have been for my family in sorting out the funeral arrangements.

My heart was racing faster than if I had just sprinted the length of Wembley, Linford Christie speed. Head more of a whirl now than ever, but everything else outside of my brain seemed to be in slow-motion. Slowly I checked myself over and apart from a few bumps and bruises everything seemed OK.

I had been given the James Bond, vodka-martini treatment. I was shaking with the sheer relief at still being alive, but normal speed had not been resumed. It took me a while to come to my senses. I could feel the blood rushing through my veins and hear the pounding heartbeat in my chest, it was louder than Bon Scott and Angus Young could ever have imagined and all I could think was: "Is this all fucking worth it."

All this worry was making me ill and it had nearly claimed my life. There has to be more to it than this. I know there is, because I have been there. I had been incredibly lucky to swig the champagne of success alongside the Gaffer and the rest of the team mates I had left behind at Forest. I had been with all of them gulping the adulation of the supporters who could not believe their lucky stars that their local team had conquered Europe twice.

That was when the European Cup was for champions, not for teams that end up fourth in their domestic leagues and fight their way through qualifying rounds to make it into the real thing. I am not bitter, far from it, but it is a fact. Only champions got in that competition. It was for the *creme de la creme*.

Fortunately there was no kerb to smash into, there was no gate barring my uncontrolled progress across the carriageway and there were no lorries laden with cargo coming in the opposite direction. I had missed everything, a bit like my goalscoring chances at United and for once I was elated that I had not hit the target.

I took five minutes to get the heart rate back down to something approaching normality and for my breathing not to sound as irregular and alarming as that of a 40-a-day smoker who had just ran up four flights of stairs. What an escape. What a slice of luck. Someone was looking down upon me that night. Someone who wanted me to get the message that football, irrespective of Bill Shankly's claim, was not more than a matter of life and death.

We can all claim to get moments of perspective from all kinds of occurrences in our lives. We all get shocked into action or brushed with uncontrollable relief at times least expected. I had just dodged a bullet, well a great big four tonner to be more accurate, and I should be grateful. I was fortunate that all I had to do was compose myself, turn the car around to face in the correct direction and start the engine again.

The remainder of the journey was probably the slowest I have ever driven back to Nottingham. I don't think I managed to get above 50mph at any stage of what was left of the distance between myself and that pint I had set off in such a hurry to console myself with.

Eventually I arrived back in familiar surroundings and made my way to the Cadland, a favourite watering hole that I used on many nights when things were far rosier in my Forest days. At last I felt safe and cocooned in an environment of friends who would comfort me now, in the same way they stopped me demonstrating effects of the Big Time Charlie syndrome when I was a player there a year earlier and polishing my second European Cup winners' medal.

On the remainder of the journey, after the close shave near Ashbourne, I had resolved not to let the United thing affect my head any more. It centred me and helped me become less intense, and the goals came for United the following season. Little did I know, though, as I contemplated my future and what lay ahead, that it would not be too long before my commuting days to Manchester would soon be over and that I would be back where my Jim'll Fix It, Roy of the Rovers true life story had begun four years earlier.

2

HOT BOVRIL
Table manners in trial and terror

'GET off my fucking table!' There was a growl and a scowl, delivered with all the welcoming friendliness of an un-trained pit bull terrier. The familiar face, thrusting through the door of the away team dressing room, caught everyone, mostly me, by complete surprise. My heart hit my boots, bounced back and nearly escaped through my cranium. Something else came uncomfortably close to hitting the inside of the virgin, white Nottingham Forest training shorts, that, despite my trembling hands, I had somehow managed to ensure were facing the right way round, when I pulled them on moments earlier for the first day of a month that was going to transform my life.

I was far more nervous than I had been five years earlier, when I had been invited to a month's trial at Aston Villa after signing schoolboy forms. That was bad enough. At that time I had been presented with the dilemma of leaving school and giving up my exams to pursue my ultimate goal. It was an agonising spot to be in. Did I carry on preparing for exams and say no thanks to Villa? Or did I put everything on the line for one month and the chance to climb on to the first rung of the professional ladder?

At school I'll be the first to admit I was not particularly academic. Don't get me wrong, I was no numbskull and I never skipped lessons, but maths and geography and any other lessons for that matter always finished a distant second to sport. I held 800m records, won the only long-distance run I was asked to participate in, played cricket and generally immersed myself in anything sporty going on. But football was the game I lived for and fortunately, unlike nowadays, I had teachers like Mr Hackett and Mr Whittaker who never missed an opportunity to encourage me and indulge my passion.

I even remember the moment I arrived at my senior school, Alderman White, that my reputation as being a bit of a decent player had preceded me.

I had only been there five minutes and I was thrown into the first team, even though I was only 11 and I was playing with and against boys five years older. Not that it mattered to me. My debut for the school team ended in a 10-1 victory and I scored the ninth goal.

School teams were valued back then. Sports competition was important and well organised and we had national heroes like Sebastian Coe, Steve Ovett, Daley Thompson and Ian Botham; genuine world class athletes and cricketers, who were the envy of every other country in the world. So many governments and local authorities since then have diluted the competitive struggle that produced such champions. They have done all they can to destroy team sports at school and to remove any lasting shred of competition in that environment. The same governments and MPs that can't wait to launch an inquest when we fail to win enough medals at the Olympics, or our Davis Cup tennis team gets beaten by Liechtenstein.

I have heard the argument, theory, call it what you like; that it is the taking part that counts and it is not all about winning. What a load of crap. Sport IS about winning. That is why they have gold medals, cup competitions and the Formula One drivers championship. They all celebrate winners. If you can emerge victorious with grace and humility all the better, but no one remembers losers. I only ever played to win and unless youngsters growing up have that competitive edge from an early age, how are they ever going to become champions in their chosen field? How are we going to produce winners of the future, sporting icons who we can aspire to be and be proud of? This country has got some hare-brained ideas.

Fortunately when I was growing up it was different. I would play three games a weekend. Saturday morning. Saturday afternoon and Sunday. I lived for it and just could not get enough. That might be considered a breach of human rights now, but back then it was the norm for me. I was even banned by the Nottinghamshire FA once for not turning up to a Nottinghamshire Schools game, because I had been told I was not playing and I went off to play for Attenborough, my club side. A silver-haired bloke called Terry Annable, who ran the Nottinghamshire FA, banned me from all games for six weeks, even though I knew I was not required to play for the county! It was an early lesson on the subject of our wonderful governing body! But that was how committed I was to playing football as a kid.

So when Villa came calling, my parents were brilliant about the whole thing. They knew it was all I wanted to do. It was in my blood. My dad Ray lost count of the number of times he suffered third degree burns on his forehead, from a ball that was as lethal as coarse sandpaper, after playing head tennis with me for hours on the beach in Wales on summer holidays. He never once reminded me of the amount of cash I cost him having to replace windows at home, as a result of me smashing around tennis balls in the back garden to improve my touch. I never practised with a full-size ball. I wanted to know I could control one of those without even looking. I even used to use a tennis ball for a warm-up in the dressing room with my amateur side Long Eaton United.

My folks could have been really tough and dogmatic about the whole thing. They could easily have insisted I remained at school like the father of one of my best mates, Martin Northfield, and complete my education. Martin was a fantastic centre half and he could have made it, but was given no choice about his future. He was made to stay on at school so he could go follow his father's wish and succeed in getting his qualifications to better himself in life. Education seemed far more highly valued then than it is now and becoming a professional footballer was a pipe-dream of so many kids who never made it beyond their first pair of screw-in studs and under-10s.

Football was not a lucrative cash-cow back then either. It was not a red carpet to untold riches and fame, but fortunately mum and dad were right behind me. They backed me all the way and I packed my bags for a month in digs in Birmingham. I spent every day at Bodymoor Heath, Villa's training ground, as a left-winger. That was my position as a kid. I bust a gut to get that big break and at the end of it, all I received was the 'thanks, but no thanks' routine from Villa. It is hard to describe the sense of utter desolation when you hear those words.

My whole world caved in. My dreams were stubbed out faster than John Robertson extinguished a sly fag in the toilets if he thought BC [[Brian Clough] was going to catch him having a drag on a Silk Cut. It was a devastating experience for a 16-year-old. I thought that was it for me. I had sacrificed my education and could not go back to school and been told I was not good enough to do the one thing I wanted to do more than anything in the world.

Within days I was at Beeston's Job Centre. That was all that was left for me to do. I had to get a job. It was as simple as that. I scoured through the vacancies and spotted one for a floor layer. It made sense to me. It was my old man's profession and he was bloody good at it. He used to go over to Northern Ireland at the time of all the sectarian troubles re-fitting shops like Timothy Whites and Boots that had been bombed, because he had the contract for those companies. He even worked away in Libya and once just arrived in time to see me complete a hat-trick for the Cubs when I won my first trophy.

So following him into the same profession seemed like the right thing. I got the job being advertised with a local firm in Chilwell, run by a bloke called Bill Marshall. My first pay-packet was £12-a-week. I thought that was it for me. No more dreams of pro football anymore. I had a trade. It was welcome to the nine-to-five grind of humping carpets and floor tiles, up staircases in buildings with no lifts, with some weekend semi-pro stuff on the side.

I travelled all over the country with Bill for contract jobs at Army barracks, turning stair carpets. The MOD liked to get their money's worth out of carpets in those days so we used to just turn them around and re-lay them so the bad tread, where everyone had trodden the pile down, was now on the vertical part of the stair. I even made sure the feet of the heir to the throne were comfortable by laying carpet in Prince Charles' quarters at RAF Cranwell. Not that he was around to let me know whether I had done a decent job or not! After a while the disappointment subsided about Villa and I got my head around the fact that I was going to be a carpet fitter for life. At least I had given professional football a go. I would not die wondering, 'what if?'.

Little did I know at the time there was to be another chance. Something far more incredible than the apprenticeship I had failed to secure at Villa Park. Something I had imagined on all those days of playing striker and goalkeeper with a balloon in my bedroom as a kid growing up. Throwing the balloon in the air, plotting the uncertain trajectory as it missed the light fitting and the head of the imaginary defender, waiting for that perfect moment to volley it before diving headlong on to my bed to tip the venomous shot from Birtles around the post.

I could hear the commentary of Hugh Johns on Star Soccer as the balloon swerved more erratically than Roberto Carlos or any of his Brazilian superstar friends could ever make a Mitre Mulitplex misbehave. Birtles the 'keeper could not prevent Birtles the striker from rounding off the perfect hat-trick. A towering header, a right-footed volley and now a wonderful lob, with the left foot, from the edge of the penalty area. An England call up could not be far away. How could my country not need the talents of this precocious eight-year-old?

Hopes. Dreams. Fantasies. Ambitions. I had them all and there they were in my sweaty palms in the away dressing room at the City Ground. All I had to do was clasp my fingers shut and grab them to make it reality. The reality was that there was no doubt in my mind as to the owner of the unmistakable, snarling voice that had just greeted me. It was him. No doubt about it. I had just been given my first introduction to Brian Clough, the man who had cornered the market in bombastic and developed it into an art form.

I had only ever really seen him on television. I had heard that famous voice countless times, doing various Brian Clough party political broadcasts, the rhetoric better than any of the Labour politicians he famously allied himself with. I had listened transfixed when he pontificated about the game he loved. His TV ratings were higher than Coronation Street in those days. He was pure box office.

Since the early 70s at Derby and now at Forest he was the nation's favourite, most irreverent, famously irascible expert. I would not insult him with the throwaway title of pundit that became the vogue. He lit up every panel, as if all the floodlights at Old Trafford had been flicked on, whoever he was sitting alongside. No one wanted to hear any of his fellow panellists speak. Clough rendered them grey and uninteresting. Listening to him toy with journalists was hypnotising. Watching him tie them up in knots and berate them, with that knowing smile and charm oozing from every pore. His sardonic demeanour that made you scream 'arrogant sod' and yet like him simultaneously. Those unfortunate inquisitors. They knew less than what would have been on the first page of BC's manual on the Do's and Don'ts of management. He rarely wasted a chance to put them straight about their lack of knowledge of the industry in which he was king and he did it with such a flourish.

Most people laughed when they saw him intimidate others. You know, that nervous laugh, when what you are fully conscious of whatever it is you are witnessing is not really funny, more like a blood sport. His argumentative streak was legendary. His domineering personality was fearsome. His tongue possessed a lethal edge. If Gillette could have marketed that, their boffins in their testing laboratories would never have had to come up with fancy gadgets like Fusion razors, with five blades all crammed together for that ultimate shave.

Clough commanded fascination and the poor bastard on the receiving end, getting it in the neck and floundering around like the victim of a giant crocodile before he goes into the death roll, begged for sympathy. You actually quivered on behalf of the sap on the other side of the microphone, who was no match. What you did not realise at the time was that the journalist in question actually felt honoured he was being embarrassed in such an excruciating manner. A rebuke from BC was a badge of honour. To receive a stinging attack of the verbals, which normally started with 'Eh shithouse, I'm only kidding. It's a term of endearment' was something to be cherished like a first love and safeguarded to tell the grand kids.

'Get off my fucking table!' was a variation on several themes and my first bollocking. I will take it to my grave. That badge of honour pierced my skin. Fleetingly, I felt like those journalists he ran rings around and anyone else who had been left with razor burn from his tongue. After recoiling, the fear hit me and then the embarrassment. The emotions poured out and my face felt as if it was on fire. It was as red as the Forest shirts worn by the first team I was trying to join in the dressing room a few yards up the corridor.

Only later on that morning did I discover I had been somewhat unfortunate to receive such a harsh welcome because next to the away dressing room in the corridor outside was a set of double doors that went through to the board room, trophy room and on to reception. They were usually locked and the Gaffer took the longer walk across the car park at the back of the Main Stand and entered through the same set of red doors all travelling opposition teams, officials and home players entered on a match day.

For some reason, on this day of all days in November 1976, they were open and he decided to take a short cut past the trophy cabinet he was soon to fill with that much silver Ray Ban considered opening a sunglass hut at the entrance because it was so bright inside. There was no advanced warning. The visitors' dressing room was nearest to those double doors. So he instinctively popped his head around the door and caught me sitting there. It was just his way of making it clear he was in charge.

Without actually saying it, what he conveyed was simple enough. The message was clear: 'You're here now Birtles. You haven't made it yet and you are green as grass. I'm the Gaffer. This is how things work and these are the rules. Blah, blah, blah. You have won yourself a month. Use it wisely and while you are here mind your manners'. It was not ruling by fear, people that dismiss his approach as pure bullying tactics are talking a load of bollocks. It was to keep me and everyone else on our toes. It was my first lesson to always be on the lookout after that. That is what he wanted. He wanted you to be constantly on your toes.

Bollockings like that were dished out to players like hot drinks in a soup kitchen. No one escaped. The bigger you are, the bigger dressing down you cop for. It was much better to hear one early on in the day, because whether you were on the receiving end or not, there was a certain comfort about them for all the players at the time. Hearing someone get an earful meant he was in the building. It was somehow comforting and a relief you knew his whereabouts. Because it was the not knowing that was worse. It was the uncertainty of his whereabouts and when he might materialise that was really disconcerting.

That game of cat and mouse made life interesting. It was like working in one of Roald Dahl's Tales of the Unexpected seven days a week. It was great. Here I was at the gate to all that. Panic stricken and butterflies churning with nerves worse than any first date. I was desperate to make an impression. I was eager to please and turn this one-month window of opportunity into a lifetime of playing football for a living for the greatest manager of his generation.

I had made an impression alright. I was lounging on his table. In his dressing room. In his corridor. In his football ground. I had managed to get off on the wrong foot even before I had tied up my boot laces. As flying starts go, I was stuck on the grid and could hear the deafening roar of the engines of all the other competitors ready to complete their first lap and come tearing past me at 200mph, while I was still trying to get the engine fired up. I could sense the trickle of the embarrassing beads of sweat on my temples.

It was bad enough that all the way to the first day of my trial I was checking that you could not smell Evo Stick on me. That was the glue I had been using to lay carpets the previous Friday. All I kept wondering was whether the Swarfega, that old hand cleaner, had managed to get all the traces of it from my fingers. Would all those household names, John Robertson, Viv Anderson, Martin O'Neill and Tony Woodcock spot it? Would they smell it? Would they smell the naivety in me? Would they get a whiff of the fact that I was some non-league footballer that had been given a punt at the big time?

Daunting was not the word. I was a £60-a-week floor layer. I had been on my hands and knees hammering in carpet gripper 48 hours earlier while they were preparing for a Second Division game in their bid to get promoted that season. What am I doing here? They must have known where I came from and my background. They could easily have turned up their noses. Fortunately, football snobbery was not so prevalent back then.

Just a few days earlier I had met the Gaffer in his office at Forest to sign the forms. It was whirlwind stuff and I don't think I had enough saliva in my mouth to lubricate it sufficiently and un-clamp my tongue. I don't think I said too much, in what seemed like a few seconds. I remember a few nods of agreement and barely being able to hold the pen to flourish my signature for the 28 days of opportunity I had just been handed. The chance to prove I was even remotely worthy of his interest. It was an interest that had come about via a bizarre set of circumstances.

At the time I was getting a bit of a reputation at Long Eaton and was scoring a few goals, but only once, since that devastating knock-back from Aston Villa, had I come remotely close to a second chance at making the grade since signing schoolboy forms for Villa when I was playing as a 12-year-old kid for Attenborough Colts and a Villa scout called Les Rowbotham, a lovely old man, spotted me.

He used to watch me play down on the pitches at Inham Nook from behind the railings, in between tending to his cabbages and his potatoes on his allotment. When you signed schoolboy forms in those days, that club had first refusal on you. You could not go anywhere else. You did not go into swanky academies then. There was none of that. Villa had put a first reserve on me, if you like, but I kept playing with all my friends at school and at representative level and for Attenborough.

Today clubs that take young kids at nine or ten stop them playing with their mates at school. They stop them representing their county and take them away from the environment they know and cocoon them in academies. It's criminal and wrong. Kids don't have a proper childhood any more. No wonder some players go off the rails later in life, because what they go through now is plain wrong as far as I can see.

How can that be of benefit to any youngster? It is just not natural. I understand that clubs want to protect their interests, but to do that at the expense of a childhood being played out the way nature intended is not acceptable. I don't want to sound like a miserable old-timer because things in the game now are far better than they were when I was playing. Many things have developed for the better, but the way kids are introduced to the professional arena is not one of them and if there was something that could be done to change that, I would be all in favour.

After suffering at the hands of Aston Villa, I was fortunate to make one of the best decisions of my young life in leaving Attenborough to go and join Clifton All Whites at the age of 18. It may sound slightly trivial that I had switched from one excellent youth team in the county to the one widely regarded as the best, but it was then I first encountered coach John Raynor, who played a key part in my breakthrough into the professional game and who became my mentor and one of my closest friends.

John was an absolutely fantastic bloke and had all the best players in

Nottingham at his club. He had a reputation for being able to spot talent and it was a compliment when he asked me to join Clifton, even if it was a wrench to leave Attenborough. It was the only team in the league that had ever been able to give John's sides any kind of genuine game and it was a logical progression for me to follow him to Long Eaton United where I could combine floor laying during the week and earn beer money in the Midland League.

If it had not been for John, I might not have ended up at Nottingham Forest at all and I would have signed for Peterborough United instead! I quickly gained a reputation as a striker with some promise for Long Eaton and several clubs were rumoured to be sniffing around, including Manchester City and Burnley, but it was Peterborough manager Noel Cantwell who made the effort to come and see me and sound me out about the step up into the pro ranks.

Cantwell and his assistant John Barnwell, who I had watched from the terraces when he was a Forest player, braved the pissing down rain to watch me train on the all-weather pitches at Carlton Forum for Long Eaton one night. At the end of the session I was in the dressing room with the pair of them and John Raynor. They wanted me to go to London Road and they had a professional contract for me to sign. Cantwell was so keen he even set me up with a house to move into as well. It was flattering and I was looking around for a pen. Even though Peterborough were in the old Third Division at the time, it was professional football, getting paid to do something I would have done for nothing.

My head was racing and all I had to do was say yes and I would have been off to London Road. No-brainer really. So I said no! My heart was screaming yes, but John Raynor told me to have the evening to think about it. After Barnwell and Cantwell left John made it clear to me that he thought there were bigger clubs out there and I should not rush into anything. As far as he was concerned it was the wrong choice for me and he told me to be patient.

Much as it pained me to do so, I listened to John and I took his advice. He had been a mentor to me. Most of what he had ever told me had turned out to be spot on. So I trusted his judgment and took his word on this one. What I did not know at the time was the plan he was hatching and the phone call he was about to make that would change my life.

Many people have tried to take the credit for bringing me to the attention of the Gaffer, but it was John's phone call, direct to Clough himself, that set the wheels in motion for my move to Nottingham Forest.

MY MAGIC CARPET RIDE

The day after Peterborough made me the offer John rang the City Ground and told BC that there was a contract for me at London Road and I was considering signing. He was told point blank to keep me where I was and not to let me put my signature on anything just yet, but it was only when the suggestion of me moving to Manchester United came along soon after that Cloughie decided to make his move.

Not too long after my meeting with John Barnwell and the temptation of London Road I was playing at Burton Albion in the third round of the FA Cup. Neil Rioch, brother of Bruce, was in charge of Burton at the time and for some reason Ian Storey-Moore was there watching. I am still not entirely certain why, but thank god he was. 'Muggsy' used to play for Forest, before the Clough revolution took place.

He actually did what most players thought was unthinkable and turned down the chance to sign for Clough at Derby County in 1972, preferring to go to Old Trafford instead. Peter Taylor had even paraded Derby's new '£225,000 signing' on the pitch at the Baseball Ground prior to a game, only to find out they had not completed the deal and Storey-Moore ended up at Old Trafford. Whatever people think about his judgment on that issue, for some reason he liked the look of me that day and I am not sure why.

We ended up losing the game 5-0. Hardly the kind of seismic performance that would have scouts rushing for the nearest pay-phone, but I had had a decent game despite all that and Storey-Moore must have seen something in my performance to decide to try to do his former club United a favour. He rang a friend at Old Trafford to suggest that they take a look at me and that I might have the potential to be something. He could have saved United the £1.25m they coughed up to sign me six years later, if it had not been for the intervention of a certain Mr Clough.

Quite by chance, Maurice Edwards was also at the game that day because the game he had been scheduled to watch in the Cup had been called off. He has since confessed he was not there to watch me. I had not been so much as a faint blip on the Forest radar at any point up until then. Maurice told me several years later that even though Long Eaton had been on the end of a good hiding, he spent the remainder of the weekend thinking about the 'young, slim lad' playing for United who caused 'all kinds of problems for Burton's defence on his own'.

A week later I scored in extra-time on a paddy field of a pitch for Long Eaton to win a Derbyshire Cup game to give Maurice another dig in the ribs, but word had already reached the City Ground that Manchester United were interested in signing a striker on Clough's doorstep and he decided it was time to intervene and find out for himself. His reaction to the suggestion of a local lad leaving Nottingham for Old Trafford was typically blunt: 'No lad from Nottingham who is supposed to be able to play the game, is going to Manchester United without me seeing him first'. It was all over the local papers at the time and it was rather difficult to know quite what to make of the whole thing.

He got a chance to see me more quickly than he anticipated, even if he did not know where the hell he was going and who he was going to watch. The following Saturday the Gaffer rang Maurice to tell him that PT [Peter Taylor] had taken the first team to Oldham and he wanted to know where Maurice was going that day. "Where the hell is Enderby Town?" was his response after being told the scouting destination. It was only when he arrived at Maurice's shop and handed over his car keys that BC discovered he was coming to watch me. "Good, I like judging centre forwards," he said.

All the talk about me not being able to leave before BC had seen me had my head in a whirl really. I was not sure whether to take him at his word or dismiss it as pie-in-the-sky nonsense. I never heard anything from Manchester United and quite frankly never really gave it much consideration. Let's face it, I was playing in the Midland League for Long Eaton United. Players from there did not go to Manchester United, or Nottingham Forest for that matter. They went to work on Monday morning, slogged it out until Friday and counted the hours until they could play again on Saturday.

Outrageous hope, the kind you have on a Saturday night clutching your ticket and watching the National Lottery, before the first ball comes flying out and you decipher, through all the gyrating, that it is not one of yours and your latest plans to buy holiday homes in the Maldives go out the window. I did not give the Forest situation much thought. My concentration was focused on more tangible matters, such as another cup game playing against another higher level non-league side at Enderby Town. I was not to know at the time, but that would be the day that changed my life forever.

All the rumours about 'would he or wouldn't he' stay true to his word and come and cast his expert eye over my spindly frame started circulating in the build-up to the match. I was never certain he was going to turn up, but the mere suggestion had the stomach churning. I could feel the contents of my bacon and eggs revolving like a roulette wheel. Fucking hell. This was it. The greatest manager ever to step into a dug-out was slumming it to watch a 20-year-old who had less meat on him than most whippets. If he was there, he must have been able to hear my teeth chattering from inside the dressing room.

The Long Eaton manager at the time was a bloke called Geoff Barrowcliffe, who used to play for Derby County. He was not one for saying too much. He was a lovely fella, very quiet and undemonstrative. There was just the odd comment that day in the dressing room. All pretty standard stuff. You know the kind of thing about getting an early touch. Don't waste the ball and we have got nothing to lose. I could hear it, but it was muffled, because of the voices that were shouting for supremacy in my head. 'How the hell can I relax now and enjoy the game when that is coursing through your thoughts. Put him out of your mind. Go and enjoy yourself. Score a goal. Help your team mates. Concentrate. Fuck off. This is Brian Clough we are talking about'.

Running out on to the pitch, I scanned the faces surreptitiously. I wanted to know if he was there, but did not want him to know I was looking for him. That would tell him all he needed to know about my concentration levels and professionalism. I could not see him anywhere. He was hardly likely to be on the front row giving me the big thumbs-up and don't blow it routine was he? Get your head down Birtles and play like you have never played.

Ten minutes into the game, with all those distractions gone, I was on the receiving end of an absolutely shocking tackle. The centre half went right through me and snapped my shin pad. I thought I had broken my leg. The pain was excruciating and I had to get carried off on a stretcher. There is always that instant feeling of shock when you get whacked. The nerve endings over your body all seem to stab at the same time, while you try to work out whether you really are seriously injured. All I could think was some hairy-arsed centre back had just screwed up my 15 minutes of fame in front of Brian Clough.

I had this huge gash on my shin, but fortunately there was nothing broken and I was able to return to the pitch. I would have crawled back out there if I had to because there was so much riding on this on a personal level. We lost the game and I did not score. So I was not in the best of moods after the game. I felt I had blown it again and my mood was not helped much by Clough's comments in the Nottingham Evening Post the following day. They reported that he had been to watch me play at Enderby and when he was asked about whether I had impressed, his reply was typically withering and comical. 'The half-time Bovril was better than Birtles' performance' and he never tired of telling people that all the way through my career.

I am glad he stayed long enough for the Bovril and it must have been good, because despite my lack of impact I must have done something right. He must have spotted something in me. Maybe it was just my sheer bravery to come back on to the pitch after getting smashed like that. He was a striker too. He would have killed to score a goal and even tried to get up and play on when he had his cruciate knee ligament severed playing for Middlesbrough. He hated seeing injured players on crutches, but he loved bravery. Maybe that was the sole reason he decided to offer me the month's trial. That day was the reason I was sat on his 'fucking table'.

Needless to say, I got off the table in double quick time, trying to hide my embarrassment at the same time as trying to hide the nerves as we headed off down the banks of the River Trent to the training pitches that were situated the other side of Boots Athletic ground on the embankment. That sense of feeling sick to the pit of my stomach started to subside the moment Frank Clark took me under his wing for that walk to the testing ground, where my ability would be scrutinised as much as any atom scientists had tried to split.

We used to run down to training in twos and it was a steady jog down alongside Frank, who was a senior pro at the time, not long arrived from Newcastle United when it looked like his career was almost over. Little did either of us know at the time that our careers, at vastly differing starting points, were about to be launched into an extravagant orbit that made space exploration of Mars look like a trip to the local Sainsbury. Frank was one of the good guys, but everyone was fantastic to me. Not a solitary member of that first team squad looked down their nose at me. Even if I did whiff of Evo Stick!

One or two might have been a little surprised at the unconventionality of it all. One or two, and if they did they kept it well hidden, might have thought I was seriously out of my depth and would not last two minutes. These days players would slaughter someone like me, a non-league player walking into a Championship dressing room. It was not really acceptable then either, but it was accepted at Forest. There were no egos. The Gaffer banned them the moment you turned off Trent Bridge and drove through the car park gates.

So there I was, training just along from the likes of Woodcock, Robertson, O'Neill, McGovern and Anderson. I was being scrutinised by the eyes of coaches like Jimmy Gordon, Liam O'Kane and Ronnie Fenton, his corps of trusty lieutenants. They could always be found in a little room further down the corridor from the dressing room. It was the coaches' room, where plans were hatched and people were discussed away from prying eyes. It was the Forest equivalent of the Anfield boot room and BC could be found in there, talking football, but I rarely found him at the training ground.

On that first day I was expecting him. He had already given me one bollocking and I was banking on a few more. Surely it couldn't be that difficult to spot him. With that loud, canary yellow rugby shirt and his white shorts and trainers. That first session I was trying to concentrate on the training routines and make sure that my first touch was good enough to impress the array of players who would soon become household names. I was sharing the same training pitch with them, but at the same time, my head felt like it was rotating 360 degrees to locate the Gaffer.

Where was he? Where was Peter Taylor? What was the point in taking someone on trial and not coming down to see them play? I had worked up all that nervous tension on the understanding that they would keep their half of the bargain and be down there, watching me like hawks, shaking their heads in unison when I had done something wrong and nodding the odd nod of appreciation when something went right. It was the least they could do to make up for my shredded nerves. It was what they were supposed to do, wasn't it?

What was the point of getting me here if they were not going to have a look? I soon learned that seeing the Gaffer or PT on the training ground was as likely as spotting a rare bird feeding across the road on the square at Trent Bridge. There was minimal contact in that month's trial. Jimmy Gordon, Ron Fenton and Liam O'Kane did the day-to-day training for everyone and intermittently, the Gaffer, PT and their dogs would be spotted walking across the training pitches.

Del was the name of BC's faithful retriever and rarely left his side. He was even more loyal than most of the players who played for him and enjoyed the greatest times of their careers under him, whether at Derby, or Forest. As a reward the Gaffer would bring Del to work in the Merc and take him for a walk down the Trent and to the training ground to catch the last bit of a session. He was not heavily involved for the vast majority of training. He preferred to let his coaches do that for him.

He would just come and supervise the last five minutes or so. He would put in an appearance with Pete, who would bring his black Labrador too, and when Kenny Burns had become bored of kicking his team mates in five-a-sides he used to give Pete's dog Bess a kick up the backside every now and then instead! Only when PT was looking the other way, of course.

So I quickly learned that the Gaffer's training methods were far from conventional. He was not your normal manager and when he did eventually wander down there was nothing like the pearls of managerial wisdom that I had been anticipating. Imagine being a young kid of that age, straight out of non-league. As well as wanting to impress, I wanted to know the secret. I wanted to see him work at first hand and understand what all the fuss was all about.

I wanted the insight into his world. The insight I assumed I would get as a matter of course, after agreeing to the trial and entering into the same world in which he shaped the careers of players like John McGovern, Robbo, Viv Anderson, transforming them from under-achieving, unknown, or under-rated, into precious gems that all other clubs would covet and want for their own. After all, that was what he was renowned for, his managerial brilliance. Surely it must all come on the training pitches. That must be the place where he hatches his plans to win game after game.

My first experience of his presence could not have been further from the truth, but if I was not prepared for lesson number one and whose table I was sat on, lesson number two was even more of a shock. If he had a reputation for being different, there was no way on earth I could have been prepared for his first set of instructions to the rest of the group and me on the training ground.

All I heard him shout was: 'Millsy get us through the nettles'. The order was barked at Gary Mills because he was the youngest, but it went for everyone and all I could do was follow the lead. There was a clump of trees in the far corner of the training ground where the groundsman used to dump all the grass cuttings. It was compost corner really and all kinds of things grew in there, especially nettles and there was a very healthy clump of them.

The instruction was simple and Millsy set off, with the rest of us following him to run through the nettles and manure. It was not a huge thicket of nettles, but it was deep enough and there was enough manure too, to ensure we came out the other side covered in stings and smelling less than savoury. That would not be the end of the instructions. When we finally got out the other side, there would be a choice of further orders. The Gaffer would either shout: 'Millsy, lead them through again, please' and we would do it all over again, just to make sure that we had sufficient need for Dock Leaves.

Or Cloughie would shout: 'Last one in the five-a-side net' and everyone would hurtle, full pelt before we tried to shoe horn 15 fully grown men into a five-a-side goal. It was carnage. Was that alien to me? Was it completely bonkers? I had just come from laying carpet and playing non-league. All of my football until that point had been having a laugh and mucking around with a load of mates. I had no real concept of what professional football was all about. So running through nettles, or diving head-long into a five-a-side net, quickly became the norm for me.

Everyone had to do it and no one was spared. John McGovern held up the European Cup twice, but he would be selected as the leader of the nettle pack. It made me laugh with utter bemusement, but I am not too sure what people like Trevor Francis and Peter Shilton thought about the whole thing when they turned up at the club later on in my career. They probably thought it was bonkers and beneath them, but they still did it. No one was too big for the nettle dash.

It was just another bizarre, off-the-wall way the Gaffer showed us he was the boss. He was in charge and his word was final. Unorthodox was a word invented for him and I, for whatever reason, had been given the privilege of a chance to become part of that incredible world. Never mind nettles, I would have run through brick walls for the bloke. He was that inspiring and I wanted a contract.

I was handed the opportunity to earn one faster than I imagined when I was named in the reserve side to play Coventry City at their old home Highfield Road in my first week of the trial, but not before I received another bollocking, although at least the dressing down did not come from the Gaffer this time. I was hauled over the coals by John Sheridan for taking a deck of cards off the team bus and playing patience in the dressing room before the game. I did not know any different. I was an amateur and it was as my way of trying to keep the butterflies still, but it didn't go down too well with the reserve team coach.

It was hardly the sort of soothing, confidence-injecting pep-talk I was looking for and I was unable to get a goal. Goals were like gold dust to the Gaffer. He would have knocked old ladies out of the way to get one. I do remember that we won the game and Sean Haselgrave scored the goal, but sitting in the dressing room after you dissect your own performance because it means so much. There is so much riding on it and I was not exactly ecstatic to say the least, but I discovered later that was the game that clinched the deal for me at Forest.

John Raynor felt PT had tried to belittle Long Eaton months later when he claimed Long Eaton were a "little club who would have been glad of £200." He had a right to be aggrieved, but it was Pete who became my biggest supporter and eventually the chief reason why I ended up signing professional forms at the City Ground.

Unbeknown to me and the rest of the lads that night, Peter Taylor had undertaken one of his frequent spying missions. The Gaffer regularly sent him on under-cover missions, but this was not him casting his eye over players at another club. It was him putting me and the rest of the reserves under the microscope Taylor-style and he had travelled to Highfield Road separately to the team bus and driven his wife to the game. He never announced himself to any of the Forest staff or players and was wrapped up in a big overcoat and hat.

Everyone knows a coach, manager, assistant manager or scout from any club can get himself into any game in the country without having to cough up a penny. All they have to do is get the club secretary to fax the club in question and get themselves on the guest list, but that night Pete paid for himself and his wife and sat up in the corner of the stand, out of the way of prying eyes, so his eyes could do the prying.

It was only some time later when I was an established member of the first team squad that Pete owned up and revealed that was the game that convinced him I was worth taking a punt on. I was a little taken aback, because I did not think I had done anything particularly out of the ordinary. I certainly did not come off the pitch slapping myself on the back, but PT loved one particular thing I had done. I had a trick, probably my only one, when I used to let the ball run across me and I would drag it back with the opposite foot and swivel away from opponents. That was what he liked. My trick convinced him 'I had a chance in the game'.

3

IN THE COURT OF KING CLOUGH
The old Palais act

DOING enough to convince PT was all very well, even if the Gaffer fully respected his side-kick's sixth sense when it came to spotting talent and players. I still had to get over the hurdle of actually being offered a contract when the end of the month's loan came around, but I was hoping Brian Clough would return the favour. After all I had signed him as Forest manager in the first place!

Just over a year earlier Forest had been looking for a replacement manager after deciding to part company with Allan Brown. The club was going nowhere in the old Second Division and I was going around in circles on the revolving dance floor, in the opposite direction to the lights bouncing at all angles off the mirror balls hanging from the roof of the Palais de Danse on Nottingham's Lower Parliament Street. It was the place to see and be seen for everyone in my pre-Forest days.

I cannot claim to have played a key role in Brian Howard Clough breezing into the City Ground in January 1975. I had not smuggled him up the A52 from his home in Derby, where he was counting his money after being paid out handsomely, following his turbulent 44 days at Leeds United fighting the ghost of Don Revie and trying to overcome the inhospitable nature of Billy Bremner and Co. If Leeds United's star-studded dressing room did not want him, more fool them and he might as well come and work his magic at the City Ground. I remember putting my name to a petition in the Palais that night to get Brian Clough as Forest's manager.

Even if I had been spinning upside down on the revolving dance floor, I would have been able to scrawl my name on the sheet of A4 paper, along with 9,999 other people who flourished their signatures on it. It had not one jot of influence in BC deciding to shake the dust from his unfortunate experience at Elland Road and become the club's new Messiah, but I can say I was one of the 10,000 that signed Brian Clough and that feels good to me. Now I wanted him to re-pay the favour.

As soon as the month's trial came to an end, I knew there would be the inevitable call into the office. Sure enough I was summoned on my last day and I have to admit I had no idea whether I had done enough to get the contract I wanted. Even if PT thought I had got a chance. I felt like I had done one of those wishy-washy job interviews and you are not sure which way it has gone. Well that was the state of mind I was in. I never thought, 'that's it, I am nailed on here'. I am a perfectionist and my own biggest critic. I always wanted everything to be spot on, whether that was laying carpets or playing football. I was never big-headed enough to think that I had sealed the deal during that month.

I always looked at the worst case scenario first. It is not that I am a pessimist. I just examined the down sides, before I imagined the best outcome. It was just the way I had been brought up as a kid. I was always taught not to take anything for granted and to work hard and appreciate what I had. I was raised on the Inham Nook council estate in Chilwell about ten miles out of the city centre. It was not the worst area of Nottingham by any stretch of the imagination, but it was pretty rough and there were some tough folks about. Families consisting of seven or eight kids were not a rarity. So it was hardly silver spoon stuff, terrific times all the same.

That was what family life was like for me. My folks had standards. My old man worked bloody hard and did everything for us and my mom ran the house and made sure we were looked after, until she got a part-time job later on when the kids were that bit older, but all my time growing up I was taught never to think I was better than anyone else. There was always discipline in our house and core values and football on the wreck playing 15-a-side from mid-afternoon until nine at night. I remember the whacks I used to get off my mother's hair-brush for coming in late. My crime was playing football all day! I had not been running around sniffing glue or taking drugs. Streets were a lot safer then, but rules were rules. The trouble was, when I was playing football, I was immersed in it and had no concept of time. All that mattered was whether I was winning or not.

I had not been on the Wreck at Forest, but that month had flown by in the same way those afternoons turned into evenings when I was a kid, but I was so intent on making an impression I had not really considered how I had done. I felt like I had made an impression, but you are never sure. The Gaffer was very particular and peculiar. So I would never presume. In the same way that I dared not ask any of the first team players on that walk along the banks of the River Trent to training every day. It was not my place to say anything. I was a carpet fitter from Long Eaton and my job was to keep my head down, not be over exuberant, get on with it and know my place.

D-Day finally did arrive and I got the call to go and see the Gaffer in his office. December, 1976. It was shit or bust time. It was pretty straight forward, either he was going to give me a contract there and then, or he was going to 'bomb me out' and I had no idea which way the coin was going to fall. I was given the all clear to go down the corridor to his office and breathed in so deeply I nearly sucked myself inside out. I knocked and heard 'Eh, come in Birtles'. I wandered in and he was sat there, leaning back in his chair, with his feet up on the table. The epitome of relaxation but he could probably hear my heart pounding.

'Son, I'd like to take you on and how does £60-quid a week sound?' was the Gaffer's very matter of fact offer and I don't think he had even got the wages bit out of his mouth and I had already said yes. The money on offer was the same wages I was earning for wrecking my knees and getting high on Evo Stick while floor-laying. Forest were anything but a wealthy club at that time. £60-a-week for a professional footballer sounds crazy when you consider the wage explosion which followed not too many years later, but to me the cash was almost irrelevant. I could not get the pen fast enough before he changed his mind.

After my little trick at Coventry, the finger post pointing to potential as raw as a baboon's backside, it was hardly the fast-track to superstardom in my early days at the City Ground. Collecting reserve team appearances and the odd goal was my stock-in-trade and I had to wait just over three months for my debut, even if that caused something of an upset with newspapers at the time suggesting that Clough had stunned fans by 'ignoring established stars favour of a 21-year-old unknown'.

This was March 1977 and if the fans were stunned, that was nothing compared to the way I felt. The team was always posted on a Friday on the little notice board in the first team dressing room. You would come back from training and it was either already there or it did not take long to appear. There were rumours that I could be playing. The grapevine always buzzes with stuff like that and I heard it all, but it was only when the team went up and I saw G. Birtles on it that I started to panic myself. Fucking hell! I even had a lager that night to calm my nerves.

All I could think about was 'what if I have a stinker?' I felt the pressure on me more, because of my inexperience, the fact that I was a Nottingham lad and the fact I did not want to let my family, friends, Cloughie or myself down. First impressions as a player are crucial, as I would discover later in my career. I did not even drive in those days, I had not passed my test, so I had to be picked up by John McGovern.

He would always in with John O'Hare from Derby and cut off the A52 to pick me up standing at the top of the road. It always stuck with me that our captain would go out of his way to pick up some young kid. It's like Rio Ferdinand driving in from the leafy suburbs of Cheshire to Old Trafford and swerving out of his way for 15 minutes to collect some reserve. Mind you reserves at United these days probably all drive BMWs as long as they are old enough to pass their test.

I never asked, they offered. Not just for matches, but every day for training and in return I bought them a bottle of every spirit going as a Christmas present. They picked me up that day for the Hull game, while all my family and my mates I had grown up with from the Cadland made their own way to the ground for moral support. They were all protective of me. That was great and they wanted me to do well. I was one of them and me succeeding made it special for them, like they had all played a part and they had. They felt it for me.

Apparently I had deserved my senior debut against Hull City for 'showing lots of promise'. Even if I was being forced to play out of position. In those days I was ordered to play in central midfield on the Gaffer's instructions. I hated every minute of it and at no time did I fully appreciate it was being done for a reason.

He made me play in midfield for the reserves to build up my strength and stamina. He wanted me to increase my lung capacity and learn to run all day, but I hated him for it and the only way I increased my lung capacity was moaning and bitching about it. I had no interest in playing in midfield. It was bloody hard work for starters and there was no real glory to be had driving through the mud in the centre circle. That was not glamorous or attractive to me. I wanted to score goals and grab the glory, but when he put me on the team sheet for the game at the City Ground I did not care what position he had given me, well that was until I realised Billy Bremner was playing at Hull in those days.

The flame colour of Billy's ginger hair might have not roared with the same intensity in those days as he was winding down his illustrious career, but he was still more than capable of leaving his calling card, an art-form he had perfected during his time as Don Revie's on-field general at Leeds United. Not that I was given any assistance from the manager in how to deal with the combative Scot. I was given no instructions whatsoever. He never said a solitary word to me. He did not even wish me good luck as it was my debut. He polled in at ten minutes to three after his game of squash at the squash club. It was not part of his make-up to sit me down and say 'Gaz relax and enjoy it'. To the Gaffer all that crap was a waste of breath.

It staggers me when I see some of the psycho babble managers and coaches indulge in now with their clip boards and magnetic markers. All those DVDs, set plays, scouting reports and pro-zone stats. Drawing lines here and making notes there. I am surprised players don't forget how to play the game. The Gaffer thought dossiers were tramps sleeping rough and he was brilliant at taking the pressure off. He was no great counsellor. He did not talk you down with words. That was not him. He knew you were probably tense and he relaxed you by not being there for ages in the dressing room before matches, filling your head full of nonsense.

That was the beauty of the Gaffer and Pete. They took all that responsibility away from you. That was their burden, not that you ever noticed them weighed down by any of it. They were masters at it. All they wanted me and the rest of the team to do was to go out and play football the way we could. Nothing else was required from us. They never said anything in the way of coaching or instructions to individuals before a game. I remember later in my Forest career the Gaffer catching Colin Barrett doing an impression of him.

Colin was giving it 'the ball is round and the grass is green now go out and kick it!' routine, mimicking the odd simple thought and sound bite the Gaffer used to give TV to explain what he said to his players before a game. It was Colin's take on the 'if God wanted us to play football in the sky he would have put grass on the clouds' routine. What he did not know at the time was that the Gaffer was within earshot.

He was in the right place at the right time to hear everything and everyone, but that did not include being in the dressing room hours before kick-off. I think he realised the damaging effect he might have had on people, being under their feet as they were preparing for games. If he had been in the dressing room for a long time before a game, what does he do? He would only be in the way and the fact he was not there gave us even more belief. He trusted us. We knew that he knew we could do it and that was great. It made us ten foot tall.

That became the norm for me the more I eventually got my feet under the table at Forest. It never seemed out of the ordinary, but that day it did catch me by surprise, because I was expecting some kind of pep-talk or slap on the back to put me at ease a little. He must have been able to tell I was nervous, but not a word and beyond that I don't really recall too much of the day I had dreamed of every day when I had been growing up and banging in goals for Attenborough and Clifton All Whites.

From a personal point of view it was an inauspicious affair. My debut for Forest passed me by and I can't remember a thing about it. All that slogging, all those hopes, all the knock backs for that precious 90 minutes of a professional football debut and I can't remember a bloody thing about it. I had spent so much time worrying about how it would go, whether I would be any good and, if not, would that be the end of me as a player. Get your first touch right. Don't be uptight. Relax. Don't be too extravagant. Keep it simple. These were all the instructions to myself. I had a million and one things going on in my head and the added complication of the best manager in the world simultaneously shouting instructions from the touchline. Compute what he is saying and relax! Forget it and I completely forgot the game.

I don't think I had any chances to score. I would certainly have remembered any glaring misses. In all it seems largely irrelevant now, but I do remember the crucial aspect. No one wants to make a losing debut and goals from Tony Woodcock and Peter Withe ensured mine was a far more enjoyable occasion and fortune must have been smiling on me in more ways than one that day. My shins were returned with barely a bruise on them -- Bremner was unable to play because of injury. But that was not the end of my good fortune, before a mad dash to the Cadland to get the beers in for a celebration.

After the game I was knackered and elated. All my mates had been there to see my debut. We had won and it had been an incredible experience that was about to get even better. The Gaffer made a beeline for me in the dressing room after the game and I thought I was about to get a pat on the back, or some kind of congratulatory morsel that would have made the day complete.

'Gaz, if I ever play you in midfield again, the chairman has told me I will get the sack'. That was my well-done-son-speech. Not very complimentary I know, but at least it meant my midfield days were over and even more reason to celebrate.

Unfortunately my first team experiences were over for the remainder of that season too as the Gaffer kept driving on his experienced players, chipping away at their bid to gain promotion to the First Division. I was not called upon for any more games that season, but I did get the welcome surprise of being called up for the squad for the end of season piss-up in Cala Millor, which turned out to be more than just a load of us letting off steam at the end of a tough campaign. We had more reason than we bargained for to get hammered, but we did not make the discovery until we were at 32,000 feet.

We were half way to Majorca when the pilot interrupted the game of three card brag at the back of the plane with an announcement and it wasn't your usual 'this is your captain speaking' message. 'I would just like to tell everyone on board the flight today that Bolton Wanderers have failed to beat Wolves this afternoon and therefore you have finished third in the Second Division and secured the final promotion place, congratulations'.

Beer was always on the agenda from the moment we boarded at East Midlands, now we had the champagne to go with it and it turned into a week of hard drinking at a club where we used to get fined for not going out to have a drink on the night before games! I was not even supposed to be on the trip. I had only played one game, hardly what you could consider a key contribution in the success and I have to admit I felt a bit of a fraud being there, but Sammy Chapman hated flying and I had been told three days earlier to go and get my passport as I was going to Cala Millor. Everyone was on the trip, including Brian's wife Barbara and the kids, including Nigel.

Cala Millor is on the east coast of Majorca, about an hour's drive from Palma de Mallorca and roughly translates means 'Better Bay'. I am surprised the Gaffer did not find somewhere that meant Best Bay, but it was his favourite summer retreat. He used it all the time he was in charge at Forest and the players loved it too – even if it almost claimed the lives of at least two players who went on to become England internationals and an integral part of the European Cup winning sides long before they had even announced themselves properly to the football world.

Whilst we were expected to do a little bit of club propaganda while out there and dine as a group with the management, mostly at a fabulous fish restaurant called The Shack, we had plenty of free time to amuse ourselves during the day and evening and it was after one late session that Viv Anderson very nearly found himself splattered all over the floor like a pavement pizza as the result of some crazy antics that fortunately he managed to survive and tell the tale. It could easily have ended in far more tragic circumstances, the final act being his funeral, minus his honour of being the first black player to represent England and his European Cup medals.

I had grown up playing against Viv in schoolboy football in Nottingham. He played for Clifton Athletic when I played for Clifton All Whites. We played against each other on a regular basis and we sometimes palled up when we came together at Forest along with another Nottingham lad Peter Wells, who was a young 'keeper on the staff at the City Ground at the time. Occasionally we'd spend lunch times in the Bench and Bar at the entrance to the Broadmarsh Shopping centre and later in the afternoon in a sports shop inside Broadmarsh.

A friend of ours owned the place and we were invited to play head-tennis over the racks of clothing to entertain the punters. It was a nice advertising gimmick for our mate and kept us out of trouble.

It was on the Majorca trip that I made a grisly discovery about Viv – he slept with his eyes open. Not a pretty sight and, trust me, a rather disturbing one. I think I was the only one who could put up with it, so I got lumbered with him.

Although we were very nearly not room mates for any extended period of time as the result of some of Viv's stupid, beer-fuelled antics just a few nights into the trip to Cala Millor and our stay at the Said Hotel. After another heavy session with the majority of the team I got back to our room to find Viv trying to climb across from our balcony into the balcony of the room next door. Now Viv had incredibly long legs which proved invaluable throughout his career in nicking the ball off wingers and flying forward on attacking raids. They earned him his nickname 'Spider'. That was where the arachnid comparisons ended. His legs were not made for leaping across balconies. Especially when we were six floors up and he certainly could not spin a web!

He was pissed and not really taking a great deal of notice of me, but somehow I managed to drag him back into the room before he ended up making a mess of the chairs and tables that were dotted around the pool down below. If he had fallen there is little doubt he would have died instantly and I still shudder to this day at how such a crazy prank could have gone completely pear-shaped. Viv dying would have been such a tragic waste and I often wonder how I would have explained the whole thing away to the Gaffer on my very first trip with the club. The good thing about it is no one saw it. There were no embarrassing newspaper reports of high jinks and no one was hurt.

If one narrow escape was not enough, the following day we hired a load of mopeds to go scooting around the island. It was just supposed to be a gentle jaunt around Majorca for a couple of hours, but that was not good enough for Tony Woodcock. He had aspirations of being Barry Sheene and thrashed the bike as hard as he could until he went hurtling headlong into a tree and smashed his moped to smithereens. He managed to walk away with barely a scratch on him, but we all had to have a whip-round to pay for the bike.

Two narrow escapes and Terry Curran made it a third when we were around the pool the following day. Terry was a bit of a wind-up merchant and he had spent most of the morning baiting 'Googie' which was our nickname for Peter Withe, after a female character called Googie Withers in the 70s prison drama series Within These Walls. Eventually Googie snapped and climbed off his sun-bed whereupon Terry threw him into the pool, inciting his drenched victim to chase him out of the hotel grounds. It was an absolutely baking hot mid-morning. Not the kind of temperatures for a slog around the island on foot, but Terry had pushed it too far.

As a winger, Terry was pretty quick and did not have much weight to carry, while Peter was strong as an ox and had a build to match. Lightning pace was certainly something he was not blessed with, but what he had in its place was a tremendous amount of stamina and a steadfast refusal to admit defeat. Googie was a stayer and there was no way he was going to let Terry off the hook as they were spotted exiting the grounds of the hotel. It was over an hour before they returned! Peter had chased Terry all around Cala Millor until they eventually returned back to the pool. Peter could have run another few laps around the resort but Terry was knackered, allowing Googie to exact his revenge and sling him in the pool for the stick he had been forced to suffer from Terry's sarcastic tongue.

Hangovers every day meant sobering up by the pool on a regular basis and it was a fantastic week to end a whirlwind couple of months, but if I thought my career at Nottingham Forest was going to be plain sailing from there on in I was sadly mistaken. The bubbles from the champagne up my nostrils were replaced by the stale odours of some football outposts as I did not kick a ball for the first team for the entirety of the following season and was confined to reserve team duties and massive bouts of frustration.

In between reserve team fixtures, whenever I got the chance I would sit and watch Woody and Peter Withe provide the spearhead for an assault on the First Division title that no one would have anticipated from a team that had just scraped into the top flight almost by default the previous season. It was not the most fulfilling experience for an aspiring rookie, watching two exceptional strikers dismantle First Division defences. Those were the days of only one substitute allowed and so I had to content myself with honing my skills in the stiffs and the dubious pleasure of getting up close and personal with BC in a manner few of his illustrious first team squad would have ever dreamed of.

I had retained my keen interest in squash and played regularly still and somehow the Gaffer got to find out about it. I am not sure how, but he knew everything about everyone who played for him. There were no secrets and he probably knew what colour socks we were going to wear each day, before we had chosen a pair out of the chest of drawers. Once he discovered I played squash that was it, he had me earmarked as his new playing partner and that might sound a privilege, but let me assure you, it was not.

The way it would work was fairly simple. He would let me go down to training and complete virtually the whole session and then, as regular as clockwork, ten minutes before everyone was allowed to pack up for the day and return to the ground an apprentice would come jogging over in my direction and utter the immortal words 'you're playing squash with the Gaffer in ten minutes'. It was never 'would you like to play squash?' Always an instruction and I would have to dash back to the ground and get myself sorted out.

There was never any time allowed to get a shower and get cleaned up. I used to have to sprint back up the banks of the Trent and get back to the dressing rooms in double quick time. The best I could hope for was to rub most of the mud off my legs and filthy training kit, before grabbing my squash gear and shifting my backside to the front of the ground where the Mercedes would be running and he would be looking at his watch. He would drive us over there and we would be straight on the court, which was where the fun began! Even though it was only a five-minute walk to the cricket ground, across Radcliffe Road and into the back of the Parr Stand and round to squash club, he insisted on taking the 'company car'.

Despite always complaining about having a dodgy knee, he was a bloody good sportsman and loved squash and tennis, but I was better than him. He knew it and I knew it, but I don't think I ever won a game! It was not that I was some pathetic brown-nose who let him win in the vain hope that might curry favour and get me in the first team. He was a terrible cheat and hated losing. So there was not a great deal I could do about it. The key strategy in squash after playing your shot is to get back to the T on the court, so you can control the rally. That positional advantage helps you dominate your opponent.

Obviously you are in a rather confined space, due to the nature of the game and how can I put this politely? Whenever I was attempting to manoeuvre myself towards the T and into the optimum position to make my next shot, I would somehow bump into this immovable object that went by the name of Clough. Or he would play his shot and accidently set up a personal road block on the exact route I needed to take to continue the rally. 'Would you like that point again son?' was his usual response when that occurred. He said it out of deference to the rules, but it was never a genuine offer and I knew it.

If I had said that I wanted the point replayed he would have said 'tough shit'. There was no such thing as a let when he was playing squash. Effectively I was left apologising for running into his racquet with my teeth and the point was his! It was a ritual humiliation I endured for an hour a couple of times a week. We had some great games and battles, but whenever it got to key points, or tight, I knew the offer of replaying the point was never far away. Cheating? He would have called it gamesmanship and he hated losing, especially to a carpet fitter.

Anyone thinking that I became one of his favourites because I was his chosen one on the squash court can forget that notion as well. It was a misconception I had knocked out of me at an early stage after the summons had come to get myself on the court one lunchtime. Even though I had trained in the morning and had a reserve team game at the City Ground against Derby County later that evening, he wanted to play squash and I had no choice. It was the usual frantic session of hard graft and being cheated out of points at Trent Bridge squash club and I thought he would take my extra workload into consideration for the reserve game. He must have known I was absolutely cream-crackered and only had a couple of hours to rest up before a 7.30 kick-off.

Reserve team games only ever attracted a handful of die-hard fans and Forest only ever opened the Main Stand for games because the demand for seats was hardly overwhelming. That was the reason there was always such a peculiar atmosphere because of the silence from the stands. On a Saturday afternoon in the First Division you could barely hear yourself think, such was the raucous nature of the crowds on the terraces. On a Wednesday night for the reserves you could hear blokes zipping up their flies in the toilet behind the stand. It was so quiet. You could hear that and one voice above everyone else. His master's voice, of course, the dulcet tones of BC would drown out anything else.

He rarely missed reserve games and could usually be spotted sitting in the directors' box of the main stand with his flat cap on and an overcoat. He certainly did not miss that night and I got the clearest reminder that I might be his squash partner, but that would not spare me the lash of his tongue. My legs were like concrete after all the graft I had put in earlier in the day and the first time the ball came up to me I failed to control it. 'Gaz, that's crap. Hold the bloody ball!' For the entire game I was under scrutiny and so much for my optimistic view that he would take it easy on me. He hammered me for the entire time I was on the pitch, his voice echoing around the empty stadium making me shudder every time he opened his mouth.

That was another lesson learned. Never presume anything. You just had to hold on tight, prepare yourself for any eventuality and enjoy the ride, but that was something I found increasingly hard to do in that second season as Forest were blazing a trail at the top of the table. There was only one substitute allowed at that time so there was no hope of getting on to the bench. I spent much of my time scrutinising the play of Withe and Woodcock, working out how they played with each other and what made them such a formidable partnership.

It was part of my education and study, just in case I was needed if either of them suffered an injury. As a Forest fan, watching the club rise from obscurity to the pinnacle of English football in the blink of an eye was incredible, but somehow it was not so pleasurable for me. I felt I was on the outside looking in. I wanted a taste of it, but all I was being fed was a diet of bland reserve team football while the rest were eating First Division caviar. My patience was being tested. I was restless and had this overwhelming sense of lack of progress and it was starting to get to me.

After months of finding my route to the first team blocked by Withe and Woodcock, I came within a whisker of cashing in my chips and calling it a day at Forest. I was not enjoying things and after one particular reserve team game at Sheffield Wednesday I had to be talked out of packing the whole game in. I was sat on the team coach, ready to return to Nottingham opposite Frank Clark, who had been playing that night. He found me shaking my head and looking really fed up with my lot. When he asked me what was wrong I just told him that I wondered whether I was cut out for the whole professional football thing. I was starting to have doubts about whether I could hack it. I could only see a very long dark tunnel because of the excellent form of Woody and Peter Withe. All the initial excitement of signing pro was starting to wear a little thin.

Frank had looked after me from the day I walked through the doors of the club and he was someone I respected because of his seniority and experience in the game. He was a top bloke and he just told me to keep my head down and keep working hard. I had to be patient. He was right and I knew I had to stick it out.

But when the first team began a run that would last 42 games unbeaten in the league, a record that was eventually beaten by Arsenal's Invincibles, it was hard to see any kind of light at the end of the tunnel and that eventually I would play a crucial part in that long undefeated sequence of matches.

4

THAT WAS THE WEEK THAT WAS
Liverpool and Jap sub sunk

'NO one has heard of this lad Birtles' were the words Richard Keys chose to describe my goal and Forest's first in the first leg of the European Cup first round against Liverpool at the City Ground on the night of September 13th, 1978. It was long before Rupert Murdoch reached for the Sky and revolutionised the way people watched football in this country and anywhere else for that matter. It was long before Keys moved to be one of his most respected and well known TV anchormen in the Murdoch satellite empire and it was the blinding light at the end of the tunnel I had been bemoaning would never illuminate my way under Clough.

'They fucking have now'. The response was instantaneous from Bill Shankly OBE, Liverpool's legendary manager. The gnarled Scot, raised in the Ayrshire mining town of Glenbuck, had spotted a few gems and polished them to a blinding sparkle in his time at Liverpool. That night in the press box he was alongside Keys as his analyst for the Battle of Britain, trying desperately to hide his obvious allegiances to the Red Machine he had created in the famous Anfield boot room. He was never one to mince his words and he might have offended a few listeners with the agricultural language that slipped past the censors, but it's hard to argue with the sentiment and Richard Keys can remind me of the story as many times as he likes. I never get tired of hearing it.

For two years I had been slogging away, trying to make an impact at Forest. I had been flogging myself trying to make the Gaffer choke on that Bovril gag he never tired of trotting out and at last, at long last, in the split second that it took me to steady myself and tap in Tony Woodcock's pass from about six yards, while Ray Clemence could only watch helplessly, everything I had dreamed of as a kid, smashed me straight between the eyes.

My head was about to explode. After all those balloons I volleyed between the pictures of Joe Baker and Ian Storey-Moore in my bedroom, before making my own crowd noises, sucking in to imitate a roar, whilst simultaneously trying to speak and give a running Match Of The Day, John Motson-type commentary, all the time milking the adulation of the fans. This was the real thing, magnified a million times.

There was no need for the artificial acoustics from me this time. The best part of the 38,318 crowd crammed into the City Ground that night were roaring my name. In the space of four games, I had progressed from the Midlands League and hammering down carpet gripper to the European Cup. That must be enough to make Roy of the Rovers look mundane. Enough to make his feats with Melchester Rovers look like a jobbing professional on the League Two circuit. I had just scored my first ever Forest goal, in only my third senior game in the bloody European Cup! I was black and blue all over my arms from the number of times I had to pinch myself.

It's incredible to think now that a few weeks earlier I was on the verge of leaving Forest to move to Mansfield Town! If my mood had been lacking optimism the previous season when Forest won the First Division, it had reached an all-time low by the start of the following season when I was not even included on the pre-season tour to Yugoslavia. Withe and Woodcock were still first choice and a young kid called Steve Elliott had emerged from the reserves and was taken in my place.

He was a Geordie lad and the Gaffer had been pushing him for England under-21s and had named him as sub in two of the three games on the tour while I was left kicking my heels back in Nottingham. I thought the writing was on the wall and that I would have to move on. That was certainly the way Mansfield Town read the situation too and they made an offer to sign me and were ready to pretty much double my wages to £110-per week.

At that stage the season had started and Forest had set about defending the title they had won the previous May and I was leaning more and more towards the idea of Mansfield when unforeseen circumstances changed the whole picture. Peter Withe thought he would chance his arm and ask for a pay rise after playing such an integral part in winning the league title. His demands were hardly astronomical, in fact the rumours were that he was only looking for an extra tenner a week! It sounds pathetic and ridiculous I know to ask for such an inconsequential amount.

It is hard to imagine anyone saying no to an extra £10-per-week in the pay packet, but don't forget this was Clough and Taylor he was dealing with. In would have come as no surprise if Peter had gone in all full of bluster and certain he was going to get his raise, after all, he had just played an integral part in helping the club win the Championship title at the first attempt. He got his pay rise, but only after he realised he was being sold to Newcastle United for £200,000, a handsome profit on the £43,000 they had paid Birmingham City for him a couple of seasons earlier.

At last there seemed a chink of light at the end of that seemingly never-ending tunnel and it was a straight choice between Steve Elliott and myself as to who would get the chance to step up. Steve was a fantastic goal-scorer and had built himself quite a reputation and BC fancied he could fill the void left by Withe's departure. All of a sudden Mansfield seemed attractive again, but for all Elliott's potential, he had a terribly unlucky run in the side, hitting the post and just about anything else without actually hitting the back of the net. His first four games were all 0-0 draws and then we managed ten goals in two games, including six in a friendly against Mansfield, ironically, but he did not manage to trouble the scorers once.

Just as I had pretty much made up my mind to leave for Field Mill, the Gaffer decided he could no longer persevere with Elliott and the Friday afternoon before we were due to play Arsenal at the City Ground the team sheet went up. There was no word of warning to me, but I scanned down the list to number nine where the words Garry Birtles had been scribbled. After all the waiting and wondering I was finally going to make my First Division debut against Arsenal. I had to dash to the nearest toilets as the nerves kicked in sooner than anticipated.

There are very few things I remember about the day. It was such a blur of excitement, fear and stomach-churning nerves. I do recall my parents being there and most of my mates from the Cadland as well as my wife Sandra, her parents and her brother David. I also vividly remember getting my introduction to life at the top within seconds of the match starting. Willie Young, the Arsenal centre-half who was to become a colleague at Forest and a very close friend, came clattering through the back of me as I went to collect my first pass and he hit me so high I got a lovely aerial view of the River Trent and Market Square in the centre of Nottingham!

Central defenders in those days had a licence to maim and it was pretty much rubber stamped by the officials. Referees even went up to well known rough necks prior to kick off and said 'You're allowed one bad one today, make it a good one!' Regulations outlawing the tackle from behind belonged to a civilised galaxy light years away and strikers may as well have worn targets on the backs of their socks, knees and shorts for that matter to help give a centre half a choice as to where he preferred to leave his six stud marks.

My job was to hold the ball up. I knew Willie's first tackle was coming and I couldn't do much about it. The rules of engagement were simple: Show no fear and show no pain. Take it and get up. So up I got, gave Willie a big smile and ran back into my position to make him have to chase after me. There was no way anyone was going to intimidate me out of the game on a debut I had waited over a season for. We ended up winning the game 2-1 thanks to a penalty from John Robertson and another goal from Ian Bowyer. I did not make the score sheet, but I made an impression.

After the match I could barely haul myself into the showers I was that tired. I had run myself into the ground, mostly on pure adrenalin, but the Gaffer made a beeline for me and told me I would be the first name on his team sheet for the Liverpool game three days later, when Forest were due to make their first ever appearance in the European Cup. Was he serious? Or was it his attempt at humour. I was not sure at the time, but I did not really care because I was still so high on making my First Division debut and I wanted to enjoy that before I even started to turn my attentions to playing against Bob Paisley's European champions.

I remember at the time of the draw for the first round of the competition everyone at the club was digging out their passports. Everyone in the squad had a favourite destination and a favourite team to play against. Giants like Real Madrid or Juventus were the popular choices for first round opposition. The European Cup was supposed to be an adventure, visiting places we had not seen before and squaring up against opponents whose names we had never heard of and couldn't pronounce. It was the journey into the unknown that provided the romance of the whole thing and the prospect of a few beers in the sun.

Getting paired with Liverpool in the first round was the ultimate slap in the face. It was such an anti-climax. There was going to be no passports. No foreign beers. No plane trip. No hotel. No sun and no experience of another culture. The only culture waiting for us at Anfield was the culture of hate from Scouse fans when we had slogged up the M1 and across the M62. We felt cheated. Our European adventure was not going to get as far as Liverpool docks. How shit was that?

They had beaten Club Brugge in May to retain their European crown. Kenny Dalglish had scored the goal at Wembley and I remembered watching it. There was a lot of bravado amongst us, but deep down we were disappointed. We had just taken their league title and beaten them in the League Cup but this was different altogether. Liverpool were the Kings of Europe at that time and were desperate to teach us a lesson for having the temerity to nick the First Division title out of the Anfield trophy cabinet.

Liverpool fans despised us. They saw us as the upstarts and at the time they could not beat us, despite the fantastic team they had. We had the Indian sign over them and they disliked it intently. Even the British media seemed against us at that time. They looked down their noses at us. There was a perception that we did not have the style, flair and class of Liverpool. We were a rag-tag and bobtail outfit, put together on a tight budget with no tradition and no history and we had a brash manager who had the ability to rub people up the wrong way. This was Liverpool's opportunity to expose us as one-hit wonders in front of the watching nation. That was how it was played out in the newspapers leading up to the first leg.

The Gaffer stayed true to his word for the game at the City Ground. Whether I was the first name he wrote on the team sheet, I am not sure, but I was on it, alongside Tony Woodcock for the first round, first leg tie of a European Cup game. Three years earlier, my last amateur game was for Long Eaton Rovers, a local Sunday side down at Victoria Embankment against an all black team called Clumber K and B. Stale bitter fumes were so powerful in the changing rooms even the whiff of the liniment being slapped all over all shapes and sizes struggled for supremacy and here I was in my third professional game contesting the giant trophy coveted from Milan to Madrid and Benfica to Barcelona.

That September night will remain with me as one of the most amazing of my career. It was a sultry late summer evening drenched with late sun-light and laden with expectation. There was the most intense buzz I had ever known at the City Ground and over 38,000 were crammed in there to see if Clough, who like the Fairy Godmother, had waved his magic wand and transformed the careers of John Robertson, Martin O'Neill, Viv and Tony Woodcock and his team could defy Liverpool again and the expectations of a nation that pretty much to a man had decided we did not have a prayer.

As a rookie I got all the usual banter you might have expected on the pitch. No one had heard of me at Liverpool and there was some piss-taking coming in my direction from more than the odd member of the Liverpool team. I half expected it. Their players did not hate us like the fans did. There was a grudging respect for what we had achieved, but I got the sense this was pay-back time, but they were not prepared for what we had to throw at them and fortunately I was switched on enough to prompt Shanks into that unfortunate outburst over the airwaves when Woody squared the simplest of tap-ins for me in front of the Trent End.

It was the sort of chance you would see gobbled up on the Embankment every Sunday morning by players still hung-over from the night before and blindfold. It was routine, but it was everything to me. Hollywood script writers would have found the idea too fanciful. Garry Birtles, scoring his first senior goal against Liverpool in a game of such magnitude was beyond the realms of dreams. I still remember the way the ground erupted, drowning out the senses and it was only when the cheers subsided that I was snapped back to reality.

'One goal won't be enough to take back to Anfield'. It was a statement spat out with contempt and derision in equal measure. The cocksure nature of Phil Thompson, the Liverpool central defender, was a jolt to the sense of euphoria. It was not arrogance. It was merely a statement of fact as far as the England centre half was concerned. It was pretty much a case of enjoy your moment in the September sun Birtles, because no one will remember you after the return leg has been sorted out. It shocked me and put a little bit of fear into my mind at the same time. We might have had one of the best back fours and the best goalkeepers in England at the time, but had we got enough?

It looked like it was going to have to be enough as time ticked away when I managed to get beyond Thompson with about ten minutes remaining after our left back Colin Barrett had begun the move in our half. I could hear the Gaffer's words, that relentless ranting on to his players: 'Get in the box, get in the box'. It must have driven me on towards the byline and when I managed to cross, there was Woody to head down for Colin, who'd continued his run forward to pounce with a volley that seared past Clemence. Cue pandemonium. People on Trent Bridge and in the Lace Market must have felt the aftershock from the reaction inside the ground.

It might have been hard to hear myself think at the time, but I could not resist the impulse swelling up inside. The first person I had to run past on the way to re-start the game was Thompson. Over the subsiding roars I shouted: 'Will two be enough then Phil?' I could not help myself and I was completely out of order. A young upstart like me should not have been saying things like that to a respected England international, but I was high on pure adrenalin. I could not resist. His face was like thunder. So much for not getting the chance to dust off our passports. We had given ourselves the ideal platform to maintain our dominance over Liverpool and their fans hated us even more.

Possibly the only club they despised more than ours at the time was Manchester United and just to round off my whirlwind introduction to life at the cutting edge of the professional ranks I stayed in the team for a 1-1 draw against Manchester United in front of 55,000 at Old Trafford. Three games in a week, Arsenal, Liverpool and United. Meteoric rise doesn't do it justice and at last I felt like I had finally made it, even if the nagging spectre of the return trip to Liverpool for the second leg was hanging over me and the rest of the team.

Liverpool were capable of amazing feats at Anfield. It was a legendary place revered by the red half of Merseyside. The fans believed it had super powers that would render opponents helpless and many bigger clubs and bigger names than ours had been swatted away or sucked in and spat out by the Kop, hypnotised by the sea of scarves and the haunting power of their anthem You'll Never Walk Alone. That swirling sea of bodies and the passion within had helped turn games on their head and it would be fair to say there was still a certain amount of trepidation, even though we had such an impressive cushion from the first leg and had not conceded the away goal.

We drove up to Liverpool on the day of the game. We left reasonably early and half-way through the journey BC shouted to Albert the bus driver to get him off the motorway because he was sick of it and he wanted some fresh air. That is after he had shouted at him to spark up a fag because he 'liked the smell'. Albert must have been the only bus driver ferrying First Division footballers around that was allowed to smoke. It probably made it easier for him to cope with being told to drive on hard shoulders, ignore motorway cones and various other transgressions he was forced into when the Gaffer decided he wanted to get home, or to his destination.

We were in the middle of nowhere on the M62 when Albert pulled off the motorway and we all were told to get off the coach. We went for a short stroll, to stretch our legs and get a break from the traffic. It must have been a bizarre sight, us in our blazers walking in the middle of nowhere on our way to face the music at Anfield but the Gaffer pulled a masterstroke of psychology later on when he decided to make ar statement.

We were still in those blue blazers and grey flannels and he sent us out over an hour before kick off to go and walk in front of the Kop as a team. He just told every one of us to get out there and stroll about in the goalmouth in front of a seething mass of Liverpool fans. You can imagine the reception that awaited us.

A vast array of missiles was chucked in our direction and I remember dodging oranges, apples and all manner of food. But for Brian Clough it was simple. He sent us out there to make it clear we respected them and that we knew all about their fabled powers, but we did not give a shit. It was effectively us saying, you can sing Walk On until you are fucking hoarse, but it won't make any difference. We are here to knock you out of the European Cup and there is fuck all you can do about it. We fronted them up and it unified us even more.

There was no way they were going to put us out that night. This was our night and we were not intimidated. The sight of us strolling around laughing and joking just riled them all the more. All sorts of stuff was hurled in our direction, including a tennis ball, which fell at the feet of John Robertson around the penalty area. Quick as a flash, Robbo flicked up the ball and volleyed into the top corner of the net Clemence was going to have to defend at some stage. Have that!

If Robbo's control and volley was instantaneous, so was the response. The Kop broke out into applause. They might have hated us, but they knew we were bloody good. It was a grudging respect, which is more than I had for the famous walk down on to the Anfield pitch. That area when you go down the steps and the This Is Anfield sign above you was part of Liverpool folklore. Every one of their players used to touch it on the way out on to the pitch. All it was was a little plaque. It had no special powers and it cut no ice with me. I remember standing there and watching them touch it and I just thought 'so fucking what?'

Liverpool threw the kitchen sink at us, the washing machine, dish washer, the tumble drier, juicer, food blender and the ironing board for good measure that night. We knew it was coming and they did not disappoint, but in just the same way we had stood resolutely in front of the Kop, we stood shoulder to shoulder on the pitch as well and the back four, led by Kenny Burns and Larry Lloyd, were amazing that night. They headed and kicked pretty much everything, repelling all Liverpool had to chucked our way and on the rare occasions the back four got breached Peter Shilton stood there like the Incredible Hulk.

Sir Matt Busby refused to pay £275,000 for Shilton just before BC made him the most expensive goalkeeper in history at the time. The legendary

Manchester United manager reckoned Shilton was 'too costly and goalkeepers do not win you games'. Sir Matt did not get too many things wrong in his illustrious time at Old Trafford, but that was a stinker of a call. Shilton made the goals behind him look the size of Subbuteo goals. Strikers running through, bearing down on him were almost already defeated by his sheer size and presence before they got to see the whites of his eyes.

If the intimidation did not get them, they spent so long trying to locate some kind of gap in the Subbuteo goals behind Shilton that while they were searching, his stealth got him into a position where he was bearing down on the striker and any kind of gap disappeared. In blind panic the striker would just shoot, cross his fingers and hope for the best and Shilton would throw out a big paw and swat the ball away like King Kong smashing airplanes on top of the Empire State building.

I remember scoring one goal against him, after he had left Forest and was at Southampton. I still regard that as one of the best I ever scored, just because it was past Shilts. It was then and still is now a non contest for me when it comes to the debate that raged at the time over him and Clemence. He was the best and I could never understand that nonsense about the two of them switching for England during that period. The managers at the international set-up at that time could not make up their minds and I could never see why.

Ray was bloody good. An exceptional 'keeper, but he was nowhere near Shilts' level. If the Gaffer had got the England job when he went for that interview, Shilton would have ended up with nearly 200 caps and David Beckham would have got nowhere near him! There would have been no fudging the issue on who was the best. A decision would have been made and it would have been the right one. There would have been no sharing duties.

If Sir Matt decided against it, the Gaffer thought he had got a bargain with Shilton and coughed up £250,000 without batting an eyelid and we were glad he did. Shilton was our insurance policy and the longer the game went on the more agitated and heated the whole thing became. We got on well with the Liverpool players, lots of us mixed together at international level. They had a lot of respect for us and it was mutual, but they just could not find a way through and the atmosphere became more horrible as the game progressed.

My Dad and several of my mates were in the Forest section of the crowd that night. They had ball bearings, darts, coins and all sorts thrown at them. Fortunately all the people I knew escaped injury. None of that was highlighted at the time. There was no Fifa investigation into the despicable antics of the Liverpool fans, but when the dust had settled we did not give a shit. We had beaten them. We had knocked the European Cup holders out at the very first hurdle and had not even conceded a goal!

The euphoria in Nottingham was to be expected and I don't think we brought too many of our own drinks in Madisons, Uriah Heep or any of the other clubs and wine bars we always used to race back to after games for quite some time, but the rest of the country did not share the same levels of approval of our win as our own fans. For some reason the media and all the po-faced columnists of the day took the view what we had achieved was some kind of travesty of justice. We were accused of doing our country a disservice. Can you believe that?

Their argument was a simplistic one. After winning the competition for the previous two seasons, Liverpool knew exactly what was required to achieve success. The self-appointed experts of the game felt Paisley's team were capable and had all the ingredients required to record a treble of English success and the common consensus was we had been fortunate and that at some stage in the very near future that good luck would run out and we had no chance of carrying the England flag all the way to the final. We were somehow cast in the role of villains! We did not give a damn. We were through and they were spitting mad. That just added to the sense of achievement.

Our reward for causing such indignation in Liverpool and Fleet Street was a pairing with a genuine legend. Ferenc Puskas, the Real Madrid striker and member of the Magic Magyars, was the manager of the Greek side AEK Athens. He was the only person we knew though. We did not have a clue about any of the opponents who were blocking our progress to the next stage of the competition. Apparently Peter Taylor used to go on the odd scouting mission to run the rule over European opponents. Either that or BC would send his trusted scout Maurice Edwards to take a look, but that was it. He certainly never went to watch opponents in action.

It seems amazing to think of now, in the days of pro-zone, DVDs, team meetings, pattern of play, set piece organisation and individual dossiers on what your direct opponent has for breakfast, lunch and dinner and how many sugars he has in his tea, but in all my time at Forest, throughout that whole European adventure, not once did we have a team meeting to tell us a solitary thing about the team we were playing against. I was never pulled to one side and told whether the centre back marking me was strongest on his left side or his right, whether he had a limp, a dodgy eye or anything. We did not even know the colour of the opposition kit until we trotted out onto the pitch.

Well at least by drawing AEK we had to reach for the passports. We were going to get a nice hotel to stay in and some sun on our backs and the odd foreign beer, but we did not have a clue what we were going to come up against. The evening of the game was sweltering on a sapping pitch. I managed to get one of the goals and John McGovern the other and the 2-0 first leg advantage was stretched into a 7-2 aggregate win after the return leg. This European lark was easy and mid-way through November in 1978 we could put the competition to bed until March the following year and a third round tie with Grasshoppers of Zurich.

In between, games came thick and fast. Our league form suffered a little bit and Liverpool at least had some satisfaction in ending our 42 game unbeaten run in the league, just after we had completed a calendar year without defeat with a 0-0 home draw against Queens Park Rangers. We also managed to make our customary progress to the League Cup final, which we had won the previous season defeating Liverpool, and I scored twice in a 3-1 aggregate semi-final win over Watford to set up my first trip to Wembley.

That was in the days when the League Cup was a trophy regarded as worth winning. Not like it became in the early 2000s when Sir Alex Ferguson, Arsene Wenger and other leading managers sent out youth sides. Mind you, winning the Pork Butchers League Cup would have been just as important to BC. He loved the smell of the polish needed to shine silverware and Forest spent as much on the stuff as they did on me during his time in charge.

I certainly wanted to win the League Cup and so did every other member of our squad, but we were not done too many favours by the Football League at the time in terms of scheduling that or any other of our matches. It would certainly not happen now. There would be up-roar from managers and players and the PFA if clubs were forced to deal with the kind of ridiculous fixture lists we had back then. In my first season at Forest we played 76 games!

If you want an idea of what it was like just take a look at our fixture list for March 1979.

Saturday March 3 – Ipswich Town (a)

March 7 – Grasshopper Zurich (h) European Cup 3rd round first leg

March 10 – Everton (a)

March 14 – Norwich (h)
March 17 – Southampton League Cup final Wembley
March 21 – Grasshopper Zurich European Cup 3rd round second leg (a)
March 24 – Coventry City (h)
March 28- Chelsea (h)
March 31 – Bolton Wanderers (h)

Nine games in 20 days, which included two crucial European Cup ties and the little matter of a Wembley final. No one batted an eyelid back then at the number of games on crap pitches in shit conditions. You were just told to get on with it and we never got any sympathy from our own boss. In fact, when we did not have games midweek, he often found that to be a good time to add to the workload! We went on all kinds of crazy friendly fixtures and played in testimonials. Earlier that season we had been to Dynamo Zagreb for a friendly in December as well as West Bromwich Albion and Exeter of all places.

Grasshopper were a good team and had a striker called Claudio Sulser who that season ended up getting nominated with me for a European award from a top Italian football magazine at the time. He was highly skilled and very dangerous, but we ended up winning the first leg 4-1 thanks to a couple of late goals. I had opened the scoring and Robbo grabbed another of his regular penalties, before Larry Lloyd and Archie Gemmill made the evening look far more comfortable than it had been. It was just the kind of result we wanted to set us up for the task of beating Southampton and retain the League Cup. How we managed to achieve that after the way we spent the previous evening 'preparing' still makes me wonder.

I have never tried to hide the fact that we loved a beer or two. We were one of the few teams in the league that got fined for not going out and sinking a few in the build up to games. It was part of our make-up as a club. It was the way we did things, but that night our pre-match livener was even more than I had bargained for. We stayed at the same hotel England used for Wembley games and we got down there nice and early the day before the game and were told to check into our rooms and report back downstairs in about half an hour.

Viv and myself went and dumped our gear and checked out the facilities before returning downstairs at the appointed time and we were all milling around in the reception area when we were told to go to a private room out of the way. It had been reserved for us for the evening and we would not be disturbed, which was just as well really, because when we got in the room, we were told that we could order whatever drinks we wanted, bitter, lager, champagne – you named it, you drank it.

The Gaffer and Pete had us in stitches telling stories from their early days at Hartlepools. PT really did make the Gaffer laugh, real belly laughs.

Less than 24 hours before a major cup final, we were throwing beer down our necks and having a right good piss up. Club dieticians all over the world would have reeled away in disgust and disbelief, but there we were, every single member of the squad tucking in with gusto as part of the Gaffer's plans to help us all relax. It relaxed us all right, so much so that my legs did not work and when Archie Gemmill wanted to bail out and go up to his room earlier than everyone else, he was told he was not allowed.

Archie had a pre-match routine of having a bath on the night before a game and had a sour face on him that would have curdled milk because he was ordered to stay with the rest of the crew, but BC made him wait for another ten minutes before we were all told to call it a night and go and get some sleep. Archie was furious, but everyone had to stick together. Presumably we all had to depart at the same time to help each other focus and get to our rooms!

I was so pissed I could not climb the stairs and I fell over and was crawling around on all fours on the way up to my room. I am not sure all the others were as inebriated but I had made the most of the invitation to have a few and had drunk more than my fair share. Suffice to say, I woke up on the morning of the final with a raging hangover and I don't think I was the only one feeling like shit either. Mind you the freezing cold and the snow the next day on that March morning shocked us back into some form of human life.

They had to clear the snow from the pitch at Wembley and it was all piled up around the edge of the pitch. But if the pitch was clear, you could not say the same for our heads, still muddled by alcohol and it took some time for the effects of the lager to wear off, which is why we played like amateurs in the first half against Southampton. It was the equivalent of a Sunday morning side going out on the lash on a Saturday night as a bonding exercise and we found ourselves 1-0 down in a game we were supposed to walk, according to the bookies.

Wembley was a massive occasion for me. Getting in the side and playing European Cup games was an adrenalin rush, but the Twin Towers of the old stadium was something else. It was the home of English football, the venue for so many famous occasions and it was my first chance to savour the occasion. The League Cup final then meant something too.

MY MAGIC CARPET RIDE

It was not a competition for Arsenal and Manchester United to give their kids some experience. It was a trophy that all clubs wanted to get their hands on, even if it did not carry the same kudos and tradition as the FA Cup.

There was no way I was going back to Nottingham with an even more painful hangover of failing to win my first ever medal and when the haze of the lager finally started to clear for most of us, we clicked into the kind of gear that had seen us win the league the previous season, but not before we had been given an almighty bollocking at half-time.

The Gaffer was never usually one for big speeches at half-time, but on this occasion he was furious with the way we had played. He laid into all of us and a mixture of that and a more sober team did the trick and we flew in the second half. On a personal note it was pleasing to play such a vital part in securing the trophy for a second season in succession. I scored two of the goals that day, but will never lose the feeling that I was robbed of the kind of milestone few players can boast about.

I should have left Wembley with the match ball as well as a winner's medal that day. I actually scored four goals in the final, but two of them were chalked off for offside. One was dubious, but the other I will take to my grave as being a goal. I went round their 'keeper Terry Genoe and he never stopped before I tapped the ball into an empty net. No one will ever convince me that the linesman made the correct call on that one. I have seen it too many times to mention and it still rankles with me. I know I should be content with winning the thing, but strikers are a greedy bunch and I only ever scored one other hat-trick for Forest.

Although I did well to leave with my medal at all. If you watch the video of us collecting medals and tankards at the end, all you can see is me bobbing up and down. I held the tankard alright. Probably because I was good at holding a pint pot, but I dropped my medal and it was rolling about on that balcony and I could not pick it up. I looked a right idiot.

Victory at least soothed the personal sense of injustice I harboured, but we did not exactly have much chance to celebrate in the proper manner, because Grasshoppers and the return leg was only four days away. We might have had a handy cushion from the first leg, but I knew and so did the rest of the team that we were flattered by the 4-1 scoreline from the first leg and there was a European Cup semi-final place hanging in the balance.

Grasshoppers second leg was one of the toughest games we played in the competition and those late goals in the game at the City Ground came in handy before we finally emerged with a 1-1 draw and a place in the last four of the tournament. The draw for the semi-final paired us against the strongest other team left in the competition and the one, if I am honest, we were hoping to avoid. Cologne was the last of the three potential opponents left at that stage who we wanted to draw, but fate decreed we would have to face the Bundesliga Champions and play at home in the first leg, where we knew we needed a healthy lead to take back to Germany.

If the pressure on us to get a good result in front of our own fans was not bad enough, we had the added handicap of being without Kenny Burns and Viv Anderson for the crucial tie on what could only be described as a paddy field of a pitch on the banks of the Trent. There was so much water and mud on the ground, you could barely see grass and having two cogs missing from our back four, which had been so resolute throughout, was something we could have done without.

I don't know if it was the occasion, the strength of the German team, the loss of Burns and Anderson or the awful state of our own pitch, but our dreams of making it to Munich for the final looked like they had sunk in the mud as we conceded two early goals and were completely taken by surprise by the Germans. Belgian international Roger Van Gool and German international Dieter Muller knocked the wind out of our sails and all that hard work at Anfield months earlier looked to have been for nothing. Over 40,000 at the City Ground certainly thought our number was up.

If we were not prepared for the way they came flying at us, they were less prepared for the incredible manner in which we fought back. Robbo was gliding over the mud, while everyone else in the German side seemed to be sinking in quicksand and Archie Gemmill had so much energy and was so light on his feet, he ran through the puddles without making a splash. It really was shit or bust and there was no way we were going down without a fight.

I grabbed a goal back to continue my run of scoring in every round so far and was involved in the build-up for further goals from Ian Bowyer and Robbo as we turned the tie on its head. It was only a slender lead to take back to Germany, but it was better than a two-goal deficit. Well that was how it looked until we were hit by a sucker punch late in the game, which gave national newspaper headline writers the kind of dream moment they yearned for as they sat at their desks in Fleet Street waiting for the outcome of the match.

The longer the game went on the worse the pitch became and that played right into the hands of Cologne substitute Yasuhiko Okudera. On any decent surface Shilts would have saved his 25-yard shot with his eyes shut, but the ball took a weird bounce in front of him and made him look like a novice as Cologne levelled the tie. Shilts copped some flak for it, but not from me, but we woke to headlines the next day like FOREST SUNK BY JAPANESE SUB.

Well before the morning papers landed on the doormat, an overwhelming air of negativity enveloped the ground, among the fans and members of the press corps. Losing three away goals and not winning the tie was seen as a disastrous result and one we simply could not hope to get away with when we travelled to Cologne. Effectively our European Cup adventure was over, even though we still had a game to play.

Everyone was writing us off and the Gaffer was stunned by the negative attitude of the media questioning in the immediate aftermath of the game. No one could find a positive in our performance and he was copping the brunt of it. Typically, he looked straight into the lens of a BBC man's camera and said: "We have to go to Germany now and win. I hope nobody's stupid enough to think we won't do it."

The Gaffer's bravado was legendary and we rarely had cause to doubt him, but I have to admit, on this occasion, his oracle-like status was under question. We were a disappointed and negative dressing room soon after the final whistle. We were down and there were some chins on the floor that would put his magic and our resolve to one of the most fearsome tests. Not that it seemed to bother PT. He was one of the funniest men in the world, even though he did not realise it and we could always bank on him lifting us when we needed it. He would have raised the mood on the Titanic and from the moment he got back in the dressing room our mood changed.

For the first time Taylor might have seen a shred of doubt in the minds of players who had made winning a habit. Did it shock him? Did it shake his sense of belief in the team he had helped assemble and take to the brink of the European Cup final? Did it hell. All he could say was 'there is nothing to worry about. We are going to beat this lot. Not a problem'. He was absolutely convinced of the fact we were going to the final.

So much so that he took confidence to a new level well before the return leg kicked off in Cologne. He was adamant we would win and put his money where his mouth was. At least that is how Maurice Edwards tells the story. Maurice recounts that he put a large bet at 4-1 to win £1,000 for Forest to prevail in the Mungersdorfer Stadium. No wonder PT had a smile wider than the Trent that night.

By the time the return leg came around our mood had changed from resignation to indignation. We did not spend too much time licking our wounds after we had read reports in the Nottingham Evening Post, written by Forest reporter Trevor Frecknall, that the Cologne players were allegedly drinking champagne on the return flight home. They thought they had done it. They thought they had booked their place in the final and were going to get the chance to win the greatest club competition on their own soil, with the final being staged in Munich. It was as if they had started ordering the Weiss beers in over-sized Steins.

The Germans have that arrogance about them on a football pitch. It was what made them such a bloody good national team and helped them win World Cups. I always admired that sense of self-belief, but when I was on the receiving end it was not quite so admirable. It stuck in my throat and every other throat in the Forest dressing room and it just inspired us to teach them a fucking lesson they would never forget. Arrogance is one thing, complacency is another thing entirely.

If drinking champagne was bad enough on the plane, matters got progressively worse as the second game ticked closer and our anger was fuelled further by Dieter Muller, the Cologne striker, who we found out had been mouthing off in the German press telling everyone that they would be going through to the final and they were confident. That was just an added incentive, but it got even better for us when we arrived at the stadium a couple of hours before kick-off and saw notices all over the place which we had half an idea what they meant. Just to be certain PT had the idea of getting them translated and it confirmed our suspicions. The posters were notices of ticketing arrangements for the final and when they would be going on sale!

Talk about putting your towels out on the sun-beds. What a fucking cheek. It transpired Cologne had booked hotels for the final too and it was all too much. Whatever happened that night in the second leg, whether we made it through or not, Muller was not going to be playing in the final. Larry Lloyd had made his mind up about that. It did not take much to upset the big man on the pitch. He is the only player I know to have been substituted during the national anthems before a game!

We were playing in Canada against Vancouver Whitecaps in a friendly and he refused to pull up his socks as they were playing the Canadian national anthem. It caused a commotion among all the dignitaries who were present for the game on one of our regular jaunts around the globe and the

Gaffer dealt with it the only way he could, by deciding to substitute him before we had even tossed the coin before kick-off.

Lloydy hated friendlies, but he hated losing more and he resolved that Muller was going to get it that night, no matter what happened. He was a man on a mission and he sorted out the German striker good and proper. There was nothing naughty. There was nothing off the ball. There were no elbows. That was not necessary. Larry just kept smashing into him and whacking him. Every time the ball came anywhere near Muller, Larry just took it as target practise and Muller did not fancy it. He had a big mouth and plenty to say for himself, but he did not have the balls to back it up and he limped off injured after 20 minutes with his tail between his legs.

That really upset the Germans and his team mates could see one of their star players had been intimidated out of the game. It got to the rest of them too. It was a crucial victory struck by Lloydy which made the Cologne fans choke on their Bratwurst and you could sense all the cockiness subside from the Cologne players too. From that point on we knew we had them, but we still needed that goal to get through.

Ian Bowyer scored a few goals during his career for Forest but he got the most important one of his life that night, stooping to send a diving header, from my cross, past the Cologne goalkeeper and send us through to the final. The winner was scored by a player nicknamed 'Bomber'. After we had been sunk by a Japanese sub in the first leg, the tabloid headline writers were on another gleefully nostalgic trip back down memory lane to the Second World War.

5

CHAMPIONS OF EUROPE
The road from Mansfield to Munich

AFTER silencing the best part of 60,000 in Cologne the celebrations were brief thanks to the wonders of the Football League fixture computer and the Gaffer deciding to take us to The Dell for his good mate Laurie McMenemy's testimonial game.

Including the semi-final success, in the build up to the biggest game of our lives we played the ridiculous amount of 10 games in 28 days! That included fulfilling a fixture that the Notts County Football Association could not even bother to postpone to assist their premier team in the county to climb to the pinnacle of Europe. Can you believe that lovely Mr Terry Annable – the one who banned me for six weeks as a teenager – wanted to jeopardise our mission to win the European Cup!

It's laughable, but the stuffed shirts in their little office in the centre of Nottingham ordered that we had to play the County Cup final before we set off to Germany. So that was one European Cup semi-final, seven league games, one friendly (god only knows why the Gaffer agreed to that at that stage of the season) and a trip to Field Mill to face Mansfield Town in the Nottinghamshire County Cup. So when do you think we should fit that particular game in? Given the fact we were playing nearly every other three days there were not too many windows of opportunity. So with the final in Munich's Olympic Stadium scheduled for May 30, we travelled to Mansfield's ground a week before we were going to face Malmo in the most important game we would ever play.

You might still be shaking your heads trying to compute that information, but it is true. Mansfield Town v Nottingham Forest in the Nottinghamshire County Cup took place on May 23 in front of 9,165 and anyone thinking the Gaffer would spare his players from the risk of collecting injuries that would put them out of the final have not been paying much attention to what kind of bloke the man who transformed the fortunes of Nottingham Forest really was. To underline his character just take a look at the team that played against Mansfield that day. The penny might finally drop.

Shilton; Anderson, Burns, Lloyd, Bowyer; Francis, McGovern, O'Hare, Robertson; Woodcock, Birtles. Sub: Clark

If you want a more contemporary example imagine Sir Alex Ferguson about to head off for the European Cup final against Chelsea in 2008 and a week before the game, Rooney, Ronaldo, Vidic, Ferdinand, Van Der Saar and the rest were all forced by the Manchester Football Association to play against Stockport County a week before taking on their Premier League rivals for the Champions League final. Just imagine how red Fergie's face would have gone in his rage to complain against the ridiculous bureaucracy of it all. Not everyone always finds themselves falling into line to agree with the Knight of Old Trafford, but on an occasion such as that, it would be fair to say Fergie would have plenty of supporters in his argument.

Did we argue? Did BC kick up a stink? Only with any member of his side that complained about having to play such a low priority match. Even Trevor Francis, our million pound man, was not spared. It was another trophy to win and Forest paid more money for tins of Brasso than they did for me during his time in charge. In his mind it was the perfect way to get the stiffness out of our limbs and blow a few cobwebs away before we headed to Munich. Mansfield were no Malmo, but we ran out 3-1 winners thanks to goals from Lloyd, Francis and Robertson. Finally we could put our feet up and try to get some rest before we tackled our 76th and final game of the season!

Well we could rest physically, but mentally Tony Woodcock and myself just continued in a state of turmoil leading up to the final because both of us were scared witless that we might not even get on the pitch against the Swedes thanks to the large shadow being cast by Trevor Francis. There had been a big hullaballoo over his signing for £1m earlier in the season. Even though BC only paid £999,999.99p because he just wanted to be awkward! He might have left a penny short, but Francis was pure class, which is precisely why Woody and myself were so concerned. You don't pay that kind of price tag for a footballer and stick him on the subs bench to be admired like a Ming Vase. Francis was not a collectible. He was a commodity that was to be used. He was signed to improve the team and he was signed to help us win the European Cup.

That was one of the manager's strengths in those times. He always knew when to strengthen and when to buy a player. It was usually from a position of superiority as a team. He never indulged in panic buying in those days. When the team was flying and looked as good as it could get, he would make sure he made it even more superior with a key signing. Francis was one such example. Every Forest fan was excited. Francis had broken into the Birmingham City team as a teenager and slotted away goals as if he was shelling peas.

When I say everyone was excited, that's not quite true. I was seriously worried. I had bust my nuts to help get the team into the final, just like all the others. I had scored in every round of the competition and there was no way I wanted to miss out on a European Cup final. Trev had been at the club since February, but UEFA rules at the time stated he was not allowed to play in the competition until the final. No manager could justify spending that kind of money in those days and not play Trevor Francis in the final. Not even BC – even if Francis' first game was for the A team and even if one of the first things he was forced to do was make us all a cup of tea! If he had been left out of the team in the final and we had lost, imagine the stick his boss would have taken.

Tea-making and running around with the youth team was just part of the initiation ceremony. He might have cost £1m, but he was just like the rest of us and not too big to put the kettle on! But his feet were under the table now and his feet were itching to get on the pitch in Munich, just like everyone's feet, including Martin O'Neill and Archie Gemmill, who were carrying injuries leading up to the final and were left out of the County Cup. While my mates were making their way to Munich, eating dog food and doing all kinds of stupid stunts to make cash on the way over to fund their trip, I was praying I would be able to perform in front of them.

On our final day of preparation the Gaffer pulled aside Martin and Archie and both told him they were fit to play. 'Gentlemen, I am delighted for you both, but you are not going to be in the team. You are both on the bench' was his curt reply. I will never forget the sheer desperation they both suffered. It was hard not to feel for them and hard not to feel selfish at the same time and glad that I was not having to endure that awful desolation. Archie was so distraught he fell out with the Gaffer big style and quit later that summer to join Birmingham City. They later patched up their differences and Archie became a trusted member of the back room staff, but I am sure he must reflect in quieter moments about whether he was too hasty in leaving. After all, if he had stayed he would have had another tilt at playing in a final.

I remember many years later, after Martin had become a successful manager at Aston Villa, that his side were mauled 7-1 by Chelsea at Stamford Bridge. He had found himself on the other side of the coin many times in that career, having to make tough decisions and leave players out, but that day in West London, in the immediate aftermath of the game, he said that was the worst he had ever felt in his entire career. After the weekend to think about it, he set the record straight and having reflected on the situation, that news from Brian Clough that had smashed him in the solar plexus 30 years earlier was still his lowest point!

The fact that Martin got injured in his next game for Northern Ireland and suffered a recurrence of the hamstring problem merely underlines that the Gaffer got it right. He made the right call in the worst of circumstances and that is what top managers have to do. Martin's injury was perfect for him too, because it meant Trevor, Woody and myself could all play in the final, with Trevor operating wide on the right. It was not his favourite position, but I would have played in goal to be part of the team and I am sure that went for pretty much everyone who stepped on the pitch in Munich that night.

But before I set foot in that famous stadium I wanted to punch the Gaffer for the way he humiliated me in front of the rest of the team as we were all sitting round, killing time in those horrible moments between the bus leaving the hotel for the game. I can still vividly picture the scene outside our hotel as if it were yesterday. We were all sat in the garden at the rear of the hotel. It was a scorching hot day and we were all in those horrible blue blazers and grey trousers, sitting in the shade trying to keep out of the heat. I can still see our team coach parked at the side of the building.

The team coach in which we had all piled our belongings minutes earlier. We were all tense and itching to get on with things and there had been no late night drinking sessions this time. I was 21-years-old and just a few hours away from the European Cup final. I was as nervous as hell and sporting a day's growth of bristle on my chin. I always had a bit of a six o'clock shadow. It was a bit of a lucky omen for me and BC never really seemed to mind, even though he liked his players to be clean shaven.

However, on this occasion, he came over to where I was sat and said: "Gaz, what is that crap on your chin?" I tried to explain, but before the words came out to contest the issue, I was ordered to "get it off!" My problem was all my kit, clothes and toilet bag were in the bus under a pile of gear. Not to be outdone, Clough bellowed out "has anyone got any shaving foam?" For some bizarre reason Chris Woods, our reserve team 'keeper, had his handy and he was sent with me, up to BC's room, where I had to use the Gaffer's razor to have a shave and get rid of the facial furniture. I was fucking furious and red with embarrassment. I felt I had been treated like a naughty schoolboy and that the rest of the lads were laughing at me. Not to mention the staff in the hotel.

It was only later that I realised he had done me a favour. His greatest talent as a manager was man-management. Management is almost 90% that if you ask me. To know your players intimately and what makes them tick. To be able to spot which one has had a row with the missus the night before, or which one has cash problems, without even having to ask the question. That day in Munich he could see that I was getting more fractious the closer the occasion loomed. Instead of putting his arm around me, he needed something to take my mind off things. Making me shave and curse him in his own hotel room mirror took me 20 minutes and took all the edge off my nervous tension. By the time I got back downstairs, the bus was revving up ready to go and so was I.

All the big boys, the types of teams we wanted to face in the earlier rounds of the competition had fallen by the wayside. Juventus, winners of the previous two Serie A titles and never out of the top two in their domestic league in seven years, had been beaten by Glasgow Rangers. Real Madrid, winner of three of the previous four La Ligas, had been taken out by Grasshoppers. PSV, UEFA Cup champions the season before, had also been dumped by Rangers who in turn were eliminated by Cologne. While they all got knocked out, Malmo, the complete unknowns from Sweden, negotiated a route past Monaco, Dynamo Kiev, Wisla Krakov and Austria Vienna to reach the final under English coach Bob Houghton.

We were overwhelming favourites to win the final and on the princely sum of £10,000-a-man to do so. That was serious money to someone earning £100-a-week at the time. It was almost two years' wages! After putting out the likes of Liverpool and Cologne, no Swedish team could be viewed as a serious threat. That was how it was being viewed. No Swedish team had ever reached the final, but Malmo were there on merit and after getting that far, we were certainly not going to underestimate their threat and lose the game through complacency.

MY MAGIC CARPET RIDE

Going into the final Malmo had terrible problems. Their two main centre-backs Bo Larsson and Roy Andersson were injured and their captain Staffan Tapper was forced to play with a broken toe. They had so many injury worries they could only name four fit subs. Houghton was a canny man and knew that if he took us on in a game of pure football they would come hopelessly unstuck. So there was only one thing for it. They were a massive team. It was like Land of the Giants and all they wanted to do was defend, defend and defend some more in the hope of nicking a set piece goal or winning on penalties.

That was why it was such an awful final. It was horrible to play in. It was like being stuck in a Swedish straight-jacket. They never came out to play and just stuck ten players behind the ball. I wanted it to be a spectacle. I wanted Forest to show the rest of Europe what we were all about and how good we were but we never got the chance. It was a grind of a game to play in and must have been awful to watch. I think I had one chance early on when I went through and lobbed the 'keeper but the ball ended up on the roof of the net.

One person the Swedes singled out for more attention than anyone else was Robbo. Sometimes he had three men around him. They knew how dangerous he could be and that he was the most likely catalyst to spark us off. All they kept doing was preventing him from attacking on the outside and kept forcing him into a packed midfield. While the Gaffer and PT sat on a bench miles away from the playing surface, we were running into barriers all over the place. Even Barry Davies, who commentated on the game for national TV, sounds as frustrated as I was during the match, at least until Robbo gave the kind of swerve of the hips his big hero Bryan Ferry would have been proud of to finally get round the back of a packed Swedish defence.

Robbo was never blessed with lightning pace, but over a couple of yards he was electric and all he ever needed was a chink of daylight to deliver the kind of cross David Beckham can only dream about.

Davies' commentary goes up a few octaves when Robbo attacks on the outside and bursts to the by-line. 'We have been waiting for Robertson to do that all game' he screeches. It is one thing being able to burst past defenders at pace, but when you are running out of pitch and the ball is about to go out of play, to be able to wrap your foot around it and tease over the perfect centre is pure genius.

But that was Robbo and we expected nothing less. I could see how the play was developing and bust my balls to get into the area as the ball came fizzing over. Almost instantly, after plotting the trajectory I knew it was going to be fractionally too high for me. Did I lunge at it? Then out of the corner of my right eye I could see Trevor Francis racing in behind me. If I had lunged I would probably have taken it right off Trev's head. I pulled out and the ball landed smack bang in the middle of his forehead before flashing into the Malmo net, accompanied by a victory role in the shot-putt circle to the right of the far post. Winning an Olympic Gold medal in that stadium years earlier could not have been any more satisfying than seeing that goal. Apart from hearing the final whistle.

If you had offered me this and said I was only going to get one full season as a pro a couple of years earlier, I would have snapped your hand off and died a happy man. The elation. Seeing mates' faces in the crowd. Tears of joy for so many that had followed us on that incredible journey was amazing. Clough the 'Fairy Godmother' had waved his magic wand. He had transformed Robbo, who was very nearly drummed out of the City Ground in 1975 because of his refuelling habits and love of a fry-up, into the best winger the game has seen since Matthews and Finney.

People like Martin O'Neill, Viv Anderson and Tony Woodcock probably would be the first to admit that their careers going nowhere and the club was doing the same. To perform such a transformation in the space of four seasons was an act I firmly believe would have been beyond the best managers the game has ever seen, bar Clough. No one else, Shankly, Bill Nicholson, Bob Paisley would have been able to do it. Even a hybrid of Jose Mourinho and Sir Alex Ferguson would have failed.

None of them would have pulled our medals off us either, within moments of having them hung around our necks! We had barely had a chance to get back in the dressing room and start the celebrations with the trophy when we were hit with a bizarre order from the Gaffer. "Right you lot, hand over your winners' medals, I want all of them," he said. I thought it was a wind-up, but he was deadly serious. We all wanted to walk around with them around our necks and sleep with the most wonderful thing we had ever won and we had them taken from us with no explanation.

We did not get them back for a week and to this day I still do not know why he took them. We all presumed it was because he wanted to get winners' medals struck for other members of the squad. That was the only explanation we could come up with and my suspicions were aroused even further when I got around to getting my medal valued when it was returned. It was worth a measly £15 according to the jeweller I went to. Maybe I got lumbered with one of the copies when they were redistributed. Not that I cared. The metal might have been worth £15, but the title European Cup winner 1979 was priceless and always will be. No one can buy one of those.

Over the years I have got tired of people having a pop at Forest and that first European Cup final win, trying to degrade its value by saying we only beat a bunch of Swedish part-timers. They were the best in their league at the time. They were champions of their country at a time when the competition only allowed champions to take part. There is no way anyone will be able to devalue the achievement for me. You can only knock over the skittles that are placed in front of you and that is what we did. We even had to fight with our own media to try and get the recognition we thought we deserved.

I still remember Robbo sat on the window ledges inside East Midlands Airport when we returned home with the trophy. He was in strident mood berating national newspaper men, claiming they had not given us sufficient credit for our achievements. He always felt they looked upon us as some raggedy old bunch thrown together ad hoc and that we had got lucky. We were not lucky. We had our moments of fortune, but we won on merit and maybe we never really did get the acclaim we deserved, but stuff them. We knew what we had done and if we had any doubts, the tens of thousands of people who lined the streets from Holme Pierrepont to the Council House in Old Market Square when we paraded the trophy just reinforced it. That is when it really hit home for me. No amount of double stick adhesive could have given me that kind of a high!

Nottingham Forest – European Kings. It had a great ring to it and it was no fluke or good fortune. Winning that fantastic giant pot is one thing. Keeping hold of it is a whole different ball game. Liverpool had done it until we did for them, but we had an English domination to uphold and you can bet that was the one thing on the Gaffer's mind as he headed for Cala Millor and time in the sun to re-charge the batteries before returning for pre-season to start the campaign to do it all over again and I headed to Ibiza for what I hoped to be a break. However, I ended up finding myself involved in the middle of the equivalent of another European Cup – this time in beach soccer!

Managers would lose their marbles in the modern day if they discovered their precious players had risked serious injury taking part in a five-a-side tournament organised by a group of foreigners when they had been laying around the pool on their sun loungers. Can you imagine Inter Milan winning the Champions League and finding Wesley Sneijder had been having lumps kicked out of him by Spanish waiters and a ramshackle collection of German holiday makers looking for a souvenir?

That is exactly the situation I found myself in when Sandra, myself, a good mate Pete Castledine and his wife headed off for two weeks of San Miguel and feet-up right after the celebrations in Munich. Most of the early days of the holiday were spent dragging ourselves out of bed once the hangover from the night before had started to abate. That was followed by some kind of omelette to make us feel human, before the San Miguel started to flow again. That was until another holiday maker recognised me in the first week and asked Cas and me if we fancied a kick about.

Before we knew what was happening we had been roped into a five-a-side team for this tournament along with Mick Leonard, who was a goalkeeper at Halifax Town at the time. We sweat pure lager in the ridiculous heat, but somehow our rag-tag outfit made it to my second European final in the space of six weeks and we looked in with a real chance of winning the thing until Mick's wife decided that her husband could be wrecking what she hoped would be a promising career with such stupid antics and he pulled out of the team. One of the German teams was good enough to loan us one of their numbers named Jurgen and we just thought we had been sold a pup.

It turned out 'Jurgen' was the German international hockey net minder and we were going to need him, because the team we were playing in the final was none other than FC St Pauli, a German second division side at the time and staying in the hotel next to us! Birtles, a salesman and someone who had not long got himself out of the pit (mining, not his bed), a German goalkeeper and AN Other against a crack second division German outfit who were desperate to rub our faces in the sand. No chance, but we held our own throughout normal time – until someone came up with the idea of settling the game with a sudden death goal and as the San Miguel took its toll we finally cracked. At least we did not succumb in a penalty shoot-out and the St Pauli players were so impressed with our performance they dashed off to the hotel and returned with two barrels of beer. It would have been rude to let them drink it alone!

As for the genuine European Cup, no one had given us a prayer of winning it first time. BC was brash enough and arrogant enough to tell people he was going to do it, but if he had claimed he was going to win it again, they would have had him carried away to a padded cell!

Especially when we got thumped 5-0 by Bayern Munich in a pre-season friendly, though normal service had been resumed by the time we met another Swedish team, Oesters Vaxjo, in the first leg of our defence of our crown. We had made a solid start to the season losing just one of our opening eight games, a 3-1 defeat to Norwich at Carrow Road in the final game before the first round of the European Cup. It was hardly the best preparation, but we put the record straight against a really dour and physical side, who kicked lumps out of Woody and me, with a 2-0 home win.

Despite the bruises two Ian Bowyer were enough of an advantage and a 1-1 draw did the trick in Sweden where Woody, who scored on the day, and me were the only two players booked. In fact, I only picked up three bookings in my entire career. One of those was for slipping over on an icy pitch and clattering into a Watford player by accident! The other was playing centre half for Notts County later in my career, when I wanted to find out what centre backs had enjoyed so much in kicking me as a striker.

The passage from Scandinavia led us to another dubious pairing in the second round with Arges Pitesti, a Romanian army side, and the chance to go hunting for Dracula in Transylvania, but not before I had stocked up on provisions to combat the dreadful food we were warned to expect. After winning the first leg at home 2-0 thanks to goals from Woody and myself, my suitcase for the return leg stank the place out because I took that much cheese and chocolate.

I was glad I made the effort, because I could not eat anything that was placed in front of me over there. It was all cabbage and clear soup and we never did find Dracula. Then we embarked on a lengthy coach trip the day before the game to an old cathedral in Transylvania, but there was no need to go hunting. I had a brought Dracula with me along with the cheese in the form of a cape, false fangs and fake blood capsules. Not that Viv Anderson was too impressed when he fell asleep and found me hovering over him dressed as the Count with blood dripping from my false fangs.

They were not the only clothes I packed. I hated tracksuits and would do anything to get out of wearing them. I fancied myself as a bit of a dapper dresser and was always in two of the fashionista houses in Nottingham, Birdcage and Lido, two men's boutiques that were the leaders in new styles. One of the guys who co-owned it was Dave Bartram, a founder member of the band Showaddywaddy. I was always in there getting suits made and had two particularly natty ones made in blue and red, both with gold checks in and blue and red shoes to match. I certainly stood out against the black and drab outfits worn by the women washing steps in Romania. No wonder so many people followed me when I stepped out of the hotel.

As the food was so rank and my cheese and chocolate ran out, there was little left to do the night before the game other than for us to plough through 16 bottles of wine in another one of the Gaffer's relaxation techniques. It did the trick, even if we had to play at 4pm in the afternoon because the Arges ground did not have floodlights. Any team without floodlights can't get into the Blue Square Conference these days, but back then it was not deemed a problem. We kicked off early enough to be able to see where we were going and I grabbed another goal, along with Ian Bowyer to make safe our passage to the third round to face Dynamo Berlin.

Domestically our league form was not quite good enough to maintain a title challenge for the second season running, but for the third season in a row we were heading towards the final of the League Cup and just before facing the East Germans we did little to improve our popularity rating in the red half of Merseyside by defeating Liverpool over two legs in the semi-final to book a return to Wembley to face Wolves. The order for more silver polish was placed before we welcomed the Germans and they took full advantage of our hospitality with Hans-Jurgen Riediger's goal leaving us with a 1-0 deficit to make up behind the Iron Curtain.

Four days before we flew out to renew battle with Berlin we had our Wembley date with Wolves and the first time we had been force fed the bitter pill of defeat in a major final for Forest. We were overwhelming favourites to win the trophy for the third time in succession, but ended up with egg on our faces thanks to a mix-up involving Peter Shilton and David Needham. The pair collided trying to deal with a ball on the edge of our own 18-yard box and Wolves striker Andy Gray never scored an easier goal in his illustrious career, tapping the ball into the empty net.

It was just one of those things. Shilts rarely came that far off his line and it would be harsh to blame David Needham. He thought he had to deal with the loose ball and tried to. It was just one of those days. I always think that Wembley almost pre-ordains the winners before kick-off. If it is meant to be your day it will happen. That day Wolves 'keeper Paul Bradshaw had the kind of game he would not have even dreamt about. He saved everything we threw at him. When he saved a shot from me by sitting on the ball, I just knew it was not meant to be that day, but it did not make it any easier to take. Leaving Wembley as a loser, just 12 months after tasting victory, was one of the worst moments in my Forest career. The Gaffer was less than impressed too.

I did not have a good game that day. George Berry was playing centre back against me and I just did not have the kind of impact on the game I wanted to. That made it worse on a personal level and it was hardly the kind of preparation for what we were being told was mission impossible in Berlin, especially as Dynamo had won their league game ahead of facing us by ten goals and Kenny Burns was suspended! There were shades of Cologne 12 months earlier about the fixture and not too many people gave us a prayer of over-turning the tie – not that the East Germans were leaving anything to chance. They even tried to kidnap Robbo on the way out there!

Communist East Berlin made Romania look more opulent than the millionaire's playground of Monte Carlo. It was the most austere of places. From the moment our plane landed and we stepped off we were greeted by police and army with enough weapons to take down an enemy battalion. No one was allowed in without being checked in triplicate and there was not an earthly chance that anyone was allowed to escape the communist regime. That was the reason for the huge military presence and we were just delighted to get through all the checks and onto the coach waiting to take us to the hotel.

As soon as we were on the coach, the head count was performed, a bit like the one when you had been on a school trip somewhere and it was only at that point we noticed there was someone missing from our party. Further investigation revealed the absentee as Robbo. After asking whether anyone had seen him, BC decided he had better get off the coach and go and find him. He was certainly not intimidated by the machine guns being waved around.

When he got back into what passed as passport control he discovered Robbo had been man-handled into a tiny room and was being held there against his will. The Gaffer was ready to take on the entire East German security contingent until he discovered that Robbo had been detained because he had been reading a book on the plane which had a picture of a Swastika on it. The East German officials took one look at that and the copy of Penthouse Robbo had for lighter reading and decided they were going to confiscate them. They very politely informed Robbo he could collect his books (sic) on his way back out to England after the game. Needless to say he never bothered.

That might have been a humorous interlude, but it was a rare one and I certainly could not find anything remotely funny on a trip to the Brandenburg Gates. Seeing the bullet holes in the walls and hearing our guide tell us how many people had been killed trying to escape the communist regime put what we were doing and our lives back in England into stark perspective. We were just trying to win a game of football. Those people were fleeing for their lives and so many failed and paid the ultimate price.

Losing a goal in the first leg did not seem quite so important as we stared at history, but to the Gaffer conceding was a major crime. He prized clean sheets more than the housekeepers at the Ritz. Before every game he would bang on about the importance of them, even more so before European games. 'I have got 180 minutes to win this game and I will wait until the last second if I have to. Just get me a clean sheet' was usually his mantra. Keeping the German side out in the first leg had been beyond us and going into the return with the dark clouds of defeat and losers' medals from Wembley weighing heavy must have been a concern, even if he did not demonstrate the fact.

There were a few knees knocking on the night of the game, but that had nothing to do with the fear of getting eliminated and losing our grip on the trophy. It was down to the fact we were all fucking freezing. I have never in my career played a game in such bitterly cold conditions as we did in Berlin and just to make matters worse he sent us out in short sleeved kit an hour before the kick-off to get 'warmed up!' I always wore short sleeves for matches. That was just a personal choice, but that evening you could almost feel the hairs on your arms and legs freezing and snapping off it was that cold.

That did not stop him making us walk from the ramshackle dressing rooms the 100 metres to the pitch an hour before kick-off and tracksuits were banned! It was another act of defiance he wanted to see from his players. We had lost the League Cup, been knocked out of the FA Cup by Liverpool and we were not going to win the league. This was all we had left and the whole season could have been put into deep freeze that night, but one person in particular was in no mood to give up the season in such arctic conditions without a scrap and Trevor Francis was awesome that night.

We had become strike partners following the sale of Tony Woodcock to German side Cologne and once Trevor moved into his preferred role he repaid every penny of that £1m transfer fee. There was some suggestion that Trevor had somehow won his first European Cup medal somewhat by default, coming in at the 11th hour and grabbing all the glory in Munich and now it was pay-back time. Dynamo just did not know how to deal with him that night and he put on a master class, scoring two goals and I got brought down for the penalty which Robbo took extra pleasure in slotting in. It was his two-fingered salute to the soldiers who had nicked his magazine! Once again we had defied the odds and it was job done. We could not wait to get out of the place and head home.

Getting out of European ties we only ever had one thought, will we make it back to Madisons in time to get a few beers in? Madisons was a nightclub in Nottingham which had become our late night drinking den, usually to celebrate European victories. As soon as our return flight touched down at East Mids, Albert the bus driver had the engine revving and drove as fast as he could to get us back to the City Ground and then it was a footrace to the cars and a race over Trent Bridge to get into the centre of town.

Pretty much every member of the team would go. We would be in there in our daft blazers having a few beers and the punters were drinking with us. They loved it and we loved it. It was part of our ritual and a good way to chalk up another success. Drinking was part of our squad mentality and Madisons was as familiar to us in those days as the four walls of the home dressing room at the City Ground. The only thing missing was his nibs, which was always a bonus!

Beating Dynamo earned the reward of a two-legged semi-final against Ajax. Fortunately a few years had rolled on from the Johan Cruyff side that dominated Europe and he had long since departed as had several of the 1974 Dutch side who made it to the final of the World Cup, but Rudi Krol remained as their talisman and Ajax were still a formidable obstacle to get over. Fortunately we had the home leg first and once again Trevor Francis was immense. He scored and another penalty from Robbo, plus one of BC's beloved clean sheets, gave us a 2-0 cushion to take to Amsterdam, but we were still not totally convinced it would be enough. Ajax were strongly fancied to win the tournament and we would still have our work cut out. It was a situation that would call for some more unorthodox man-management skills to nudge us into a second successive European Cup final and you could always count on Clough and Taylor to find them.

CHAMPIONS OF EUROPE

Now as most people know, Amsterdam is famous for one thing in particular and it is not clogs. De Wallen forms part of the Rosse Buurt (red light district) which tourists and revellers flock to see when they are in the city and we were no different. So when the Gaffer called us for a walk after dinner on the evening before the second leg, he decided it would be a great idea to go and have a stroll by the side of the famous canals to have a look in the windows! Can you imagine Carlo Ancelotti leading John Terry and Co in their Chelsea suits, peering in at scantily clad prostitutes of all shapes and sizes before a game in the Amsterdam Arena?

Apparently that was not unorthodox enough and PT decided he wanted to liven up proceedings even more and he broke away from the party and headed towards this place which was clearly a sex theatre and he was having a lengthy conversation with some burly looking bloke on the door. If transpired shortly after his return that if he could have negotiated a satisfactory group rate, the Gaffer and his European Cup semi-finalists could have spent the night before facing Ajax watching a live sex show! Instead we ended up wandering for a little while longer until we found a bar and BC led the way in.

It's crazy when you think about it, but there we were, sat in some bar in the red light area of Amsterdam having three or four beers in total anonymity. Not one of the locals or people wandering around knew who we were. Just imagine how much the pictures would have been worth to a freelance photographer if he could have got them back to Fleet Street in time. BC and his players drinking beers in a den of iniquity, so close to the European Cup semi-final. It would have been priceless to an eagle-eyed snapper. Mind you the Gaffer would probably have got us to pose for pictures if there had been any long lenses around!

Ajax's OIympic Stadium was not a place for faint hearts and there were 65,000 in there, most of them Dutch expecting their team to turn the tables. After all they had put 16 goals past HJK Helsinki and scored ten in one game against Omonia Nicosia and Rudi Krol and Co could not have done much more in their attempt to do so. They absolutely battered us and when we needed them most our back four and Shilts were incredible that night but despite Ajax getting a late goal, we managed to hang on for dear life. We had earned the right to defend our title in the Santiago Bernabeu, home of Real Madrid and if critics reckoned we had it easy against Malmo a year earlier, they must have been delighted with the fact we copped for Hamburg and Kevin Keegan 12 months later.

Now those who had spat bile at us winning in Munich against no hopers were going to get their revenge and Keegan, who had signed two years earlier for Hamburg after deciding to leave Anfield and his German team mates were going to teach lucky Forest a lesson. Their confidence was bolstered by the way Hamburg reached the final, over-turning a 2-0 defeat against Real in the Bernabeu in front of 100,000 in magnificent style with a 5-1 win in the Volksparkstadion, to the amazement of 65,000 Hamburg fans.

To help Hamburg's cause we played nine games between our trip to Holland on April 23 and our last game on May 16, a friendly. Yes I said friendly against our friends up the road at Leicester City! We even managed to play a friendly in France against Brest on the day Trevor Brooking headed the FA Cup final winner for West Ham United against Arsenal and completed our Nottinghamshire County Cup final duties against Notts County!

We played 80 games that season including pre-season and friendlies. We even trekked to Cairo at one stage. We were trading on our title as European Cup winners and the justification for it was to raise funds for the club. To me it was sheer bloody madness, but no one questioned a thing at the time, but I will always maintain the crazy schedule that season, which continued right up to the final cost Trevor Francis his place in the team for the final and handicapped Forest even more than ever before.

What was being billed as Keegan's European final had everyone believing that the former idol of the Kop would crown his second successive 12-month stint as European Footballer of the Year for 1979 by lifting his second European Cup, after his earlier success with Liverpool. Even with Francis, our odds were long ones according to the experts. Then he heard the tell-tale gun-shot go off at the back of his ruptured Achilles tendon during a 4-0 win over Crystal Palace at the City Ground on May 3. His season was over and he would not be part of our armoury in Madrid.

John Robertson scored over 20 goals that season and finished top scorer. Not bad for a left-winger, but few did more in the games against Dynamo Berlin and Ajax than Trevor to get us to the final and to see him carried off, his season in ruins, was terribly sad. Everyone felt for him. I don't care what anyone says. There are no words of consolation. All that bollocks about we will win it for you Trev is simply that. Bollocks. The Gaffer did not want him around the place hobbling on crutches. He had a real thing about seeing injured players around. It must have been a reaction to his own time in plaster and on crutches when his cruciate ligaments exploded playing for Sunderland. Trevor was pretty much banned from the ground.

He was certainly not invited with the rest of the squad to Cala Millor which was precisely where we headed straight after our last game on May 16. The final was 12 days away and we were going to spend seven of them in Majorca getting a sun tan and playing tennis, in between a few trips to the Shack and several beers. No one could believe that the Gaffer was taking us away for a break before the final. Everyone thought we were on a jolly up and not taking the final seriously. There were more than a few eyebrows raised over our preparations.

Yet to our manager it was simple. All he wanted to do was get us out of the way. He wanted to find us a place to relax and get away from the hullaballoo of the whole thing. If we had stayed at home in Nottingham for a week it would have been bedlam. The attention and focus from fans, media, everyone would have been intolerable. We would have been unbearable to our nearest and dearest. So the easiest thing was to escape the lot and to the place he knew best and felt most comfortable. There was hardly any training. It was very much rest and relaxation. Mind you, if we were not match fit after 79 games, we were never going to be fit in our lives.

It was the perfect way to prepare and when we flew back to Nottingham to get our gear together to fly out to Madrid for the final, we had unwound wonderfully and re-charged the batteries with a bit of sun on our backs. Cala Millor had healing properties I am sure of that. We were so laid back we did not even kick up a fuss about the choice of hotel ahead of the final. Well not until we had got there that is.

For some reason best known to the Gaffer, he picked an old converted monastery about an hour out of Madrid as the venue for our team hotel ahead of trying to knock the European Footballer of the Year crown off Keegan's head. It was so far off the beaten track and such a spooky place, I was expecting Lurch from the Addams Family to open the door and take our bags up to the rooms. I swear the place was haunted. After all the soothing charm of Majorca, now we were going to get scared out of our minds by having to sleep for a couple of days dodging Morticia and a collection of apparitions.

It really was an awful place and so far away from the Bernabeu that we never even trained at the stadium before the game. It was part of Uefa regulations that teams should be able to train at the ground where they were due to play 24 hours before the match. We never set foot in the place until we turned up to play the game. Uefa regulations cut no ice with the Gaffer. Regulations full stop cut no ice. It was a case of fuck your regulations. If we want to train we will. If we don't, we won't.

So from the moment we arrived in Spain a couple of days before the final we did not so much as practise a set piece. We never pulled on any training kit. Well everyone apart from Peter Shilton that is. Shilts was the consummate professional and while the rest of us were happy to put our feet up and rest, he wanted to do some training routines before the final. The only problem was, there was no way he was going to Madrid on his own. So he had to look for an alternative venue and PT came up with the most bizarre you could imagine.

Picture the scene in the middle of a traffic island somewhere on the outskirts of Madrid. The green oasis in the centre of the busy road was covered in grass and Shilton was throwing himself around like a maniac with PT and Jimmy Gordon, our trainer, going through a training routine for the benefit of the rush hour traffic! Absolutely bonkers and completely true. It was the only patch of grass nearby that we could find and it was bibs, balls and cones on the contra-flow! Like I said, total professional Shilts and we would not have had him any other way. Even without Trevor and Woody, with Shilton in goal, we always had a chance.

Hamburg were overwhelming favourites to win the title. They had a fantastic team and Keegan gave them that X-Factor that the pundits, almost to a man, believed would swing the tie in favour of the German side. Keegan's name was all over the place in the build up. It was almost as if we were not playing at all. We were there just to make up the numbers. It was incredible really. We were the reigning champions, looking to retain the title. Only seven clubs other than Forest had ever achieved that feat. AC Milan and Inter Milan. Real Madrid, Bayern Munich, Benfica, Ajax and most recently Liverpool. That was the kind of illustrious company we were trying to emulate and it was as if we did not merit a mention.

Keegan was such a dominant factor he even managed to get inside the head of the Gaffer. For the one and only time in my career as a player under him he mentioned an individual who played for the opposition. It was the only time I ever heard him say that an opponent needed sorting out and he made it crystal clear to Larry Lloyd and Kenny Burns that Keegan was not to be allowed to have any kind of influence on the game that would be detrimental to our chances of victory.

Now Kenny and Larry rarely needed an invitation to be scary and to intimidate. Normally just one withering look from either of them was enough and they took great pride in their ability to scare the living shit out of opponents, but the pair of them, along with Bomber, who could also do his fair share of leaving his studs where they were not welcome when necessary, hatched a plan which would ensure Keegan was to become a complete non-entity in the game.

It started as we lined up in the tunnel. Larry knew Keegan from their time together at Liverpool and gave Kev a warm welcome and a pat on the back and some chat. 'Hiya Kev, nice to see you, but keep out of my way, because if you don't Kenny is going to get really angry because he doesn't like you'. Keegan took one look further down the line and Kenny had taken out his false teeth and gave him that gap-toothed smile that made the bravest of strikers quiver. That was the opening gambit and from the moment the referee blew the whistle Kenny, Larry and Bomber took turns in booting Keegan. It was fantastic to watch how they rotated the strike and maintained this constant mood of aggression which drove Keegan deeper and deeper in the game. It was genius the way they achieved it and poor Kev became less and less of an influence and increasingly frustrated and agitated, until it got the better of him, but that was not until a masterstroke from the bench had given us the platform for more glory.

In the opening ten minutes of the game, while Keegan was getting his early bruises we were getting overwhelmed by a superior German team in midfield. As well as Keegan, Hamburg possessed the likes of Felix Magath, Manni Kaltz and Willi Reimann and because of the absence of Trevor Francis and the sale of Tony Woodcock, my mate Gary Mills had been pressed into service alongside me as the spearhead of our attack. We only ever played 4-4-2 and that was the best option available for the task ahead. Seeing that we were struggling to gain a foothold in the game needed drastic action and in a flash the Gaffer read the situation and reacted before it was too late.

Much is made of formations and tactics these days, but back then, 4-5-1 was unheard of at least until that night in Madrid. Millsy was ordered to withdraw from his supporting role with me and to drop back into a five-man midfield, leaving yours truly as Tonto, minus the Lone Ranger, flying solo up front. People tried to make out long after the final that we started with five across the middle, but that was not the case and I have never run so much in my entire life. I loved running and was fit as a flea. I even ran on my holidays during the off season, but Raul, who played for Real for the whole of his career, will not have covered as much grass in that citadel of a stadium as I did in 90 minutes. After the game BC reckoned I had run more miles than the famous long distance runner Emile Zatopek!

I ran myself to the point of exhaustion. I have never been so shattered and I even took my shin-pads off before the end of the game. Normally that would have resulted in a bollocking from the Gaffer, but not this time. My socks were round my ankles at the end and I could barely walk, let alone run. My remit was to close down all four of their defenders and when the ball got knocked up to me, I had to hang on to it like it was a Faberge egg and wait for help. For the first 20 minutes we barely got out of our own half and I had Ivan Buljan, the huge bearded Bulgarian international playing centre half for Hamburg, kicking lumps out of me.

Hold it and wait for help. Hold it and wait for help. That was all I could think of when Robbo cut in from the left. PT always fancied he had the beating of Kaltz and when he followed his pass into my feet it was obvious to me he was looking for the ball back. As it came into me, the Bulgarian was all over me and I lost my balance. There was no foul but as I was falling I somehow managed to swivel on my arse and lever the ball back into the path of Robbo's run. I was looking through opponents legs as his right foot shot curled around the goalkeeper Rudi Kargus and into the net off the base of the far post.

Robbo had grown up in Scotland watching Real Madrid and Puskas and Di Stefano and all that. That night he joined those legends. He might have been a left winger, but he was like Ronnie O'Sullivan. He could play with his left or right. It was immaterial to him. From that point on it was a rearguard action. Shilts made one incredible save to tip away a Magath free kick and Reimann had a goal ruled out for offside, but Keegan was still on the retreat and playing right back, he was so deep and fed up of getting booted. Eventually as we tried to kill time he snapped. I was at the corner flag, running around in circles shielding the ball as Keegan tried to win back possession, but he couldn't get the ball. In sheer frustration he ripped the corner flag out of the ground and hurled it.

That was it for me. They had snapped and that gesture was as much one of surrender as of frustration. Our superior tenacity, work rate and ability to counter attack and strike before falling back to give BC the clean sheet he probably cherishes the most, had won the day. We had done it again and this time against the odds. Everyone had written us off without Trevor and against the might of Keegan and Co and we had defied them all. This victory was certainly more satisfying than the Malmo one. The champagne tasted that much sweeter. Well it would have done, if I had any energy left to drink any!

There were no medals confiscated this time, before we headed back to the Adams Family residence, but there was another instruction. Every player was to go back to the hotel, even though wives, girlfiends and family were staying in the centre of Madrid. No one was allowed out to party. That went down like a lead balloon with several members of the team. So a plan was hatched to get back to the hotel and sneak out and get taxis back into the city centre and meet up with our partners. Lloydy, Needham, Frankie Gray, Martin and Robbo were all part of the escape party and ordinarily I would have been climbing out of the window first.

The problem was I could barely put one foot in front of the other. I wanted to party and celebrate. The mind was willing but the flesh was weak. I had no energy left at all and could not get out of the chair I had slumped in the moment we got back to the hotel. While they went out and partied, I celebrated with Peter Shilton the only way I could manage. I could just about lift playing cards for brag and drop the counters down the chute to play Connect Four. That was my celebration for the night. To make matters worse, the escapees returned just in time for breakfast and Peter Taylor thought they had been up all night 'partying' with Shilts and me. The fact I would have got away with breaking the curfew made it hurt even more!

6

THEATRE OF BAD DREAMS
Golden Shot meets Blankety Blank

IT took some time to recover from the exhaustion I suffered in Madrid, but I was helped by an unexpected call-up by England manager Ron Greenwood for the squad to go to the European Championships in Italy. It was so unexpected England had to track me down in a farm house in the wilds of Lincolnshire at Chris Woods' parents house to let me know I would be needing my passport and Italian phrasebook. At the time I had no idea my selection was to lead to an angry exchange of words with the Gaffer and the parting of the ways at Nottingham Forest.

I never thought for one minute I would be involved and shot off to Lincoln for a few days when the squad was being announced. No one from the FA had given me or Forest any indication I would be involved. Apparently it came down to a straight choice for the final place between myself and Bryan Robson and I had got the nod, just because of my experience at Forest. I was totally gobsmacked when Woodsy's mum told me the FA were on the phone.

I had played for England only once, a friendly against World Cup holders Argentina, when I made my debut at Wembley against Daniel Passarella and the rest of his hard-nut mates. David Johnson, Paul Mariner, Eric Gates, Tony Woodcock and Kevin Keegan were all ahead of me in the pecking order most of the time, but I got the call for Italy and even though I had finished the season exhausted with blood blisters all over my legs.

It was my country calling and I would have crawled on hands and knees to get on the plane. At the very least it showed I was getting noticed and it was a chance to showcase all my outrageous clothes in a country which appreciated fashion!

I had yellow trousers, purple shirts. All kinds of odd stuff. My clothes were so loud and colourful I nearly blinded Bobby Charlton when he interviewed me during the tournament. He could not get over the state of the gear I was wearing. Neither could my old mate Woody.

The temperatures were ridiculously high in June and I still insisted wearing a heavy wool suit and bow-tie one day. I would have sweated less if I had been stark naked in a sauna! Woody wet himself as the beads were careering down my forehead and bouncing off the pavement.

I did not sweat much in the first game. I was not even in the squad as our opening draw with Belgium was marred by hooligans and the police had to hold up the game for five minutes in the first half. Not bad considering there were only 15,186 fans in the Stadio Comunale in Turin. No one gave a flying fig about the tournament unless Italy were playing.

At least there were more than 50,000 in the stadium for the game against Italy when I was chucked in at the deep end by Ron Greenwood, the man the FA appointed England manager because they feared they would not be able to handle Brian Clough. Ron was a safe pair of hands, but no managerial genius. I came in from the cold and got a warm reception from Claudio Gentile, the most inappropriately named man I have ever come across on a football field.

He gouged my eyes, kicked me, punched me, grabbed my balls, spat at me and would have been an absolute lethal cage fighter if the sport had been invented back then. I was black and blue by the time I was subbed in the second half. We ended up losing 1-0 to a late goal to Marco Tardelli – the Italian midfielder who ended up winning the World Cup for his country two years later and was famed for that eye-bulging manic celebration.

I was not even in the squad for the final game against Spain, which we won thanks to goals from Trevor Brooking and Woody, but Belgium and Italy drew 0-0 in the final group game. Both teams secured four points and went through. Now there's a shock! All that was left for us was to do what we were good at and have a bloody good party at the team hotel after the Spain game. Keegan paid the resident DJ to get lost and he took over the decks for the night playing all our own music and generally getting pissed.

There was to be one last game for England, 1-0 World Cup qualifying defeat in Romania in October later that year. I reckon I had only been selected because the locals remembered my coloured suits from when Forest played Arges Pitesti and they had a campaign to get me back!

I never really felt part of the international set up and never felt I was given a proper chance, but maybe being away with big name players had an influence on my way of thinking when it came to my own finances and how far down the pecking order I was in terms of wages when I looked around the England dressing room. Never mind the England dressing room, I was miles behind in my club dressing room too and I had heard some whispers Manchester United were interested in me, which would give me some leverage.

I might have won two European Cups, but I was still on £175-a-week at Forest and comfortably the worst paid player. I knew I had to tackle that situation. It was time to ask for a pay rise. It was time to open negotiations with the man who drove the hardest bargain this side of the Blue Bazaar in Istanbul. Haggling was his second sport and very few players emerged from his office punching the air in celebration. He was like the bloke in Oliver Twist who roared 'MORE!' when the poor kid asked for more food!

Squaring up to him and demanding more money was not something I was particularly relishing, but the time had come. My salary had increased from the £65-a-week I had signed four years earlier, but I had more than outlived the Gaffer and Peter Taylor's wildest expectations. That £2,000 they paid for me was chicken feed now and my pay-rate of £175-per week meant I had to work almost three months to earn the same amount I had cost Forest.

They were the basic terms. Obviously they were heavily incentivised in bonuses. Finishing in the top three made all the players significantly richer, based on the bonus sliding scale which rewarded us for where we finished in the final standings in May. Obviously the bonus from winning the European Cup was very welcome, but this was a point of principle with me now. I knew I was well down the pecking order when it came to basic salary. Players talk all the time. Everyone gets to know to within a few quid of what their team mates are earning.

I knew Peter Shilton was on good money and why not. He was the best goalkeeper in the world and deserved that. Trevor Francis was another one earning well and again, I did not have a problem with it. After all, we had signed him for £1m. He was hardly going to turn up at that price for £200-a-week. I understood all that but I was no longer the novice that had wandered in a few years earlier trying to hide the smell of Evostik. I felt I was under-valued and had made my mind up it was time to do something about it. I felt I deserved a bit more.

After all my research into the club's salary structure, I was convinced I was the lowest paid player at the time. Whether the figures were correct or not, from what I was led to believe that certainly seemed the case. I was not looking for an outrageous pay hike, but I warranted more for what I had put in. That is only right. So I managed to get an audience with the Gaffer to discuss the matter. He might not have ruled by fear alone, but he could be the kind of dictator that made Lenin and Stalin look like pushovers when he felt like it.

There had been no rehearsing speeches in the mirror beforehand. It was a daunting situation, but I had a clear idea of what I wanted to say and how it had to be put across as I wandered down the corridor, past the secretary's office and the chairman's to the real throne of power. I was polite, not greedy, and reasonably forceful with my delivery. We had discussions and I made it clear I was not looking to leave. They knew about United's interest, but instead of trying to keep the kid they found in a bargain bucket, I was told by the Gaffer that he was unable to do it. Forest could not give me the pay rise I was looking for. They could not afford to pay me more than £175-a-week! I was staggered and hurt.

Cloughie knew that United were there in the background waiting for me. He knew they were ready to pay £1.25m. In a flash he could make a huge profit. The £2,000 punt he took on me came at odds of 625-1 and I had just come in! I thought he would fight harder to keep me, but maybe he thought that after two seasons it had all been a flash in the pan and I would not be able to do it all over again. Maybe he looked at the fact that I had come from non-league and just thought he had had a really good run out of me and that all good things must come to an end.

I had a feeling they might have been cashing in too, because the club needed the money and the books had to be balanced. The £1m transfer fee for Trevor Francis was unheard of in football and unthinkable for a club the size of Forest. They paid big money for Peter Shilton, too, and were paying the pair wages to match their star billing.

Perhaps it suited the club. I will never know, but their offer was not good enough for my thinking. I had no desire to leave, but said I would take my chances elsewhere. It was the only time in my relationship with him that we really fell out.

The club was so successful. They had just retained the prestige trophy of European football and Nottingham was my home. BC was building a dynasty and I thought I was going to be there a long time. Why would I want to leave? I had not long bought a new house and that was part of the reason I was looking for a pay rise. Those are not the actions of a man who was looking to move away from Nottingham.

I had other offers. Italian club Napoli were interested, yet even though there was no offer of a pay-rise I was still leaning towards staying put until the final straw came. The Gaffer decided to give an article to Shoot magazine. He did an interview about me expressing his disappointment that I wanted to leave. His argument was that he had discovered me and rescued me from a life of carpet fitting. He had given me the platform and he had given me this and that to go with it. He felt I should have been more loyal and not rocked the boat. It was classic Clough. That was his modus operandi. He was brilliant at using the media to get what he wanted, but it upset my mum and dad. That did not help and I ended up on the transfer-list.

In the interview Clough said: "The time has come for Garry to take stock of what the game has done, or more significantly what Forest have done, for him. He really upset me a few weeks ago when he said he felt he should have more than three weeks' holiday. He did not say anything about wanting more time off before he shot off to Italy with England. I did not ask him to go to Italy.

"And I did not ask him to be best man at Chris Woods' wedding when he returned and I did not ask him to buy a bigger house. So, as I am prone to do on occasions, I went beserk with Garry and told him if he felt he was being hard done by he might be better off finding another club."

That was it, he was telling me to go. I had pissed him off playing for England and moaning about having more time off. I had gone to Italy to represent my country. At the end of that season the club doctors took one look at the blood blisters on my legs and told me I was physically exhausted and needed rest and if you can't be best man for your mate at a wedding, then that is a pretty poor show. They were crap points he was making and I just felt they wanted me to leave.

I was grateful for all they had done for me and for giving me the chance, but it was a two-way street. I had repaid them. I scored 26 goals in 54 games in my first season although the Gaffer might be quick to point out I only managed 16 in 64 the following season. I was grateful to swap £65-a-week carpet fitting for the same amount playing for Forest to start with. It was what I wanted to do, but I couldn't go on with that attitude forever. It is a

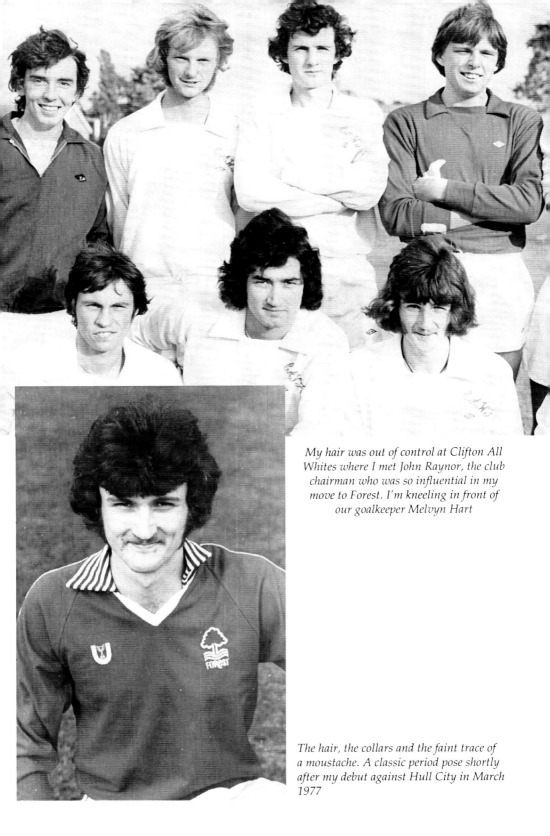

My hair was out of control at Clifton All Whites where I met John Raynor, the club chairman who was so influential in my move to Forest. I'm kneeling in front of our goalkeeper Melvyn Hart

The hair, the collars and the faint trace of a moustache. A classic period pose shortly after my debut against Hull City in March 1977

George Berry's afro got the better of me here and I tasted defeat for the first time in a major final, losing to Wolves 1-0 at Wembley in the 1980 League Cup

If the devil could have cast his net! A Christmas reunion in John Robertson's pub The Greyhound at Aslockton, Notts around 1989 when Robbo had finished in the game. The players are, from left to right, Ian Bowyer, Gary Mills, me, Robbo, Gary Fleming, Franz Carr and Stuart Pearce

I seem slightly less ecstatic about winning the European Super Cup in Barcelona than Kenny 'the gap' Burns in February 1980

After beating Liverpool in the first round, we played against one of the game's true greats in Ferenc Puskas, the AEK Athens manager. I scored this one in the away leg and we eventually cruised through 7-2 on aggregate

Me and my cousin Sherrie Hewson, of Coronation Street and Loose Women fame, with their grandmother in 1993

The shirt is red but it is me in Manchester United colours getting in between Brian Kilcline and Tristan Benjamin at Meadow Lane. Not for the first time my header failed to hit the back of the net, this time superbly saved by Notts County goalkeeper Raddy Avramovic

George Best was one of my great heroes so it was a real honour to meet him at the Century Radio Awards where Martin O'Neill presented him with the 106 Century FM Lifetime Achievement Award. Century's Darren Fletcher is on the left showing a bit too much of his dentist's handiwork

My last appearance in an England shirt, in Romania October 1980

September 13 1978 and the moment I shall never forget. My first Forest goal on my European debut against Liverpool. Phil Thompson, Emlyn Hughes and Ray Clemence are helpless but Woody is on hand to make sure the ball crosses the line. It did -- and the holders were on their way out of the competition at the first hurdle

We made sure of progress to the third round to play Grasshopper Zurich by polishing off AEK at the City Ground, this one counting in a 5-1 victory

Emlyn Hughes appears less than happy but I can't restrain big Larry Lloyd as he dashes after the Liverpool captain to say 'bad luck' or something like that at full time at Anfield. Liverpool could not get past Larry or Shilts and we deserved our 0-0 draw that denied the Merseysiders a third successive European title

We were a little fortunate to survive a battering by Ajax in the second leg of our semi final in 1980. Me in flight had nothing to do with our evening in Amsterdam's red light district the night before the game

Goals rarely come as sweet as
this one, against Manchester
United of course in 1986

The European Cup final against
Malmo in Munich was never a
classic. This aerial ballet did not
enhance its quality either

I am not sure how I managed to lift the trophy and complete a lap of honour in Madrid. Pure adrenalin probably. Martin O'Neill, Frank Gray and Viv Anderson can't contain their joy either

When we finally sobered up at half time and after an almighty rollocking from the Gaffer, we eventually got the better of Southampton in the League Cup final of March 17 1979. I'm in there somewhere after scoring in the 3-2 win, one of my two goals although I'm convinced it should have been a hat trick

short career and people have to make the best of it. I had a duty to look after myself and stand up for myself.

There is only so long you can have an inferiority complex about signing from non-league.

There have been times when I have looked back and thought that maybe I let them down and that I disappointed the Gaffer, but I was not the first player he had fallen out with over cash and I was not to be the last either. It was not just peculiar to Forest either. It happened at all clubs. We could not find a middle ground and that was the end of it. Manchester United wanted me. It was hardly as if I was being shipped out to some unfashionable backwater. United were the second biggest club in the land at the time, behind Liverpool. And they wanted me!

I had a real thing for United. Most of it was purely down to George Best. Every kid my age that liked football had wanted to be him, tried to imitate him and he was the real reason I had ever started to play football. I idolised him. He spawned a generation of wannabee footballers in the way he glamorised the game and made football sexy. The David Beckham of his day, but with more sex-appeal. Much more.

I recall the day so that I walked around the County Ground in Northampton when Best scored six against them in an 8-2 FA Cup win. I never saw a second of the match live because I had not been able to get a ticket but felt I was part of the whole thing just walking outside the stadium. Just listening to the roars was incredible. I could imagine what Best was up to. Him, Charlton and all the others playing that day. I had been bought up on the Busby Babes by my Dad. He never tired about telling me how good they were and what a terrible tragedy it had all been.

So when a team with that legacy, such depth of tradition and sheer size made it clear they wanted me, there was not much of a choice to be made. Now I could understand what Ian Storey-Moore had felt all those years earlier, when he turned down Derby County and said yes to Frank O'Farrell. When United made him the most expensive player in British football history at £225,000, well before he got around to recommending me.

In comparison to Forest and the City Ground, United dwarfed them in every aspect, apart from the trophy cabinet. That was where I was supposed to come in. The sheer size of everything was incomprehensible. It felt as if I had drunk some of that potion Alice in Wonderland discovered and shrunk in size. United today is a global phenomenon with billions on their balance sheet, but even at the start of the 80s they were huge, albeit a club in transition frantically trying to remove the huge shadow that was being cast relentlessly by Liverpool.

People ask me if I was tapped up. Everyone thinks football is a shady business and it is all cloak and dagger stuff. Well, I hate to disappoint, but it was nothing like that at all. There were no unrecognisable blokes hanging around the exit to the dressing rooms at the City Ground with collars turned up, handing out telephone numbers to call. It was all straightforward and above board. Dave Sexton phoned the Gaffer and I had an agent called Dennis Roach at the time. So I had nothing to do with the negotiations once I had made my mind up to leave. Haggling over my transfer fee was none of my business.

The situation dragged on for a while. There were even suggestions I had been banned from the City Ground, denied by the Gaffer. They were resigned to me leaving but still they played me right up until September and I scored nine goals at the start of that season. I was flying, but not flying high enough to prevent Forest going out of the European Cup in the first round, losing to CSKA Sofia. That really rankles with me still. I never wanted to leave like that.

BC dug his heels in and made it clear I would not leave until he got the fee he was looking for and had lined up a replacement. Eventually those two criteria were met and I was allowed to talk to United about the move. The only involvement I had was ensuring I got the kind of remuneration I was looking for when it came to my salary, signing-on fees and bonuses, and there was nothing like the bartering required at Forest. It could not have progressed more smoothly. A meeting was arranged with the United manager Dave Sexton at Mottram Hall in the leafy suburbs of Cheshire.

The Grade II listed building had been erected in the 1750s and the Flemish bond orange bricks made it an impressive sight. It reeked of class, just like the pictures of local artists that were hanging tastefully on all the walls. They were fabulous works and Dave Sexton handed me one as a present, before I had even mentioned figures or signed on the dotted line. It was for me, whether I signed or not. It was a touch of class and made me feel even more wanted. He was a lovely man. He was quiet, unassuming and a true gentleman. I wanted to play for him.

Within half-an-hour I got the kind of financial deal that made my Forest pay-packet seem almost like a sick joke. From the moment I scribbled my signature on the contract my basic wage had shot up to £800-a-week. That was not counting the bonus structure built into the deal. There are no too many incentives in football these days. Everything is loaded on the front and the extras are almost not worth having when you are on £150,000-a-week, but every point we collected over 45 in the season was worth an additional £1,000 to me. That was an incredible amount of money for someone who four years earlier was fitting carpets.

While leaving Forest had been prompted largely by money and a feeling of being under-valued, signing for United was not driven by avarice. I was never that kind of bloke. I was not ruled by cold, hard, cash. This was about opportunity. It was about joining a side that boasted the likes of Steve Coppell, Ray Wilkins, Joe Jordan, Lou Macari, Gordon McQueen, Sammy McIlroy and Martin Buchan. This institution in transformation wanted me to be part of new dynasty. They were all household names and it was an incredible incentive to go and play with those people.

Perhaps some of the players were mostly the old guard and the club was not enjoying the best of times but they were still Manchester United. I was honoured that they thought that highly of me. Swapping the cramped corridors and pokey dressing room at Forest, where you had your own peg and that was about it, for the opulent spacious dressing rooms at Old Trafford where you could have a quick five-a-side before kick-off on the marble floors, was something else. It was daunting and sent a tingle of excitement like a 1,000 volt shock down my spine.

I remember being amazed by the choice of floors the lifts had to stop on at Old Trafford and all the different banqueting and marketing suites. The contrast could not have been more vivid or immense. You could walk around the City Ground in 15 minutes. To negotiate all Old Trafford had to offer you had to take the morning off work and even then there was no guarantee you would be back at your desk on time to start the afternoon shift.

The leap from Forest to Manchester United was on the same scale of me leaving the Midland League and Long Eaton United for the City Ground. I am not exaggerating. Old Trafford symbolises class; a place where everything is geared to be the best. At Forest I used to travel to games eating soup and sandwiches on the team bus. At United we had a three course lunch served by a waiter in a bow-tie. We had the choice of the best hotels, the best equipment, the best of everything. It appeared that even the loos had gold taps. It was like being in a palace at Old Trafford. It was an overwhelming and overpowering place. In fact my last game for Forest was against them and I drew a blank on that day. We lost 2-1 at the City Ground and Ian Wallace scored Forest's goal.

I did not have a particularly good scoring record against them. Some clubs get a fixation about players who regularly do for them with goals. I managed one in five games against United in my two-and-a-half seasons at Forest. So it was hardly what you could call prolific. Perhaps they should have got the message loud and clear! I presumed they had just seen I had scored a few goals for Forest and had won European Cups. They had seen I had come from nowhere and must have thought I had a talent and hunger they could develop further. They wanted to help me to help them and maybe hoped some of my winning habits would rub off on the rest of the players.

It seemed like a sensible and plausible plan and hand on heart I never really thought about the size of the £1.25m transfer fee. I know it was well before fees rocketed out of all proportion and that it was a phenomenal amount of money in 1980. At Forest there had been no pressure. I was the equivalent of a round of drinks for the Gaffer. This was different. This was pressure and I could sense the fans' eyes burning into me with expectation. Everyone who signed for United had to deal with that, especially when the club was at such a low ebb. They wanted a saviour and I was happy to take up the challenge of delivering the goals they craved to initiate some kind of Phoenix-style rise.

Consciously I did not think about the money they had paid for me. I did not go out in games with this imaginary tag weighing heavy like the yolk and collar the old Shipstones dray horses used to carry when pulling those kegs of best bitter round the streets of Nottingham. It never crossed my mind. All I wanted to do was play and score goals at the Stretford End. Years later, I looked back and was willing to admit that sub-consciously it affected me more than I ever knew.

At the time, though, it seemed the ideal moment to go. United were struggling at the start of that season. They had gone out of the League Cup to Coventry City in the second round and to make matters worse they had been knocked out of the UEFA Cup in the first round by

Widzew Lodz. Naturally, I believed things could only get better and I could play a part in any revival. It was not arrogance on my part, it was just footballing logic to me.

Dave Sexton wanted me. He sold the club to me and sold me to the club.

It was so easy to get in to the dressing room and become part of things. I confess, I was crapping myself at the start but everyone made me so welcome and there were no cliques whatsoever. I was part of things from day one.

The one problem I did encounter was getting a house sorted out. It took me over four months to find a place in Wilmslow, next door to Asa Hartford.

The country was in a dreadful financial state at the time. The rate of taxation was sky high and mortgage rates were ridiculous. I still had the house in Long Eaton and spent ages trying to get a bridging loan for two properties. Football logic might have said it was a good time to move to United but in terms of real life and the costs it entailed it was probably the worst time of all and those outside issues did not help my state of mind. Neither did the fact that I did not have a solid base in Manchester.

I spent the first four months of my time at Old Trafford commuting. I drove throughout the winter months through the back roads of Macclesfield and Ashbourne. I lost count of the number of times I was up at 6am scraping ice off the car before setting off. I never thought for once that it was having a detrimental effect on me. In hindsight, travelling over two hours to training and driving back every night cannot have been good. I never felt settled in Manchester to begin with and to be honest I was a little homesick and could not wait to get back to my mates.

I still feel that the burden of the transfer fee manifested itself much later in my United career, short and anything sweet as it was! At the beginning I felt like I had been unleashed on to the biggest stage with the biggest spotlight in the world and it was a pure adrenalin rush. I have never bungee jumped or thrown myself out of a plane at 10,000 feet hoping that a parachute will open and slow my descent, but I can't imagine it is more of a buzz than running out for your first game in front of a packed house at Old Trafford.

I only had to wait a little under two weeks for my United debut against Stoke City and I will never forget it, for one reason in particular. Strikers remember all the goals they score and are like fishermen about the ones that get away. They can exaggerate the painful times when cruel misfortune strikes. My debut went reasonably well, but it would have been that much better but for an old Spurs full-back called Ray Evans. He had recently returned from playing over in the States but a short spell with California Surf apparently had taught him a few water tricks that spoiled my entrance into the United spotlight.

I cannot remember the supply line for the chance, but clear as day I remember running free of the Stoke defence and rounding their goalkeeper Peter Fox on my right hand side, my weaker side, which forced me to shoot with my right foot. I always favoured my left foot and just did not get the perfect contact on my shot. I scuffed it, maybe in my eagerness to shoot, or the fact it was the leg I used for standing on. It was a combination of both. Still I thought I had got enough on it and the ball was heading for its intended target. Would it have sufficient power to get there? I was going to score on my United debut and go one better than I had managed at Forest. Sadly, it had been absolutely bucketing down at the old Victoria Ground and the surface was as slick as the ice Torvill and Dean skated on a few years later in Nottingham.

I was getting ready to celebrate a debut goal when from nowhere, Evans came skimming into view. He did not have a surfboard – but he was aquaplaning on his arse. The wedgie he must have given himself, shorts like a thong up his backside, in his determined attempt to deny me must have brought tears to his eyes. I could only watch, helpless, cursing the fucking rain for making the grass so slippery. Even though we won 2-1 with goals from Macari and Jordan and I had made a winning start, I could not help cursing Ray Evans. If he nearly strangled himself with his jockstrap sliding to deny me, that was nothing compared to what I wished him at the time.

Every striker wants to score on his debut. I know that sounds so bloody obvious, but no other player is scrutinised like a centre forward on his first game for a new club and no matter how good your all-round performance might be, fans only think along straight lines. 'Did Birtles score? No he did not'. That goal would have made me an instant success. I would have heard the fans muttering universal approval. Birtles would have been 'just the thing we have been looking for some time now, a genuine goal scorer'."I can't tell you how much I craved that. I had had adulation at Forest and I wanted it at United.

Another chance to make up for misfortune always comes along swiftly in football and Everton were in the firing line as my potential first victims. Once again I was sent clear, like on so many occasions for Forest when I could have scored wearing that blindfold Anne Aston placed on contestants on the Golden Shot. My recollections are not helped by the fact I later became friendly with Seamus McDonough, the Everton goalkeeper that day.

As part of the banter that goes on among players, for years I was able to remind Seamus of how easily I sat him on his arse and swerved around him to open up my target. Left a bit, right a bit, fire! I curled my shot around him and was ready to acknowledge my first goal only to see the ball bounce off the post and away to safety. I could have had two goals in two games, which is usually entered into the category known as 'dream start'. Instead I had two hard luck stories and they were not about to stop there. Even beating Liverpool in my third game, which always means so much to United fans, only marginally took the edge off my bitter disappointment.

Being unable to score goals was of no use to me. That is what I had been signed to do. United paid all that money for precisely that reason. It is the most difficult art in football and I was supposed to be reasonably good at it. To make matters worse I suffered an injury early on in my time at United which set me back even further. It was a really bad problem at the time. I had this issue with my pelvis and I was in all kinds of pain. That was something else alien to me. The previous season at Forest I had played in all 42 league games in the First Division. I was as fit as a flea and was never injured, but it got to the stage where I could barely walk and I was in no proper state to do myself justice. It must have been linked to all the pounding of pitches I had done in Forest red for the previous two seasons.

Despite the pain, I tried to play through it in my eagerness to impress and go some way to justifying the financial outlay United had made. I wanted to succeed for me and for Dave Sexton who had put his reputation on the line, but after a while it became pretty clear that I was not fit enough to be out on a pitch. Somehow, and I am not sure how, I had a hairline fracture of the pelvic bone and I was told I could not do anything for six weeks after drawing another blank against Southampton at the end of November. So after joining a couple of months into the season and playing only eight games, I was forced out of the team at precisely the time I was desperate to make an impact.

I was not allowed to train for that period. Injured footballers are a moody specimen at the best of times. When things are going well in the team, those stuck in a treatment room or hobbling around on crutches are not wearing the same smile as the regulars who are stacking up victories and win bonuses to go with them. You can always spot injured players at any club. They are the ones with a face like a wet weekend and who are unable to muster any kind of words of congratulation for their team mates.

My state of mind was far worse than your average crock. I was barely able to walk and for six weeks I had to deal with the physical pain and the mental anguish of not playing and of seeing the wait for that first United goal extend further and further. Question marks about my fitness, my ability and suitability for United made the situation even more unbearable. My anxiety gorged on all of it like the lions at feeding time at Chester Zoo.

Ray Wilkins had had a similar injury problem so I was given the total support and backing from the entire club's staff as I tried to regain fitness. Still, it felt as if things were conspiring against me. What was going on here? It was almost as if some external force could sense my desperation to do well and to score goals and was putting up all the barriers it could muster to ensure that I failed in my quest to satiate my predator's hunger.

I finally got back in a United shirt at the turn of the year for the FA Cup tie against Brighton at Old Trafford, the only thing that spared my embarrassment at not scoring again was that we somehow scraped a replay in a 2-2 draw and that led to me finally breaking my duck at the Goldstone Ground. It was not the glamorous citadel I had dreamt of to record my first United goal. By that stage, however, I really couldn't have cared less. I was up and running and hoped I had turned that mythical football corner we always hear players and managers talk about.

I turned a corner right enough. Just to find another brick wall blocking my way. I stayed in the side for the remainder of the season but no matter how hard I tried, I could not find another goal and my state of mind deteriorated as the search dragged on.

Despite all the problems and the weeks that passed without me scoring the fans never turned against me and I will always be grateful for that. I have seen players crucified at clubs when they have not lived up to their billing and price tag. Supporters can be a cruel and very unforgiving lot, but those accusations could never be levelled at United's followers -- and trust me they had more reason than most to complain, whinge and generally dislike me.

Of course, there were more than the odd few dissenting voices. They would not have been human otherwise. It is the nature of football fans to complain. They pay their money and they are entitled to vent their spleen, but I genuinely feel that they could see I was working my balls off for the team and that it was just not happening for me. At no stage did I seem to get the rub of the green. Everything I had touched at Forest had turned to gold. I don't know what the opposite of the Midas touch is, but I had it down to a fine art at Old Trafford.

The fans respected me for my effort and I ran myself into the ground chasing everything. That was reassuring and somehow comforting -- but it was not enough for me. I just could not relax, because when you are not delivering the hatful of goals you were signed to deliver, even the strikers with skin as tough as Rhino hide feel the pressure eventually and I was far from the hard-nosed, hard-hearted kind that could just shrug off the tension.

Mind you, that was not helped by the fact I had priests praying for me on daily basis. Everyone knows United is a religious club and all that goes with that because of the Ireland connection. My plight reached such a stage that every time I used to go to the Cliff for training the club reverend was at the training ground saying prayers for me, begging for some divine intervention. I am not sure how much holy water I used up during that time, but he was constantly telling me not to worry. God was on my side and everything would be all right.

I even remember going on club tours to Ireland and the supporters over there were incredible. Often it would take us nearly an hour to weave our way from the dressing room back to the team bus. We signed that many autographs we had writers' cramp and they were all so supportive of me. Everyone kept telling me to keep my chin up and that they were saying prayers. If I had been handed a pound for all the times I received the chin elevation advice from fans and my team mates, I would have been able to pay back the £1.25m transfer fee as refund out of my own pocket. That would have eased my sense of guilt and I would still have had more than enough to live on for the rest of my life.

Just like the fans never turned on me, there was no whispering in corners of changing rooms from my team mates, either. You know the sort you encounter in the work place when you wander into a room and are convinced co-workers are talking in less than complimentary terms about you in a huddle. You can tell they are by the way the conversation comes to an abrupt halt and everyone starts staring at their shoes or out of the window. No one will make eye-contact with you. There was nothing like that in the dressing room. It was quite the opposite.

Ray Wilkins was fantastic. Bryan Robson, when he arrived, was one of my biggest supporters, along with Frank Stapleton. We used to hang around together with our wives and often go out. Those three were constantly massaging my severely bruised ego. I was never a big time Charlie with an arrogant streak when I had been so successful at Forest. My self-confidence was not fragile, but it was certainly not indestructible either. No matter how much backing I received, it did not ease my anxiety.

The games continued to come and go without a goal and my luck was empty. I bet red it came black. I bet odd and it came up even. I went near post and the ball hit the back stick. I pulled away to the far post and tap-ins materialised 12-yards in front of me. The longer it went on the more I started to analyse. It dominated my thoughts and I can't have been too much fun to be around. I just began thinking far too deeply about what I was doing. I was trying to find a solution oblivious to the fact that I was exacerbating the problem.

I felt that I was under the microscope from everyone and I tried searching for excuses too. When I signed for United, they played a different style to the one I was used to at Forest. Everything they did went through the Scotland striker Joe Jordan. It was a far more direct style. He might not have had too many teeth at that time, but that made him all the more menacing as he dominated central defensive markers with his superiority in the air. I don't think I saw him lose too many contests over high balls in any area of the pitch.

It worked for United at that time. They had Steve Coppell on one side of the pitch to supply ammunition to Joe. He was a fantastic crosser of the ball but I had been signed from a team that played under Brian Clough's rules. He would have introduced a law against the ball going over head height if he could have done so. Everything had to be played into feet and that was one of my strengths, holding the ball up after it had been delivered to me along the floor. Let's not forget I went to bed with the words 'Gaz, hold the fucking ball' floating around my brain for long enough.

If you think Arsene Wenger is passionate about playing in the correct manner and creating intricate passing patterns and identifying and creating angles that many managers do not know exist, never mind cannot spot, BC would have killed us for smashing the ball in the air and running after it. To him that was a crime against the game. Quite simply, United were more direct and it was strange for me. I did not feel like I was becoming depressed about life at Old Trafford, I always tried to brush it aside and get on with things.

But that evening when I was driving through the back roads of Macclesfield and Ashbourne, after Billy Wright, the Everton centre back had finally allowed me to climb out of his back pocket at the end of a 1-0 win at

Goodison Park in March, was probably as low as I got during my entire time at Old Trafford. With all due respect to Billy, I had come up against, scored against and got the better of central defenders far better than him during my time at Forest. I was really down and it played on my mind that much I almost crashed my car and could have ended up killing myself. Just because I was so absorbed in thinking about my crap time at United.

That was not the only close shave I had at the wheel, but another incident when I lost control was more to do with the fact I had just come back from a trip with United during that dreadful run of no goals, which eventually stretched to 28 games. All I had to show for my efforts in the first season was one goal in the FA Cup against Brighton. Even own goals finished higher than I did in the United scoring charts that season. Not a bad return on a £1.25m investment. It was embarrassing and my face developed a deeper shade of red, but not quite as dark as my mate Trevor Moores when I hooked up with him after another dash back to Nottingham and the sanctuary of my mates after returning from a United club trip to Malaysia.

My good mate Trevor paid the price for my decision to have a drink and drive when I was jet-lagged and if I wanted a signal as to how unfortunate my dream move to Old Trafford had become, this was it. A professional punter would have gone broke if he had endured the same kind of losing run with his investments as I had in front of goal at United in my first season. I had got more duck eggs to my name than some of the three-legged nags I used write on betting slips. That was bad enough, but my shame was about to plummet to a new low. After my TVR, Trev and myself had plummeted through a hedge and into someone's front garden in the early hours after a drinking session in the city centre.

There was claret all over my mate's face and the car dash board was spattered with the stuff too. It looked like he had broken his nose when he shot forward, probably because he was not wearing a seat belt. There were no annoying car computers then or alarms that beeped tortuously because you had not belted up for the journey. All we had to bother us were a series of ad campaigns urging to 'clunk, click every trip'. Not too many took any notice and there were no on-the-spot fines from the police for failing to wear one.

The sound of nose bone crunching on the dash occurred I opted not to home to an empty house on my return from Manchester airport. My missus Sandra was in Spain with her mum and dad so I decided to drive into

MY MAGIC CARPET RIDE

Nottingham for a few drinks with friends. I usually drank lager but for some reason that night I was drinking Southern Comfort. I had a few and as it was approaching midnight I complained of feeling tired. I needed to get home and get some sleep.

I knew I'd had too much to drink and that I would be over the limit, but that did not stop me getting in to the car and turning the ignition. Loads of people drove with too much alcohol in their system. That is not an excuse. I knew I was breaking the law but I could hear that voice in the head saying: 'You'll be OK. You don't have far to go, just take it easy'.

I took it easy all right, so much so that I fell asleep at the wheel. Even with Led Zeppelin blearing on the car stereo. That is quite a feat when Robert Plant is in full flow of Communication Breakdown.

I only woke up when the front end of the TVR smashed into the kerb on Toton Lane forcing the car to veer horribly to the left and smash into a lamppost with such force that it snapped the axle leaving me completely powerless as I tried to wrestle back control. I was wrenching at the wheel, but there was nothing I could do to prevent the car from careering into a nearby garden and eventually coming to a juddering halt before it reached the front door. It was at some point during that sequence that the nose snapped as well. Fortunately I worked out I had escaped without any real physical damage by the time the couple who owned the house shot through their front door to find out what was causing the commotion.

Imagine their shock as they found me the worse for wear and shaken up and poor old Trev covered in blood. We must have looked a right sight. Quick as a flash they ushered us inside and got to work on clearing up the blood while I was in the kitchen drinking as many pints of water as I could, in the vain hope that when the police arrived I would have diluted the Southern Comfort that was polluting my blood stream.

The lady of the house must have been in the kitchen earlier, because there was food all over the place. She was preparing a packed lunch for her husband to take to work the following day. She waved her hands frantically at the food urging me to eat whatever I could and. I crammed all kinds of things down my throat. It can't have been pretty to watch. I was like a hunger-striker who had just given up his protest, ramming sandwiches, tomatoes and lettuce in my mouth with both hands, hoping it might sober me up. I was not roaring drunk, but I knew I was over the limit. I would have eaten horse manure if I thought it meant I would have blown a negative breathalyser.

THEATRE OF BAD DREAMS

It was not long before the flashing blue lights lit up the kitchen. Fucking hell, this was it. I was going to get bagged and fail. If things were not already bad enough at United, this would be the final straw. The policemen came into the house to survey the damage to my mate's nose and they could probably smell the alcohol from the moment they walked through the front door. I waited for the familiar: 'Have you been drinking Sir?'

What's the point in saying no? I had been brought up to tell the truth and I admitted to having a drink and my heart was pounding as they pulled out the breathalyser. 'Blow into the mouthpiece sir. One, long, continual breath until I say stop'were the instructions. I sucked the air in and hoped that somehow I was cleansing it of the alcohol as I blew out until I was told I could relax. 'That's fine Mr Birtles you are under the limit. Can I have your autograph please?'

I could have killed someone. Looking back it was not big or clever. It was being stupid and it is not something of which I am particularly proud, but right at that moment, I could not wait to sign my name and get the hell out of there.

The policeman must have been a Forest fan. There is no other explanation for my incredible escape from punishment and a driving ban that could have finished my United career quicker than I was trying to end it with my lack of goals. The police even dropped me off at my friend's house where I had to explain to his parents why his nose was spread all over his face and his clothes covered in blood. It was not the kind of example a million-pound footballer should be setting. I was hardly a hell-raiser. I was shame-faced at the trouble I had caused.

So what is unlucky about all that? While I was passing the breath test and signing autographs, I was completely unaware that travelling in the opposite direction when I had hit the lamp post was a car carrying a freelance photographer. Those snappers are never off duty and always seem to have a nose for a pay cheque. So the person in question hung around and waited for the tow-truck to turn up and followed it to see where it was taken. He must have snapped off a whole reel of film taking pictures of the broken TVR.

Those pictures certainly looked good on the news pages of The Sun the following day. The headline? What else but Birtles Hits The Post Again. It was all over the newspapers and that photographer must have paid his mortgage for a few months on the back of my misfortune. I can laugh about the whole episode when I look back now, but at the time it was just another low-point in a series of soul-destroying events that I never anticipated once I had made the decision to quit Forest.

There was another thing I did not bargain on happening before the end of my first season. Dave Sexton, one of the finest gentlemen I ever met in the game, was sacked. My ally, the manager who signed me and paid all that cash was told he was no longer required at United after four seasons without winning a trophy. That is a whole career in comparison to how itchy the trigger fingers in the boardrooms became after I had retired from the game.

You can't imagine anyone lasting that long at United these days when so much is expected of people. Nevertheless, Sexton's sacking was a blow to me despite winning our last seven games, including a 1-0 win at Anfield, to finish eighth in Division One. That was scant consolation. We ended up 12 points short of the champions, Aston Villa, and just to rub salt into the wounds a little more Forest finished a place above us. That would have given the Gaffer reason to smile. I needed a holiday and I needed to get away and sort my head out. There was no way I could go back for pre-season training at the Cliff in that state.

7

BIRTLES SCORES!
Iran hostages relieved

'WE have all had our fair share of laughs at the expense of Garry Birtles since his £1m transfer to Manchester United. Poor Garry has had no alternative but to grin and bear it as the jokes about his lack of goals have flown fast and furious. Forget the fact that he managed just one goal in about five months last season. I am backing him to get a bucketful this time. It hasn't taken me long to realise that we are talking about a super lad and a tremendous professional.

'In a strange sort of way the departure of big Joe Jordan to Milan could help him. Because Joe was undoubtedly the king of Old Trafford it may well have been that Garry became a bit inhibited. I am more than delighted at the potential of his link up with Frank Stapleton. Here we have two strikers who have both mobility and a real appetite for hard work – a deadly duo.

'In fact, I have so much confidence in the ability of Birtles that although I am probably the leading member of the Trevor Francis fan club, I decided not to make strong overtures for him. Not too many so-called experts have Manchester United in their selections for the championship fight. Well I have already stated that my aim is to win the title in my first year as manager'.

Good old Big Ron. He soon had the national press in the North West eating out of the palm of his hand feeding them the snappy quotes and giving Manchester United the kind of PR and spin Alastair Campbell gave Tony Blair's Labour government. He was a natural at all that. He had the gift of the gab almost as much as BC and not too many came close when it came to the matter of charming reporters and making sure they swallowed every mouthful of the propaganda they were being fed.

The press pack in Manchester were delighted to see Ron, who was in vivid contrast to his more reserved predecessor Dave Sexton. They gobbled up every quote and naturally I was a major question he had to answer on his arrival at The Cliff. How did Ron see my future? Did I still have a future? Was I the unluckiest striker ever to play for United? Or was I the worst striker he had ever seen? Good old Ron. He went for the positive spin and bulled me up good and proper. It was the arm around the shoulder routine, when he could have cut me adrift and told everyone that I was a sitting duck. I will always be grateful to him for that.

Mind you, Ron was great at playing the journalists' political games. He was great at ducking and diving too and what he failed to mention was that for most of the time since he had arrived as Sexton's replacement he had been trying to get rid of me! All that flannel about what a great striker I was and how many goals I was going to score was a sham. For the previous month he had been busting his gut to do a deal with Forest, of all teams, and sell me back to them along with goalkeeper Gary Bailey in exchange for Peter Shilton and Trevor Francis!

By the time he was singing my praises in an exclusive interview he gave to his mate Joe Melling, of the Daily Express, it was almost the end of August and Joe's article, from which the quotes about me are taken, was published the day before we launched Big Ron's brave new world with a 2-1 defeat on the opening day of the season at Coventry City. He also omitted to mention his overtures for Shilton and Francis had been rejected in no uncertain terms by Forest and that he had no alternative but to start the season with his 'deadly duo' Frank Stapleton, a £900,000 signing from Arsenal and myself, the not-so-proud owner of one Manchester United goal!

I had heard all the rumours doing the rounds about swapping me for my old Forest team mate during the summer. While nothing had been said to me directly by Atkinson or anyone else at Old Trafford and no mention of it had reached my ears from BC, or anyone else at Forest for that matter, the grapevine was buzzing and there was no smoke without fire. It was hardly the kind of resounding vote of confidence I was looking for from my new boss at Old Trafford. Not after a summer recharging my batteries and resolving to put behind me the nightmare I had suffered the previous season.

It's amazing what the sun can do for the power of the mind. The Gaffer always came back from his summer break in Cala Millor looking a million dollars. Sun-tanned, shorts and a bounce in his step as he chucked a tennis ball for his faithful retriever Del to chase halfway around the City Ground car park as he headed to his office. By the time pre-season arrived at United in my second season, I was refreshed and had come up with a catalogue of arguments for myself which justified to me precisely why I had been forced to endure such a torrid and embarrassing first season at Old Trafford.

So many factors had counted against me. I had not done a pre-season with my new club 12 months earlier because I signed in September and was not able to have that bonding time slogging around in July and August. For the first four months I had nowhere to live in Manchester and commuting from Nottingham on a daily basis was bad for me. Spending that amount of time behind the wheel of a car every day was ridiculous.

The team were playing the wrong style of football smashing the ball up to Joe Jordan and my pelvic injury just added to the problems. No wonder I had not scored hardly any goals. When you total up all those excuses they make a pretty compelling argument. Every argument had a credible thread and that is why I resolved to make sure the new season was not going to be a repeat, especially under Ron Atkinson. He had come in like a whirlwind and created this refreshing and exciting vibe around Old Trafford. I wanted to be part of it. After all Ron said he wanted to win the league and so did I. That was the reason I had moved to United in the first place, for a bucketful of medals.

Whether Big Ron genuinely wanted me there as part of his team or not, he really did not have much choice by the time the season was about to launch. So he turned on the charm offensive. At least he made me feel as if he had some faith in me. That is always a good start for any player and he might have had a point about Joe Jordan leaving for AC Milan. At least Ron was a football man and wanted to play the game the right way. After all my schooling at Forest and days of five-a-sides and little else, it had to be a step in the right direction.

Whatever Ron's image at the time, and it was a flash one to say the least, I have to say categorically he was not a triumph of style over content. Dave Sexton, despite his name, was not sexy. He was not much of a PR man and that was how United justified his sacking. They wanted someone with some panache, who was flamboyant and wanted to play the game in an exciting way. The power brokers at United felt Sexton was dull and Ron was the Viagra needed to put the sexy back into United, well before Ruud Gullit started talking about it and made it fashionable with Chelsea.

It might have looked a stunt on the outside, but for all his brash talk and bling, Ron was a top manager at the highest level. The previous season he had guided WBA to fourth in the league and to the quarter-finals of the UEFA Cup, which was far more than we had managed at United. His barnet might have been a little dodgy but you could not say the same about his results or the way in which he liked to play football. His Three Degrees at the Hawthorns - black stars Lawrie Cunningham, Cyrille Regis and Brendon Batson, were part of a stylish side which also included the highly-talented young midfielder Bryan Robson, who was certainly one person Ron wanted alongside him.

So he had credentials and he had ambition. Whatever he had been trying to achieve during the summer in terms of shifting me on was history. He failed with his bid for Francis and I was still at Old Trafford. It was up to me to prove I belonged there and make the most of another chance. My mind was clear and I was determined to make an impression. I had scored six goals in pre-season and felt as good as I had ever done in terms of fitness. Whatever Ron thought of me, I loved his way of working.

He was brilliant in that respect. All the training changed. It was all five-a-sides and football, just like it had been under my previous manager. There was no running a million miles in training and never seeing the ball. I could never understand managers that did not let their players have the ball when they were training. It was the tool of our trade. That is like asking a painter and decorator to practise without a ladder and a paint brush. You have to enjoy what you are doing and training is enjoyable if you are playing football, not running marathons.

Ron loved his five-a-sides even more than I did. He thought he was a player, even though he only ever played for Kettering Town! He joined in and he would knock a ball and say 'that's a Beckenbauer ball'. He had super-star names for everything he did with the ball in training! It became known as Ronglish, or Big-Ronisms. But no matter how much I was enjoying all that, I had to go out and face the Old Trafford crowds again and somehow try to put an end to this miserable goalless spell.

I had trained superbly the previous season too. I played one practice match and our team won 5-0. I scored four of the goals. I practiced my finishing drills religiously, but no matter what I did on the training ground they would not go in during matches. Gordon McQueen and Lou Macari never stopped taking the piss out of me. Gordon always reminded me about the game against Crystal Palace towards the end of the previous season at Old Trafford.

BIRTLES SCORES!

I hit the post that day and had a goal ruled out because of an infringement by another player. I was livid. It would have broken my duck. Gordon ran past me and said 'you are never going to score for us are you?' He had a great big grin on his face. I feared he might have been right at the time but I had to get back out there and rebuild a reputation that had taken a jolt since being part of England's European Championship squad a year earlier.

I had run out of excuses and knowing Ron was looking around for another striker just added to the pressure as we headed off to Mottram Hall the night before we played our first home game of the season. The opponents? Nottingham Forest. While that just added spice to the fixture for everyone else, it just cranked up the pressure a notch higher for me. It is only human nature to wonder why BC said no to taking me back and letting Trevor Francis leave. Did he think I was no longer the player I once was too?

At least at Mottram Big Ron tried to put me at ease. He even came over to the dinner table and acted as drinks waiter, bringing me a pint of lager. I never had to ask. He knew I loved a beer and made it perfectly clear that it was acceptable. There had never been much of a drinking culture at Old Trafford. The players did not really go out that much the previous season. I never found myself in a night club once with any of my United team mates. There would have been a major steward's enquiry if that had ever happened at Forest. Mind you, given the troubles I had suffered, being unable to hit a cow's arse with a banjo, I doubt too many United fans would have been queuing up to buy me a beer.

On the other side of the fence, I could probably have got pissed most nights on beers brought for me by Manchester City fans! I am sure they would have loved me to stay at Old Trafford and continue my woeful run for the rest of my career. The beer at Mottram was a nice touch and I certainly don't have any recollections of feeling anxious or nervous the night before the game. As far as I was concerned, last season was history and this was a fresh start for Ron Atkinson and a fresh start for Garry Birtles. So much for bloody clean slates.

After all the fanfares leading up to Ron's Old Trafford debut, we let him down and drew a blank against Forest. There were no howling misses from me, but just another game without a league goal. It was a huge disappointment and I could sense the groans creeping in already. Last season fans had been prepared to give me the benefit of the doubt and stick with me. They stayed with me for the comedy value, but this time around it was not going to be the same. I had to deliver, or they would rip me to shreds. The benevolence was not going to last forever.

My mood only worsened when we lost our following league game at Old Trafford 2-1 to Bobby Robson's Ipswich Town. It was hard not to start thinking here we go again. If the fans had been good to me last season, their patience would snap eventually. I thought I was entering another of those dark tunnels with no light at the end of it. It is amazing how quickly all your enthusiasm and aspirations at the start of a new season can turn to rubble.

By the time Swansea arrived at Old Trafford for the fifth game of the season we had not won a match and had two points. A disappointing start does not even come close and it was really starting to get to shit or bust time. My sense of humour and that of the United fans had been stretched to breaking point. Opposition players were giving me stick again and taking the piss. All I could do was suck it up and get on with it, but it was growing increasingly hard to smile. A couple of lagers at Mottram Hall on the Friday night did not help me sleep much either. The tension in me must have been tangible for the rest of the dressing room, no matter how hard I tried to hide it.

I had to keep laughing at myself. Everyone else was, so I might as well join in. Even when I finally did break my duck for United after 323 days it did not stop the joker in me. I gave every end-of-pier and Liberal club comedian enough material for a tour from Aberdeen to Land's End. Apparently, if I had shot John Lennon he would still be alive today! I suppose because I hardly broke any goal scoring records at Old Trafford, that the afternoon of 19th September 1981 sticks in my mind so vividly.

The United fans had been more patient than saints waiting for me to show just why I had cost £1.25m and I can only hope the goal that ended the wait against Swansea at Old Trafford was worth the ridiculous delay. For me it will always be one of those Phoenix From the Flames moments Frank Skinner and David Baddiel used to re-enact. I am surprised they did not pick the moment when I very nearly caused the roof to come off Old Trafford and land on Sir Matt Busby Way. It still feels like yesterday, the memory is that crystal clear.

Someone fired the ball up to Frank Stapleton on the edge of the penalty area. It was flying at him like a missile. One of those thankless tasks strikers get with a pass they can't head and can't control with their feet, but Frank was so aware of what was going on around him. He had a complete picture of the pitch in his head and who was where. The vast majority of people may think that a strike partner such as myself and the run I was on would be the last option to pass to, but Frank never lost faith in me, thank god. Even if I might have lost some faith in myself.

He could see the position I had taken up and made the decision to chest the ball down into my path with perfect pace and direction. As the ball was coming down to me, I was tearing forward to meet it at full pelt. As I approached the bouncing ball I could almost hear the groans from all sides of Old Trafford. Only the Swansea fans were encouraging me to let fly! United had been there so many times before and someone had already left the Stretford End to run over to the square at nearby Old Trafford cricket club to bring the ball back. The rest would have been shielding their eyes out of embarrassment for me as I prepared to pull the trigger.

The pass from Frank hit the pitch just as my left foot swung through the hitting zone. Anyone that plays golf will know the feeling when they nail a driver off the first tee and it flies with that wonderful gently rising trajectory, while you can still hear the fizz of it flying off the tee peg. My left boot gave me exactly the same sensation as I smashed the ball on the half-volley. I don't think I have struck too many sweeter shots in my entire career than that one and the ball just flew in past the Swansea goalkeeper.

The poor sod must have thought he was the unluckiest man alive to have conceded a goal to Garry Birtles playing for Manchester United at Old Trafford. He should be honoured, they are collectors' items. Some clever journo worked out it had taken me 44 hours and six minutes to break my duck in front of my own fans. That was longer than the average working week back then! Old Trafford just exploded with emotion. Although I am still not convinced how many people actually saw the ball fly in or were looking away in premature disgust.

Fans were rubbing their eyes in stark disbelief, checking they were not dreaming, unable to believe it was me that had scored. There was just an outpouring of sheer relief. The fans went bananas and I thought the roof was going to come off. I have never heard a noise like it as a player. I think they were just so delighted I had finally got the mother and father of all primates off my back. Above all the roaring and laughter from the fans who can count themselves lucky to be able to say 'I was there the day Birtles finally scored at Old Trafford', I could hear my heartbeat louder than anything. I thought it was going to burst through my rib cage.

MY MAGIC CARPET RIDE

People have ridiculed my time at Old Trafford. I kept getting phone calls all the time from journalists when Diego Forlan had his rotten time with goals at United asking me to tell everyone what the Uruguayan was going through. Even the United fans called him "Diego Birtles" the poor sod, but I still finished way above him in a poll conducted by the Observer back in 2001 when I was listed as the third biggest waste of money in the football transfer market.

A few straightforward calculations in 2001 had me behind Steve Daley and RaFael Scheidt (transferred from Brazilian club Gremio to Celtic for £5m in 1999) as the third biggest white elephant professional football had ever seen. Based on the number crunching at the time my transfer fee was worth £3.2m (calculated on the rate of inflation between my original transfer and the 2001 market). In the 2001 market apparently I would have cost £23.8m (calculated as a percentage of the record transfer fee at the time and levels in 2001).

Forlan cost a fraction of that at £7.5m from Argentine club Independiente and endured some of the torture I went through suffering 25 matches without scoring a goal, but that must have felt at least double under the scrutiny of Sir Alex Ferguson – even if the Uruguayan only made eight starts in that period of time. Every match that went by someone else would ring and ask me what the turmoil was like to suffer such a drought. I got to relive my failings at United on a regular basis thanks to Mr Forlan. Not that he intended it.

When he finally grabbed his first goal, no one was more delighted than me and I gave my final musings on the subject to David Meek, the hugely respected Manchester Evening News journalist, who covered United for decades and had to endure all my goalless games for the club. I remember telling him thank goodness Diego has scored, because it meant my phone would not be ringing anymore with questions about how it feels to go so long at United without a goal. It was a bloody relief for me and for Forlan no doubt. Forlan subsequently went on to prove himself as one of the game's most lethal and intelligent strikers in Spanish football and at an international level, form confirmed during the World Cup in South Africa.

United fans kept faith with Forlan in the same way they did with me and whatever the stick I took from opposition defenders, media and fans, no one can ever take away the incredible feeling I had that day against Swansea. It was a priceless moment in an incredible theatre of a stadium and something

BIRTLES SCORES!

I had dreamt of from the moment I walked through the gates at the Cliff. It was just a shame I had to wait such a long time to taste the ecstasy.

If it was big shakes for me, it was massive news in Manchester for the whole weekend. They even had me on TV the following day. Elton Welsby had a sports show in Manchester at the time and invited me on to talk about the goal. I jumped at the invitation, mostly because I could not resist the chance to turn the jokes back on myself and show that I had never lost my sense of humour. After all I had kept every comedian in the country in gags for almost 12 months.

One of the favourites doing the rounds at the time was linked to the Iran hostage situation. A group of Islamist students had captured 53 Americans and held them hostage in the American Embassy for 444 days from November 4, 1979 to January 20, 1981, in support of the Iranian Revolution. The episode reached a climax when, after failed attempts to negotiate a release, the United States military attempted a rescue operation which was given the dramatic name of 'Operation Eagle Claw' on April 24, 1980.

That failed and resulted in the destruction of two aircraft and the deaths of eight American servicemen and one Iranian civilian before the siege was brought to an end by the signing of the Algiers Accords in Algeria on January 19, 1981 and the hostages were formally released into United States custody the following day, just minutes after the new American president Ronald Reagan was sworn into office in the White House.

Before any hostage could ask whether Reagan had been elected, apparently the first hostage to be released asked was: 'Has Birtles scored for United yet?' I took the piss out of myself and repeated the same gag for Elton. If you can laugh at yourself and take extract the michael out of yourself, even when things seem at their most bleak, then you have got half a chance.

Thus, after so many dark days I could see a ray of hope for me at United and the surge of confidence the experience against Swansea gave me was incredible. It was time for my career at United to really take off.

Big Ron's words about Frank Stapleton and myself did have some ring of truth to them throughout the season and we did develop some level of understanding that justified Ron's confidence. Partnerships are vital to strikers and for the first time at Old Trafford I felt I was part of one. In the following game against Middlesbrough I repaid the favour for Frank and scored again. Two in two games. The fans probably wanted me dope testing! I genuinely did start to get the feeling we could work together and score plenty of goals. It was as optimistic as I had ever been since the day I signed.

My self-confidence had taken a battering so the other side of the coin was a more than welcome change and when you start getting advice and backing from such United legends as Denis Law you can't help but feel 100ft tall. Denis took the trouble to go into print to back me even further, making the point to United fans that read his every word that I should carry on what I had started and learn to be more selfish and forget about the team. That was always something that was unnatural to me. I had always been a team player at Forest. So to change my style overnight was never going to be easy. On top of that, Denis never had to endure almost a year without a goal for United. The longest he went was a couple of games, but it was nice he cared and certainly helped me.

After a plodding start, which set a few alarm bells ringing for Big Ron and everyone, we suddenly seemed to click and I did not have to wait long for my next goal in a 5-0 thumping of Wolves at Old Trafford. If it was notable for Sammy McIlroy's hat-trick something far more significant happened on the pitch, before we had even kicked a ball against the team that robbed me of a second League Cup winner's medal and gave me one of my true low points in the game.

Prior to kick-off, ever the showman Ron had a smile wider than the Manchester Ship canal, but for once he had to vacate the spotlight in favour of someone else. Someone who was to become one of the most important signings the club ever made. Step forward Bryan Robson and the £1.5m signing of the West Bromwich Albion midfielder who would help transform the club. The amount of flashlights going off from photographers' cameras made Halley's Comet look like a Swan Vesta sparking off!

Ron had been after him all summer. He had unearthed him at the Hawthorns. He knew his true value. His fearless nature, superhuman powers of endurance and incredible leadership qualities. All summer he had been desperate to lure Robbo to Old Trafford with him to inject his special talent into the squad he had inherited from Dave Sexton. The transfer fee mirrored just how highly Ron valued the youngster. When you look back now at some of the outlandish fees that are paid for players, signing Robbo for £1.5m was ridiculous.

According to those who know, from the moment Ron had been given the hot seat at Old Trafford, Robbo wanted to follow him.

BIRTLES SCORES!

I had seen Robson up close in a few games against WBA and he looked a great player. That cannot be denied but I had never worked with him on a training ground and I had never been in the same dressing room with him. From the moment he walked through the gates, it was blatantly obvious why Big Ron had made such a fuss and had been so desperate to get him to the club.

Robbo was perpetual motion. Whether it was in games, or in training I have never seen anything like it in my career. He could drink like a fish and trained harder than Daley Thompson. I always prided myself on being good in training and being fit. I loved it, but Robbo made me look like a 40-a-day smoker with one lung! He looked like he could run forever and never showed the effects of training hard. His sheer will was a force I have never seen in others.

From the moment he joined Remi Moses, his old WBA buddy, in the centre of the Untied midfield the pair were incredible. They had only been there a few minutes in comparison to most of the squad, but they looked like they owned Old Trafford. It was just what we needed. We were flying and that title winning prediction of Ron's looked less fanciful now. It rubbed off on me and everyone else at the club, helping us to victory at Liverpool with goals from Arthur Albiston and Kevin Moran. We had made a statement.

True we went out of the League Cup at the hands of Spurs yet we went on a run in the league which coincided with me scoring in four successive matches, including a 5-1 win at Sunderland. In October United were top of the league and it was a position we managed to hang on to going into the following month too. Things had transformed so drastically, I was even being talked about as a genuine contender for a recall to the England squad during the qualifying campaign for the World Cup finals in Spain the following summer of 1982.

If someone had mentioned the words Birtles and England in the same sentence a year earlier they would have been dismissed as stark raving mad. If I had been the last striker on the planet there was no way I was getting an England shirt to pull on. I had not played for England since a 1-0 World Cup qualifying defeat in Romania in October 1980. It was over a year since I had been in the international set-up – a penance caused by my woeful first season with United. Now they were talking about me being part of Ron Greenwood's squad for the 1982 finals in Spain. How things change and it just proves what a fickle industry the game is, but I did not give a toss. It was great to be back in the limelight again.

Mind you, all the clamour for my England recall might have come to an abrupt end if I had been arrested by the Greater Manchester constabulary on suspicions of being a burglar at the delightful Gawsworth Hall, an ancient manor house in Macclesfield. The Tudor Manor house was well known for its fine paintings, antique furniture, sculpture and stained glass and I was fingered for casing the joint, which would have gone down well at FA headquarters at Lancaster Gate.

I have always been fond of old buildings and history and one afternoon all the family visited Sandra and me in Manchester and we decided to go out for a spot of lunch. On the way, we stopped off at Gawsworth House and had a good roam around. I spent most of the time with Sandra's brother David having a look at things and commenting on the cameras that were clearly there to protect the valuables. Once we had decided we had seen enough and hunger had taken hold, we set off up the road to a lovely pub for lunch.

I still had my TVR at the time and we had barely sat down and picked up the menu when someone came to ask me if the TVR in the car park was mine. After confirming that it was, I was asked to go outside where two police officers were waiting to speak to me. Apparently the people at Gawsworth had become a little twitchy at Sandra's brother and me pointing at the cameras as well as the paintings. They thought we were putting together a list of things to steal! The policeman asked me my name and when I told him he asked me what I did! He could not apologise enough when he realised the mistake.

Times were so good we even managed to get a bit of a drinking school going. Robbo, Frank, Ray Wilkins and myself would always tend to go out in the suburbs with our partners and wives and have a few beers and with John Gidman, a replacement for Mike Duxbury at right-back, I finally found someone who enjoyed a night out clubbing as much as I did and loved a drink just as much. Giddy had arrived from Aston Villa and he was my room mate, so I decided to take him under my wing!

He was a good looking sod. He had loads of dark black hair and was always flicking it about. He was far too handsome for a defender, but he was great to go out with for a drink and he was the one I hooked up with during a trip to Bournemouth to play a bit of golf. I think we were kindred spirits because we both loved our heavy metal music and he was the person who introduced me to Jim Steinman and Meatloaf at the start of an afternoon session that meandered into the very early hours.

After drinking all day and seeing which of us could put away the most pints of lager, we ended up in this club in Bournemouth. By this time we had turned into big time Charlies, utterly inebriated drinking champagne by the bucketful in the VIP area with the Nolan Sisters. We thought we were so flash as the strobe lights made it even more difficult to focus, bouncing off the angles of the silver tubing tables with glass tops on them. The beams of light were blinding us and Giddy had a bottle of Dom Perignon in his hand as we were struggling to stay upright. He was so disoriented that he went to lean on what was a beam of light and ended up falling just like Del Boy in that famous episode of Only Fools and Horses, straight on top of one of the glass tables and smashed the whole thing.

He went right through the glass and ended up with his legs bent over the silver tubing, laughing his head off. Not a drop of the champagne spilt...a true professional. I managed to drag him to his feet and decided it was time to leave. We were that drunk we could barely see and couldn't walk. We were feeling our way in the darkness, around the walls of the club, pulling down great big carpet curtains at one point. Any footballer since the turn of the new millennium to do something like that would have found themselves plastered all over the front pages of national newspapers the next day.

Someone would have cashed in on the debauchery and tipped off the papers. The only tip we got was where to get a cab to get us back to our hotel. No one batted an eyelid when we returned in such a dreadful state. Not a word was said. I never did find out what happened to Scott McGarvey's attempt to pull Colleen Nolan, which had not gone down well with her sisters earlier in the evening!

If Scott's tilt at Colleen did not meet with much success, the same could not be said of United's challenge at the top end of the table. By the time the end of February came around we were third in the table with two games in hand and just six points adrift. However, any hopes I had of being part of a title-winning team received a major blow when I suffered a recurrence of the pelvic injury that had blighted my season the previous year, during a friendly against Barnet.

I came off in agony in my stomach and the whole thing caused a lot of worry as well as pain. I remember going to Elland Road and was unable to play because of the shooting pains. I could barely sit down in the stand to watch the 0-0 draw. My whole right leg used to go numb from thigh to toe and I knew that other players who had been hit with a similar problem had spent as long as 12-months out of the game. You wonder why I sometimes wonder whether my time at Old Trafford was cursed!

As it was I ended up missing a month of the season, probably the most crucial part, from April to May. Being out of action coincided with United's title challenge stuttering and with five games remaining we were ten points adrift of Liverpool and it was too much of a gap to make up. Another of my footballing low points occurred at the same time as one of the happiest moments of my life, the birth of our first child Natalie in a Manchester hospital. Nothing can compare to seeing your own child being born. Not even playing at Wembley or winning the European Cup comes close to the emotion of seeing that 7lb 10oz little bundle come screaming into the world.

The fact I had to keep my feet up for the next three weeks, on doctor's orders, at least got me out of nappy duty! But that was no consolation for me. I set my heart on a comeback against Forest on the May 5 but did not make it and by the time I got back for the final three games our challenge for the league title was over for another season. At least I managed another goal in the 3-0 win over WBA at the Hawthorns, which was just a special return to his old stomping ground for Big Ron. I think I helped him fully justify his decision to leave Albion to those home fans who had been less than impressed with his decision to desert them the previous June.

It took my total for the season to 11 goals in 35 games, which was hardly prolific I know, but certainly a vast improvement on the previous one and Frank Stapleton only finished two goals in front of me and played six more games. After the turmoil of my first year, it was a reasonable return and something to build on, although not enough to earn me that call-up for the England World Cup squad to Spain later in the year.

The final game of the season was against Stoke City at Old Trafford. Little did I know at the time that the wheel had turned full circle by then. Ironically the team that had been my first opponents of my United career were going to be my last. Perhaps it was somehow fitting that my final game in front of United fans finished without a goal. I might not have scored, but some bloke called Norman Whiteside did and if Robbo had made an impression earlier in the season, the kid they called the Shankhill Skinhead caused a tremor that measured almost as high on the football Richter Scale.

BIRTLES SCORES!

Norman had come to Old Trafford after being recommended by United's Ulster scout Bob Bishop. United trusted Bob's judgment implicitly, probably based on the fact that he was the bloke who had spotted George Best and Sammy McIlroy! He became the club's youngest ever player since Duncan Edwards when he had appeared the previous season and now he was being groomed for a far bigger impact and as a centre forward!

He and Mark Hughes were making waves for the reserves and people at the club were well aware of what potential they had on their hands. Although from what I gathered from the backroom staff, they never really fancied Mark Hughes too much. They got that one wrong, but they got Whiteside spot on. Mind you, some bloke who had just landed from the moon and had never heard of football would have realised Whiteside had the lot to go to the very top of the game – as he subsequently did.

The fact that he had such immense promise and talent was bad news for me and the beginning of the end for my time at Old Trafford. My fears were confirmed as we headed out for a pre-season tournament in Spain at Zaragoza. I was joined in transit for the tour-team warm-up tournament by another Manchester-based journalist Peter Fitton. He was to become one of Big Ron's closest confidants and I had already seen all the paper talk about United wanting to sign a host of strikers including Kevin Keegan, Andy Gray and even Lee Chapman and my old club Forest being interested in giving me a fresh start.

With Whiteside on the horizon and United having such lofty ambitions I confessed to Peter that the game was up. I told him I had always been a fatalist and if the time had come for me to go, then the time had come to go. All I could do was knuckle down and do my bit while Ron searched everywhere for other strikers. I scored goals in the tournament and only just missed out on finishing top scorer. I remember one flying into the net and Ray Wilkins turning to me and saying: 'That's the Birtles we know and love'. Unfortunately there was no love left for me at United.

In the final build- up to the 1982-83 season we played a testimonial against Bolton Wanderers at Old Trafford. The United fans were caught up in the excitement of Whiteside's emergence and I only got on for the last ten minutes of a meaningless game. I missed a few chances and the flak started flying from the terraces. It knocked all the stuffing out of me and I never got my head up again. When the team was announced for the opening day of the season against Birmingham City, I was not in the squad and Whiteside started in a 3-0 win. United were up and running for a season which eventually saw them win the FA Cup, but by the time they were doing a lap of honour around Wembley, I was long gone and United could not wait to get rid of me – even if it cost them £1m.

Martin Edwards was the United chairman. He had stepped up in place of his father Louis, who had died aged 65, and Edwards junior, who failed the entrance exam for Stowe School and ran United with six O levels and no A levels, could barely contain his delight at chucking such a large amount of cash down the drain to get me off the books. When Brian Clough confirmed Forest's interest he snapped their hand off. Edwards would have carried me on his back over broken glass across the Pennines back to Nottingham. He told the world: I've absolutely no regrets. We just gambled and lost."

"Obviously this has got to be the club's most disappointing transfer deal, but some you win, some you lose. I'm philosophical about the whole situation. Frankly it makes sense for Garry to go. He worked extremely hard to make it a success, but sadly it did not work out. I don't want to make any criticism at all of Garry. We have written off the money without any regret." That was it. As simple and as callous as that. I was gone and with some personal cost to myself also.

United might have written off £1m, but they made me waive any rights to the remaining three years on my five-year contract which would have been worth £40,000. That was a huge amount of money back then, but Edwards made it abundantly clear I would not get a penny. It is a far cry from the way players sign five-year deals in the modern era, move on to a new club and still get all their cash from the club they leave behind.

But at the time the Inland Revenue were scrutinising all United's financial transactions and Edwards used that as an excuse. I tried to keep what I was entitled to but Edwards insisted that United had to have the money. I even had a representative from the Revenue call at my house in Chilwell long after I had returned to Nottingham. He told me the club was being investigated and they went through everything with a fine-toothed comb to ensure everything was above board.

Added to the fact that I wrote off £40,000 in monies that were contractually owed to me, I also lost £5,000 on my Manchester home, which I had bought for £65k less than two years earlier. Two years after I had packed up the last box and headed back to Nottingham the same property, thanks to a boom in the housing market was sold for £250,000. So that will give you a good indication of the financial penalties I suffered too. If a massive institution like Manchester United could afford to write off £1m, I was not in the position to be able to kiss goodbye to what was effectively almost a third of that.

It was a massive financial hit to take, but all I wanted to do was play football and the opportunity to return to Nottingham Forest, where it had all began for me. It was a was a pull of gravity far too strong to resist. I was going back to my home, my family, my friends and my club. In the end I left United with just 11 goals in 54 matches. It will not be remembered as the best phase of my career, but I have no regrets about the choice I made and I will be forever grateful to the United fans and to the club for doing all they did for me, even if some people felt it might not have been enough.

Steve Coppell was certainly one who believed that some people at United, within the playing squad, could have done more and he said as much in his column in a national newspaper at the time, whilst lamenting the departure of my outrageous dress sense. "For the players he left behind there will be one lasting memory of Garry Birtles. His weird, way-out gear. The fancy bow ties, winged collars, spectacular suits that no one else would wear without the courage of four bottles of wine," he said.

"And that is really only one of the great tragedies of his short-lived career at Old Trafford, because this man can play, score goals and be as exciting as any front runner in the First Division. He will, I promise you, prove that once more at Nottingham Forest.

"With a little more help and understanding from his friends – the rest of the first team squad – he might just have done the trick at United. Instead Garry suffered a nightmare experience for two years that would have broken 95% of top footballers.

"He was a success at Forest because their counter attacking football suited his style perfectly. Because United are a team who are expected to pressure all the time, we never used the Birtles secret. We played to his feet and tried to turn him into an orthodox target man and he looked completely stranded."

The last time I had been in the offices at Nottingham Forest, face-to-face with The Gaffer and Peter Taylor, they were celebrating for some reason and they called me in and made one final attempt to persuade me not to leave. The offer they made to try and get me to stay was derisory and I was so eager to get to Old Trafford I almost pulled the door to the office off its hinges in a rush to set off for Manchester and the verdant grass on the other side of the Pennines. Unfortunately it never turned out to be greener.

MY MAGIC CARPET RIDE

Earlier that season I had pulled on a Forest shirt at Notts County's Meadow Lane ground in a testimonial for their wonderful old boss Jimmy Sirrel. It was a pleasure to help Jimmy and it was more of a pleasure to meet up with some good friends and familiar faces in that Garibaldi red again. At the time I said it was like I had never been away and how wonderful it was to be back. Little did I know it was just a fitting for the new shirt I would be wearing for Forest the following season, once BC pulled his finger out and finalised the deal.

I know there was a little ill-feeling when I left Forest and a few things had been said, which upset my parents and me. I know there is a saying in football that you should never go back, but to me it was the most logical thing in the world to re-sign for Forest. I would have climbed off Martin Edwards' back and crawled over broken glass, on Snake Pass, myself to get back to the City Ground. You can take the boy out of Nottingham.....

8

THE PRODIGAL RETURNS
Back in the old routine

I TOOK my outrageous clothes, my wife and baby daughter back to Nottingham and not before long I was pictured in the Nottingham Evening Post with a dodgy suit and even more dodgy bow-tie, holding a pen, hovering above a piece of paper on the desk in front of me. It was a snap designed to portray me signing my new contract at the City Ground and I was flanked by you-know-who. He had a great big grin on his face and still had that rugby shirt on. It was as though I had never been away from the place, apart from the fact Forest secretary Paul White had grown a rather hefty beard in the intervening period.

After a period of bluff and counter bluff, with BC haggling over the price, United were bartered down from an asking fee of £300,000 to £250,000 and there was smug sense of satisfaction with the Gaffer. It wasn't so much that he had talked his way around Martin Edwards and reduced the transfer fee, which would have given him a great sense of achievement in itself. It was more like he was pleased by the fact he had been proved right about his misgivings on my decision to leave Forest a couple of years earlier.

In the lead up to my return, he had wasted little time in giving his opinion on the whole affair with United and about my problems, claiming that he thought 'Birtles would like to come back to Nottingham'. In one of his regular pieces with the local paper he went on: 'I don't consider that Manchester, the city, suits him. He was far better off here getting into his car at the end of the day and going back to his roots in Long Eaton. That is where his home and his friends are.

'I simply believe that Garry made the wrong decision a few years ago. He would have done much better following Tony Woodcock's example. I don't mean moving to the continent. Tony thought through things before he went and Garry should have done the same. The end product speaks for itself. Tony managed his affairs properly'.

Sometimes his arrogance knew no bounds. I had made the club almost £1.25m and he still could not help rubbing my nose in it. Hearing someone say 'I told you so' is one of the most infuriating things. People being wise after the event are right clever so-and-sos and his attitude would have been enough to put most people off going back. I could think of more than a few players who would have took one look at what he said, stuck their noses up in the air and stuck two fingers up as well, but I was not one of them. I even took a pay cut to go back!

When I left United my basic salary was £800-a-week. Not only had the Gaffer got me for knockdown price, he got me to sign a contract for five years that was worth an initial £400-a-week and the wages would go up by £100 a week each year. He robbed United and he was robbing me too, but I really did not give a damn. Of course I could have done with the money and taking such a hit in the pocket was not pleasant, but I did it without batting an eyelid. I liked Nottingham. I was from Nottingham. My daughter had just been born and I jumped at the chance to go back. Sandra and I celebrated with the Gaffer in his office eating fish and chips and drinking champagne.

It felt good, even if the salt and vinegar just made the open wounds in my wallet that little bit more painful and it soon became apparent as to why BC had haggled in such a miserly fashion for the transfer fee of £250,000 and just why he had been so tight with my wages. Above the picture of me in the dodgy suit screamed a headline in letters almost two inches high: 'We're Broke'. It transpired the team I had helped win the European Cup twice a couple of years earlier barely had a pot to piss in. It is a staggering indictment of how Forest failed to capitalise on their stunning achievements. Can you imagine teams like Manchester United, Liverpool, Chelsea and Arsenal failing to make amazing amounts of capital out of such success? It just would not happen, but it had happened at the City Ground.

Two replica European Cups in the trophy room and no cash. That must be the reverse of having a Porsche on the drive and sod all in the fridge. BC had to get the begging bowl out to get me back. He qualified the word broke and suggested it might have been a little bit strong, but they quite simply did not have the money to pay for me and he was having to beg local companies to sponsor the signing in one way or another. Whether it was someone offering to cough up for each goal I scored, buying an executive box or anything. He had to do his best advertising pitch to get some business in. He even offered to be sponsored to keep his mouth shut. Not that that would have generated much cash.

All Forest had to pay up front was just over £100,000 as part of Football League rules that stated 50% of all transfers had to be settled immediately and not only were they skint, someone was missing! Peter Taylor was no longer there lighting up cigars in the Forest dug out. He had 'retired' at the end of the 1981-82 season. He reckoned he had 'shot it' yet six months later ended up the manager of Derby County. It seemed like Trevor Francis, who had departed not long after me for Manchester City, allied with my decision to leave for United, had started the problems and PT had been the one saddled with the immense pressure of finding replacements.

In trying to fill the void, Forest had gambled on players such as Peter Ward from Brighton, Ian Wallace from Coventry and Justin Fashanu from Norwich City. The latter both cost seven figure sums and had found it a desperate struggle trying to adapt to life at the City Ground and working with BC. They struggled to fit in, and in Justin's case, were just not up to the task. That was a problem for him and for Forest. Unlike Manchester United, who could gamble and lose on people like me, Forest could not afford to make such expensive mistakes. The club which spent the first million pounds in the transfer market on Francis had been repaid in spades with the European Cup twice, but they could not repeat the feat.

Fashanu was a case in point and some argued it was his failure to adapt to life at Forest which was the final straw for Taylor. Some cracks had appeared in their relationship in 1980 when Taylor had a book published called With Clough by Taylor which he had done without consulting The Gaffer. That was papered over because BC knew he needed Pete's eye for a player. PT had barely made a mistake in the transfer market during the European Cup seasons. He had the Midas touch for a talent spotter. Everything he touched turned to gold, in a very similar way it had done when they had been building Derby County into league champions years earlier.

The Gaffer even admitted he was 'not equipped to manage without Peter Taylor. I am the shop window and he's the goods in the back' was his self-effacing analogy for the way the pair worked in tandem. Taylor modestly reckoned he 'filled in the gaps' and 'spotted talent'. The truth was that he was a master at it and rarely made mistakes. So Forest trusted him and the Gaffer when they made Fashanu the first £1m black footballer in 1981, largely on the back of his 1980 BBC Goal of the Season, a spectacular volley against Liverpool, from the corner of the penalty area (go and have a look on YouTube!).

Unfortunately Fashanu proved a major mistake and a very expensive one and it is thought that weighed heavily on Pete's mind and was the final straw which led to his leaving Forest. Fashanu returned just three goals in over 30 appearances and Forest finished a miserable 12th in the league. He had been signed to replace Trevor and was simply not up to the task. Very few people in the game would have been capable of it and Fashanu deserved some sympathy for his plight, but got very little. Later in life, nine years after his arrival at Forest, he came out as gay in an interview he gave to a national newspaper, but the rumours had been circulating about him for many years before.

In his autobiography, Clough recounts a dressing down he gave Fashanu after hearing rumours that he was going to gay bars in Nottingham. "Where do you go if you want a loaf of bread?" I asked him.

"A baker, I suppose."

"Where do you go if you want a leg of lamb?"

"A butcher."

"So why do you keep going to that bloody poofs' club?"

Not very politically correct and that was not one of BC's fortes either. However, one of his mantras was when you make a mistake, the best thing to do is put it right as soon as possible.

Colin Walsh, another of my new Forest team mates, tells a story too just to underline how BC wanted him out. Walshy reckons he was in Clough's office one day and there was a knock at the door. When he bellowed 'come in' Fashanu entered. Justin was a deeply religious lad and this was during the time it had been made clear to him that his future lay away from Forest. He came into the office and told BC he had spent the weekend consulting with God and that God had told him the best course of action was to remain in Nottingham and fight to prove his worth. Quick as a flash Clough countered: "There is only one God around here, that's me. And I think it is best that you leave the club."

That is where I came in. Fashanu had to go and I was the one lined up to replace him. Our time only overlapped for the short period of a week and we were never on the same pitch for a game, but it was still long enough to see my one and only ever arrest of a professional footballer on a training ground. From the end of the previous season Fashanu had been on borrowed time. No one could cost that much money and not deliver for Brian Clough. I might have got away with it for a while at Old Trafford, but Forest and BC in particular were nowhere near as lenient.

By the time the following season was underway, the Gaffer was so intent on getting rid of him he told him in no uncertain terms that he would never kick a ball for Forest again and that it was best for him to start looking for another club. He was so adamant that he issued a threat to Fashanu, telling him that he would be arrested if he did not obey instructions to keep away from the club and from training. If he was seen on the premises at any time, the Gaffer told him he would call the police himself! He was not a man to make idle threats.

It was only a couple of days into my return, training down by the banks of the Trent, when Fash turned up and to make matters worse he had his masseur with him. Word obviously filtered back to the Gaffer and within minutes a police car came scorching across the training ground and Fash and his masseur were bundled into the car and removed from the training pitch. Within days he had been loaned out to Southampton and he never returned to Forest though he did return to Nottingham to sign for our neighbours Notts County across the Trent.

Fashanu's was one departure which was not lamented to any great extent but I certainly noticed the difference without Pete. It was just not the same without the man who had played such a role in getting me into the Forest team a few years earlier. The same man who had fought my corner when BC fancied Steve Elliott. How could it be the same? Morecambe would not have been the same without Wise and neither would Abbot without Costello. When something like that changes, it cannot be the same. Trying to replace Peter Taylor was impossible.

Of course there was continuity, people like Ron Fenton and Liam O'Kane, trusted members of the backroom staff, stepped up. Still, some of the fun had gone. Even the Gaffer said he could never replace him. Some days he would spend less time at the ground than it took to smoke one of his favourite cigars and the suits in the committee room always wondered exactly what it was PT did. To put it simply, Pete had that X-Factor.

The suits did not have a clue about the chemistry between the pair of them and how it worked, but they could not help but keep sticking their noses in. Fortunately, BC consistently told them to mind their own damn business.

MY MAGIC CARPET RIDE

The pair had been together in management since they started at Hartlepools in 1965, apart from a break when they left Derby. That happened because of the Gaffer's fit of pique and a resignation letter to chairman Sam Longson, which Clough believed he would reject. He got it wrong and despite players going on strike, they never did get their job back. PT was incensed. He went and got them a job at Brighton but BC was approached by Leeds to take over from Don Revie. PT refused to go, but the pair were re-united at Forest in 1976, after a separation of around two years, and they worked together again constantly until 1982.

That is the best part of 15 years working alongside each other. They knew what each other was going to say, before a word was uttered. They were like a married couple. They knew each other inside and out and realised exactly what they could give each other. I suppose it came from knowing each other from childhood and being family-oriented people.

They transformed Forest into a family club and when someone leaves the family it is hard to cope. Taylor had gone. The European days had gone and there were only a couple of players left with whom I had shared those glorious evenings of May 1979 and May 1980. Robbo , Viv and Bomber were still there, but the rest had all departed. The club was in transition and facing a rebuilding process. That would normally have been a process that Pete would have masterminded single-handedly. They say it is only when you lose something that you realise how important it really was.

Well that was certainly the case with Pete. It was a massive loss and without him you fully appreciated what a massive part he had played. To make matters worse, the pair fell out not long after that. Within six months of his retirement Pete became the manager of Derby County. But that was not the reason for the acrimonious fall-out which led to the pair never speaking again! Pete even knocked us out of the FA Cup in the third round at the Baseball Ground in my first season back and that did not spark the disagreement. It just ended up with the Gaffer going crazy at us after the game and calling us 'gutless'. He hated losing, but losing to his mate was too much!

It was Pete's decision to sign Robbo the following season, when his former sidekick was out doing a walk for charity, that caused the bust-up. The Gaffer never blamed Robbo for the deal. John was coming towards the back end of his career and he was looking after himself and his family. BC knew the way things worked and it was one last pay-day that would give

Robbo some financial security. Instead he blamed Pete and made no bones about it either.

Pete had never talked about the transfer with his mate and that rankled so much BC branded him a 'rattlesnake' in national newspapers. He went even further and claimed that the pair passed each other on a regular basis en route to work along the A52, the road linking Derby and Nottingham, but if Taylor ever 'broke down and I saw him thumbing a lift, I wouldn't pick him up, I would run him over!'

It was a sad way for it all to end and I know that BC regretted the irreparable parting of the ways later in life. He confessed as much on numerous occasions. He even says in his autobiography with John Sadler that Pete told him he would not laugh so much without him by his side. 'He was right;. The laughter was missed by everyone. I can remember the earlier times when BC was just doubled up in laughter and could barely catch his breath. Pete was such a funny man and he never really realised it. The Gaffer could be bolshie and arrogant and Pete tried it and he could just not pull it off. Even that was funny. He was always the good cop and he had this smile that was never off his face.

One day at the City Ground two fans wandered into the trophy room, right in the middle of a team meeting, wearing scarves and hats, carrying rattles. We thought it was a wind-up and the look on Pete's face was priceless. Especially as he had already done his famous security check of the building. He was like Basil Fawlty ensuring sliding doors were closed and popping his head out of windows to make sure there was no one ear-wigging private team business. So to see these two fans just calmly wander in was hilarious. All the players were just crying with laughter and for once Pete was speechless.

He was a calming influence on the Gaffer and was integral in all that was done at Forest. That is why BC had asked the Football League for special permission to allow Pete to walk out with him at the head of the team when we played Southampton in the League Cup at Wembley in 1979. It was his way of getting his mate's work recognised, but the League refused. They hated the Gaffer because he was always so outspoken and anything they could do to get at him they did it. It was a dreadful shame, because Pete would have loved that walk. He deserved it.

It's not a secret that he loved a punt and he was regularly talking about money. He loved the stuff and the more successful we were in the early days the more it used to generate. I remember him going around the dressing room using it as a motivational tool, saying: 'If you are doing well, we will shovel the money to you. We will shovel it – in proportion'. He would be pointing fingers around the dressing room. Going around the squad one-by-one. 'You will get it. You will get it'. Then there would be a pause, followed by 'you won't get so much!'

He just had this matter-of-fact way about him. He was warm and funny and just could not help blurting out blunt statements which had folks in stitches. Few can forget the second European Cup final against Hamburg. We were one short on the bench to begin with because Stan Bowles had refused to get on the plane, livid that he had not been selected in the side. I remember his bag going around the luggage carousel in Madrid airport. One of our subs was a young kid called Brynn Gunn and Frank Gray got injured towards the end of the game. The Gaffer and PT had some frantic discussions, accompanied by some head nodding and head shaking over the options of a replacement, before BC decided Gunny was the best option. Pete's response? 'God we are in the shit now!' Nothing like having your ego massaged in the biggest game of your life and Gunny still laughs about it to this day.

It was so natural between them. They never had to work at it. They rolled up at the City Ground every day for six years and did what they did. It just worked. It was not fortune. It was alchemy. You don't get lucky and win two European Cups and a First Division title. The team had its moments of luck, but that was out of their hands. If you could bottle what they had, if you could find a chemical formula to recreate it, you would be a very rich man in the Premier League and Champions League land of milk and honey.

In my first spell I never questioned what they did. I just got on with doing what I did and just accepted they were a genius partnership. Without Taylor there, I sensed a change in the Gaffer. It was nothing momentous. It was entirely natural. He no longer had his sounding board. He no longer had that special person to bounce off and the laughter was not so regular anymore, but even so Forest were not in a bad state. They were still regarded as a decent side and apart from the fact there was no PT anymore, the environs of the club and the staff were just the same. It felt as if I had never been away.

It was not long before I was back in the old routine, scoring in my fourth game against Watford. Everything just seemed to slot into place. I had never really lost faith in my ability. I just felt I needed the correct environment to bring it out again and I had rediscovered it, among a couple of familiar old faces and a crop of new arrivals and graduates that hinted at good times ahead for the club.

Des Walker and Steve Hodge had emerged from the junior ranks on the start of their rise to become England internationals enjoying World Cup appearances, while the experience of Colin Todd had been purchased too. On the debit side, the likes of Shilts, Kenny Burns, Larry Lloyd, John McGovern and Martin O'Neill had all departed. It was a rapid change around and any club that has to deal with such alternations in the space of two years would struggle, but the signs of re-growth were encouraging.

Sometime later in life, BC confessed to me that he broke up the European Cup winning side too soon. Perhaps, but he had made the decision and now it was time to live with it and prove he could survive without his former best mate. Peter Davenport, Hans Van Breukelen, Kenny Swain, Chris Fairclough and Paul Hart all became central characters in the squad. It was a drastic change and a transitional period that would require some patience, but it did not seem to prevent me from enjoying a seamless return to my roots.

After four goals in my first four games, the last being in a 6-1 Milk Cup rout of West Bromwich Albion, BC was working his magic and made sure it was time he let everyone know how well I was doing. Bobby Robson, the new England manager, had been at the City Ground for the game to compare me with Cyrille Regis. We were two potential candidates to rival Paul Mariner for an international spot for a forthcoming game with West Germany. Just for a change BC was in no doubt and revealed that he had tried to prevent me getting a second cap from Ron Greenwood at the 1980 European Championships.

He told reporters: "Bobby Robson watched that game against West Bromwich at the City Ground and you can't do better than play brilliantly and score when the England manager is watching you. I rate Birtles as better than Mariner and I'm certain he is playing better now than he was when Ron Greenwood called him up against my advice for his second cap against Italy in the European Championships in 1980." It was nice to know that he had poured cold water on my England chances two years earlier. This time he was full of it about my prospects and Robson promptly ignored the advice, just like Greenwood had before him.

Not that it bothered me too much. I was back doing what I did best where I was happy and Dave Sexton, who had become the manager of Coventry, started singing my praises too. He reckoned it was only a matter of time before I had the England kit on again. I was scoring goals and felt it was certainly a possibility if I carried on at the rate I had hit since returning to Forest. I might have cost United almost £100,000 a goal, but in 17 matches since re-signing I scored 12 goals and formed a great understanding with Ian Wallace. I was feeling as good as I had ever done, until I was struck down with a back injury that forced me to miss the last two months of the season. So began a battle of almost two years which could have ended my career six years prematurely.

I was out of action from March and was in agony. I could not sleep and I could barely sit down in a chair. The only position I could find any kind of relief in was standing up. Which was a bit of a problem when it came to sleeping. My eyes looked like they had two suitcases under them because of all the sleep and rest I lost. I kept waking up in the middle of the night in such excruciating pain and I was prescribed complete rest by the doctors and specialists. The problem with back injuries is that people think you are faking it. They cannot see any real damage. It is not like broken bones and ruptured ligaments and people just reckoned I had got lumbago.

Looking back it was all the pounding of pitches I had done for United and more significantly Forest. The relentless number of games under BC did not abate. In my first season back we played no fewer than 14 friendly games after the season had commenced, including trips to Kuwait, Algiers and Saudi Arabia. Not to mention Gateshead, Kettering, Poole and Darlington. The club was still in financial dire straits with an £800,000 overdraft and the vast majority of the £1m balance on the new Executive Stand still owed. Lucrative friendly games, using Viv, Robbo, Bomber and me as European Cup winning exhibitions were a way of generating cash.

We were paraded all over the world for matches. Any trip we got, no matter where it was, the four of us had to be on it. I loved a trip, but that did not stop me getting thrown off the team coach one morning as we were heading to Kuwait for another money-spinner. It was early one Sunday and we were all sat on the bus waiting to set off for the airport when the Gaffer turned up late with a pile of newspapers, crisps and sweets as per usual. I should not have even been on the bus, I was injured at the time, but it was a three-line whip for members of the European Cup winning team.

I was moaning before BC arrived and I carried on moaning as the bus pulled out of the car park and did not stop until he snapped. 'Fucking hell Gaz, what's the problem. Come on, out with it, let's have it.' I just pointed out that I was injured and was being hauled halfway around the world for a game that I could not even play in. To my mind it I would have been better served staying in Nottingham and getting myself fit to play league games. It had nothing to do with the fact that I wanted to be in the Cadland by 12 noon for a Sunday session!

I thought he would see right through me, but he just said: "Son, you have got a point. Albert, stop this fucking bus." Good old Albert always did as he was told and brought the bus to a halt on Wilford Lane, which is about a ten minute walk from the ground.

The Gaffer jumped off the bus and was in the middle of the road on the opposite side. He stopped the first car heading in the opposite direction and some poor old guy, who was probably on his way to church, had to slam on the brakes.

The driver was shocked enough to be flagged down by Brian Clough and quick as a flash I chucked my bag in the back of his car as BC told him to take me back to the City Ground. 'Please!' I was cheering all the way back to my car in the car park and counting the hours down to when I could knock on the door of the Cadland and meet up with the lads. Brilliant. They're off to the desert and I'm off for a session. It was only when I got a phone call later from Ian Wallace that I realised I missed what could have been a major security incident.

I thought Wally was ringing from Kuwait until I realised he was at home too, as were the rest of the travelling party. It transpired the plane had tried to take off and been forced to abort the procedure which did not go down too well with the Gaffer. He was a nervous flyer at the best of times and he did not like the situation one bit. As soon as the plane was back on terra firma, he told one of the stewardesses to open the exit door because he wanted to get off and take his players with him.

You can imagine she was rather perplexed and said that was not possible, until he bellowed: "Young lady, open the door because we are getting off." Reluctantly the doors were opened and he marched the players off the plane, across the tarmac and back into arrivals. From there he hired a coach and got them all back to Nottingham. No one went, including me, but I was paying for all the other jaunts we had undertaken all around the globe in the name of raising money for the club. My back was in a mess and all those games must have taken their toll and caused so much wear and tear.

The specialists did as much as they could and fitted me with a special surgical corset. I was ordered not to play any squash for a year and told to rest completely if I wanted to have any chance of reporting back for pre-season training. The only exercise I was allowed was an occasional walk and I swam three times a week. Even BC noticed I could 'barely sit up on the team coach' and praised me for doing so well for so long despite being in pain. At least I had made a contribution and I felt back to my old self. If I needed a carrot, we went on to finish fifth in the league that season, a considerable improvement on the previous effort and that earned us a place in the UEFA Cup.

I had left Forest after we had been knocked out in the first round of the European Cup by CSKA Sofia and that rankled with me at the time and several years on it still did. If I needed an incentive to follow doctor's orders and make sure I wore the daft surgical corset and behaved myself that was it. The opportunity to go back into Europe again with Forest was fantastic. It felt like starting all over again with that European Cup tie against Liverpool. I wanted another adventure and so did the club and more importantly so did BC. It was a chance for him to prove something without Peter Taylor at his side.

For the entire summer, I did as I was told. I did not even play cricket, which I used to do. I followed all the doctor's orders and made sure I was fit to start the season. The recovery was that good I scored six goals in pre-season games and while the League was always the priority, I was looking forward to that unmistakable buzz you get from European nights and the UEFA Cup campaign which started with a comfortable win over East German side Vorwaerts.

I did not play in the first leg which was won with goals from Hodge and Wallace but was back in the side for the 1-0 away win earned by Ian Bowyer's strike.

By the time the second round tie against PSV Eindhoven came around I was struggling with my back again and missed the first leg. Peter Davenport and Walsh scored in a 2-1 win in Eindhoven and Davvo followed up with the only goal of the return leg when I returned to the subs' bench.

The reward for the victory was being paired with Celtic in the third round for one of those fiercely competitive but rare contests – a European battle of Britain.

The first leg was at the City Ground and should never have been played. Ken Smales, the former Forest secretary, published a Forest bible several years ago detailing all the games and alongside the entry for this fixture it states 'icy conditions'.

There were penguins on the pitch that night it was so cold. The pitch was lethal but 10,000 Celtic fans made the trip south and the game went ahead, probably out of fear for what they might do if it was called off. Miraculously no one was seriously injured in a 0-0 draw, which gave Davie Hay's side great encouragement for the return at Parkhead. That was until BC pulled another master-stroke, probably the first that the crop of new kids on the Forest block would have seen.

We drove up for the return game the day before and instead of heading to the hotel, the first port of call was a pub in the centre of Glasgow. It was not just any pub, it was owned by the Celtic manager and the Gaffer wanted to buy him a beer! So he made Albert drive around until he found it and though Davie was not in the message was soon conveyed to him and he turned up to have a beer with us. The subliminal message was more sinister. It was just BC's way of letting Davie know that we are here, in the middle of Glasgow and we are going to beat you. We are not bothered about Parkhead and your incredible supporters, even if they hate the English.

If the message did not get home off the pitch, it was rammed home on it. Hodgy and Walsh scored in the second half and Murdo MacLeod's 80th minute goal was no consolation. It was at this stage I started to get a feeling about more European medals. It was also at this stage, shortly before we were due to play Austrian side Sturm Graz in the fourth round, that we realised we had no European bonuses written into our contracts. We were doing sterling work in the UEFA Cup and not getting a penny for it. If we went on to win the thing, we would not be rewarded. Seven years earlier I had got £10,000 for winning my first European Cup!

Naturally there was a lot of talk going on in the dressing room and it was decided that a deputation had to be sent to see the Gaffer. I can't remember who got charged with the unpleasant task but the upshot of the meeting was there was no way they could retrospectively write European bonuses into our contract. The best BC could do was to offer us a deal in the game before we played the first leg. It was pretty simple. He said there was £3,000 a man on offer if we did not lose our First Division game against Wolves before facing the Austrians.

That seemed fair enough and we were virtually counting the cash as the game slipped towards stoppage time at 0-0. Then out of nowhere Paul Hart conceded an own goal and saved the club over £30,000 and our UEFA Cup bonus went up in smoke. You can imagine he was a popular bloke in the dressing room. The least he could do was score the only goal in the first leg against Graz to keep our hopes of winning the trophy alive ahead of travelling for the return tie where we were to administer over a dozen knockout blows.

BC's training methods of running through nettles and diving in five-a-side goals have been well-documented, but you always had to be prepared for the unexpected with him when he was in motivational mood on the morning of the game against Graz.

He took us for a walk to stretch our legs in this park near the hotel, he loved to have a stroll on match days so it was pretty standard stuff. What followed was not. After a short time in the park he stopped beside this tree and we all came to an abrupt halt.

'Do you know what kind of tree this is lads?' he asked and all he got in reply was a sea of bemused faces. Not that he was bothered and he proceeded to tell us all that it was the famous 'Austrian Punching Tree. Now I want you all to come up and punch it!' Another mad-cap request to a bunch of grown men and not one dissenting voice was heard. An orderly queue formed and one-by-one we wandered up to the tree and smashed our knuckles on the bark. Even our goalkeeper Hans Van Bruekelen did it too! Utter madness, but it was Colin Walsh's penalty that made sure we administered the real killer punch and we were on our way to the semi-finals against Anderlecht.

The best thing about that was we had been kept apart from Tottenham, who had made it through into the last four. They were drawn against Hajduk Split, keeping alive the possibility of an all English European final, which was an added incentive for us and when Steve Hodge scored twice to help us win the home leg of the semi 2-0 we as good as booking flights for the final. We had no idea we were about to become the victims of a bribery scandal at the hands of Spanish referee Guruleta Muro that stank out the whole of Belgium and Europe.

I did not play in the first game and was back on the bench for the trip to Belgium. I don't remember the build-up to the game at all, but the match itself sticks with me for very bitter reasons. Anderlecht were a decent team with internationals like Enzo Scifo and Franky Vercauteren, but we fancied ourselves to get a goal there and finish the tie off. We were just hoping that Spurs could make it through to meet us, but from the moment we got in the dressing room before the game the Gaffer sensed there was something not right. Our dressing room door was always closed for matches.

Not that he had anything particularly secret or special to protect. It was just our private place and he did not want folks wandering in and out like an open house, but that night our door was kept wide open on the Gaffer's orders as he was more interested in watching the comings and goings outside in the corridors. The referee's dressing room was right opposite and BC told me later in life he always felt there was something fishy going on before we kicked off because people kept going in and out of the ref's room.

It was like he had this sixth sense even if he could not quite put his finger on it. I never twigged anything at the time and I'm pretty sure none of the others did either. We were too wrapped up in getting ready to get to the UEFA Cup final. His concerns did not register with us until we were in the middle of the game and we found ourselves the victims of two shocking decisions that convinced every player in a Forest shirt that the referee had been bribed.

Anderlecht scored two perfectly legitimate goals on the evening, but the penalty they got to make sure they overturned the tie 3-0 was nothing short of scandalous. I was on the bench and can still see the penalty as if it was yesterday. I can still picture the referee too. He was typically Spanish, olive skin and a really thick head of jet black hair. He was a right pompous and arrogant bastard and pranced around as if he owned the place. The fact was Anderlecht owned him and the penalty he awarded for Kenny Swain's 'foul' was a total travesty. Kenny was nowhere near the guy. There was complete daylight between him and the Anderlecht player he was supposed to have brought down.

Not one of us argued. We were not allowed to disrespect officials but we knew we had been done. If we had any doubts it was confirmed when Paul Hart scored a fantastic header to give us an away goal and we were all jogging back for the re-start celebrating when Anderlecht players came flying at us. The goal had been ruled out for a push. Harty jumped for a free header there was no one near him and he won't have scored many better goals in his life. Amazingly, it was chalked off and we were out. Anderlecht had bought their place in the final. It was so blatant that a UEFA official came into our dressing room after the game and told the Gaffer he had grounds to complain. He was told to go away because we do not complain about officials!

Even recalling the events of that night brings the unmistakeable taste of bile from the pit of my stomach. I had been to finals before. I had medals to prove it but for people like Hodgy and youngsters starting out in their careers they had been cheated out of a momentous occasion for themselves and the club they had sweat blood to represent. I felt awful for myself but felt far worse for them. What made it even harder to swallow was that Spurs beat Hajduk Split and it would have been a fantastic night for English football.

Instead, what happened was a shameful chapter in Belgian football, the full details of which only emerged many years later when Anderlecht dragged up the whole affair themselves.

They complained to the Belgian police that they were being blackmailed by two men, one of whom was claiming to be the intermediary who helped 'fix' the second leg against Nottingham Forest. They claimed they had been paid 56 million Belgian francs, which was about £1m in hush money. That prompted a police investigation which blew the whole scandal wide open.

The Anderlecht chairman at the time was Constant Vanden Stock and he had protested for years that his club was innocent. He had persistently denied bribing the referee, but when the blackmail issue was raised, Vanden Stock's son Roger was forced to admit that the Spanish referee had spoken of financial troubles before the game and had asked for and received £27,000 as a 'loan' prior to the second leg taking place.

An Anderlecht official, Raymond De Deken, confirmed that the cash had been handed over in an envelope and that he did not know whether the loan had ever been paid back. That is unlikely as the referee died three years later in a car crash and I can't say I shed any tears for that man. My only sympathy is with the players he robbed that night in the name of personal greed and fraud. I just wish we could have been granted some form of compensation for what he did to us. We did try and English solicitors believed we had a very strong case.

I even went to Charleroi with Hans Van Bruekelen and Ian Bowyer many years later to publicise our case in an attempt to shame Anderlecht into paying compensation directly to us. We had a massive dossier put together. Players had been deprived of money, kudos and the chance to enhance their careers. Apparently we had a fantastic case if it had been heard in England. Anderlecht did not want to know and we ended up issuing a writ demanding something in the region of £200,000 per-man in the Forest squad, but nothing came of it. Under Belgian law the statutes had elapsed and we were wasting our time. Even the one-year ban they subsequently were handed for bribery was over-turned.

The only thing left for us at the time was to get roaring drunk. The end of the season club tour to Australia gave us the chance to do that in some style. Three weeks Down Under meant three weeks of getting smashed. Australia were in the World Cup and they needed some warm-up opponents. We were more than happy to take them on, at drinking, in what was one of my best three weeks on tour.

Basically the club told us there would be money for us to go and there would be money for us when we got back. It could not get much better than that.

The first thing I had to do was ditch the horrific tracksuits we were handed to tour in. I hated tracksuits and never wore them. If I had to have one for Oz then I was going to get my own and I went to my mate's shop in Hockley and got a shocking purple one tailor made! I looked a right prat. Not that I could tell the colour of it, or anything else for that matter after a 36 hours flight to Australia that basically consisted of relentless drinking punctuated by the odd nap. We had an added reason to celebrate too. The Gaffer's fear of flying had struck again and he was not on the plane!

At one stage I remember getting woken up by Harty carrying a tray of glasses of red wine. Apparently we had drunk the flight dry of Swan lager and may well have given legendary Aussie drinker David Boon, who set the record for 51 tinnies consumed during the flight, a run for his money.

The last thing I remember is two guys waking me up walking down the aisles of the plane spraying insecticide all over me and looking at Bomber with a massive red wine stain all around his mouth! The tone had been set for the remainder of the trip and we had not even set foot on Aussie soil at that stage. Driving round Perth on a bus trip in the persistent rain with a hangover was hardly the best way to begin our tour. But it did get better, much better.

Once we arrived at the hotel, Ron Fenton, who was in charge of the trip, called a team meeting to lay down the rules of the three weeks. We were told in no uncertain terms that although the domestic season had finished we were on club business, representing Forest. In short, it was a working trip. So there was a midnight curfew imposed and serious fines for anyone found transgressing.

MY MAGIC CARPET RIDE

Message received and understood. We all trooped in the following morning at 5am after a night out on the lash in Perth!

My problem was that I had no trouble with the drinking, but I was still getting serious pain with my dodgy back. After the Anderlecht debacle I played against Stoke in a 0-0 draw and remember being doubled up in agony over the wash basins in the dressing room. I was having to get epidurals, the same epidurals women use to alleviate the pain of child birth, to enable me to get through games until the end of the season. The only issue was that with each epidural I had I became more tolerant of the effects and they did not work as well in quelling the pain.

I really should not have been on the trip. The specialist who was treating my back problem wanted to operate rather than allow me to go to Australia. Now being one of the four remaining European Cup winners was a bonus. My presence on the trip was required. I could have the operation later when we got back, which was something of a relief in one respect, because although my back was a major concern I did not want to miss the chance of three weeks in Oz. I was just hoping that my back would enable me not to have to play in the games. There were five of them scheduled. One against Western Australia, two against Australia A, one against Australia B and another against Manchester United who were out in Oz at the same time.

The venues were Perth, Adelaide, Brisbane, the SCG and the MCG. I played in the first game and somehow managed to limp through the second. There I was with a back in bits and Davvo was allowed to miss one game with a sore calf and Harty never played a game on tour because he pulled a muscle climbing up the steps of the plane at Heathrow!

Neither of which particularly caught the imagination of the locals as barely 10,000 turned up in total for the first two games. So much for the European Cup winners. The Aussies did not want to see us Poms, well not until we got to Melbourne and the vast bowl of a cricket ground to take on United. 21,000 made the effort for that one, which is probably two-thirds down on an Ashes Test match.

The pitch was where the wicket would be and it was rock hard, which was not exactly going to do my back any good, but jarring the lumbar region while running on it became the least of my worries when Remi Moses, my old mate from Old Trafford, came and cut me off at the knees. Remi was a lovely lad off the pitch and never said a word. On it he was a totally different kettle of fish and I came flying down and banged in shorter than a Brett

Lee bouncer. I could not get up and was in absolute agony. I just could not move. I was near to tears because of the pain. They must have been worried because Big Ron came dashing on and had to help carry me off.

Despite the agony I still played in the fourth game against Australia A and by the time less than 4,000 turned up at the SCG I was a physical wreck. It was obvious I could not play another game. Epidural, or no epidural.

By the time I returned to Nottingham, anaesthetised by Swan lager, there was nothing left for it other than surgery -- or retire. But first someone had to diagnose correctly exactly what the problem was to prove I was not faking it with lumbago. I was sent to the Queens Medical Centre for an examination and had purple dye injected into the problem area and had to wait for three hours before I was sent for a scan. I could see that the nurse who had performed the scan was looking a little concerned when I was getting ready to leave and I asked her what it was looking like. She basically said that she was not allowed to tell me anything and it was down to the consultant to let me know. I have to admit I was scared witless and could see my livelihood disappearing before my eyes. I begged her to tell me what was going on. 'It's looking really bad' was all she would say. Thanks for that.

Under the lights of the scanning machine and thanks to the dye, my back lit up like the Aurora Borealis. There were multiple fractures all over the place at the base of the spine. No wonder I had been in such a mess and barely able to sit down at times. I was only 28-years-old, at the peak of my career and immediately I feared it was over. It's only natural that your mind leaps to the worst case scenario. Fixing broken legs for footballers was pretty straightforward, but messing around with the spine was a scary business.

The consultant who gave the sharp intake of breath when he saw the results of the scan was a Dr Webb, who became famous for operating on Prince Charles to fix his broken wrist. So I guess I was in good hands. If he was good enough for royalty then he was good enough for me, but neither of the options he presented me seemed particularly appetising.

Initially he wanted to go into the spinal canal to cure the problem. My problem was that would necessitate a two-year recuperation period! Two years out of the game, just short of my 28th birthday meant that my career at the highest level was effectively over, if I opted for that route.

He understood my predicament and came up with another option. It was one that he felt did not carry the same amount of success rate guarantees as the spinal canal route, but he was willing to attempt a spinal fusion. Basically that involved taking a piece of bone from my hip and grafting it onto my spine with a load of metal work to hold all the fractures together. Without the operation there was not much point in me carrying on playing. So the date was set and prior to the operation I had to spend another day at the hospital to have more tests, a lumbar puncture which entailed staying in overnight.

To perform that operation you have to be placed in the foetal position totally naked. Then you are placed on this machine that tugs you up and down before whacking a needle in the base of your spine. It is the worst pain I have ever felt and I woke up the following day with a raging headache on one of the hottest days of the year. It was Wimbledon men's final day and I felt terrible. All I wanted to do was go home and I insisted on going

I drove myself, I was that desperate to get away. The temperatures were well in to the 80s yet I was freezing cold and I was shaking so badly I could barely grip the steering wheel. I went straight to bed and watched John McEnroe thrash Jimmy Connors in straight sets.

It was not too long after that when I was booked in for ten days at the Park Hospital and Mr Webb worked his magic on my spine. It is not too dramatic to say that he prevented my career ending six years earlier than it might have done. After the operation he basically told me that if the procedure had been postponed any longer than another couple of weeks I could have spent the rest of my life in a wheelchair.

That is how bad it was. The metal work would remain in place for the rest of my life and the operation would be of huge benefit for Mr Webb too. He carried the X-Rays of my operation around with him on seminars all over the place for the rest of his working life.

I was allowed home on my 28th birthday with strict instructions not to do anything more strenuous than lie on my back for six weeks, in what would be the start of a six-month recuperation period. I could hardly move my legs but my fingers were tightly crossed praying that the operation had been a total success.

9

RED LETTER DAY
Black and white revival

IN my two spells with Forest I have been dragged all over the world for friendlies. I only wish they did air miles back then. I have flown in the private jets of Saudi princes and have watched the locals in Abu Dhabi stare in amazement at the first sight of snowfall they had ever witnessed. I have seen the delights of Kuwait and Australia too. I have been forced to stay overnight in Jordan, en route to Oman, we were not allowed to fly over Iraqi airspace at night because of Middle East conflict, and I have seen near-to-death beggars lying on the side of the road during a trip to visit the Pyramids in Egypt.

As a player I had enjoyed a terrific time. If this was going to be it, I could pack it all in safe in the knowledge I had played hard and partied harder! I broke every rule in the book in terms of preparation for games. Dieticians would have had fits at the way Forest and Liverpool players drank in the halcyon days. God knows what we would have won if we had stayed sober before games! I remember being captain for a game in Majorca when BC asked me what time the curfew should be. I hesitated and suggested it should be left up to the individual.

"Gaz, you're my skipper, give me a time!"

"How about 2am, gaffer?" I said, fingers crossed.

"Done. Be good!"

I still came in at 5am and that was nothing compared to the madness of the game. The Spaniards were lining up to take pot shots at us and booted us all over Majorca. The referee never did a thing to protect us and the Gaffer was going mental on the touchline. I got carried off injured. Ian Wallace had to come off for his own good. He was out there looking for retribution and the Gaffer was frog-matched to the dressing room by a policeman with a gun because of the way he was complaining.

On one of the random jaunts forced upon us, we checked into a hotel in Baghdad and the first sign we saw in the hotel lobby was an arrow pointing towards the hotel's air raid shelter. Two weeks later Glasgow Rangers stayed in the same hotel and a rocket blew up about 100 yards from their bedrooms. We didn't get much sleep during our stay but that was probably nothing in comparison to their nightmares.

Many years later, in the early 2000s, any kind of terrorist threat or prospect of such unrest and danger, and teams simply withdrew from scheduled competitions. They refused to travel and cricket tours to Pakistan were cancelled without a second thought. Player safety was the paramount issue. Not back when I was playing. The mantra was get on the plane, fly in with your Forest blazers, play the game and fly home again. If you were lucky. Well at least life was never dull.

Thanks to football there are not too many countries I have not visited. If BC could have negotiated a friendly in the Arctic Circle, playing in crampons against the local polar bear XI, he would have done. I have visited some incredible, far-flung places and loved every minute. As I lay flat on my back, in the July of 1984, I had never felt more jealous of missing out on the first pre-season friendly of the season – against Keyworth United – a local Nottinghamshire amateur side. Never mind warm-up games in Sweden, Belgium, Holland and Greece. I would have given my high teeth to play in any of them instead of spend six weeks staring at the ceiling, not knowing whether I would ever play again.

The doctor's orders were so strict I had to get permission to get off my sick bed to attend the birth of our second child on the night Sandra thought she had given birth to an alien! During the last couple of months of the pregnancy we became avid watchers of the TV Sci-Fi programme 'V' which featured green aliens. When Sandra went into labour, her father Frank drove the two of us to hospital. Hours earlier we had been watching the latest episode of V when James emerged into the world a rather disturbing shade of a similar green! Apparently he had urinated in the womb shortly before entering the world which accounted for his odd colour. Eventually, when all cleaned up, he was a more re-assuring shade of pink but even then I was not allowed to pick him up. I couldn't even lift the kettle at the time.

I have never been so bored. I watched so much TV my eyes were square.

I was that pissed off I was even doing jigsaws and I had never done one in my life until then. All I could do was cross the days off the calendar for the first six weeks until I had to report back to the specialists to see whether the operation had been successful and we could move on to the next step. Crossing the days off is all very well but when that day finally arrives you wish it was a million years away.

The not knowing was always more pleasurable than the prospect of turning up at the hospital that day and being given the 'sorry Mr Birtles' speech. However, my fears were unfounded as I was given the go ahead to start some light training, light being the operative word. I was allowed to join in training sessions with the rest of the players and walk through them. Running at that stage was out of the question.

At least just being back among my team mates raised the mood. It gave me the incentive. There was, at long last, after some very dark days, some light at the end of the tunnel and just being able to pull on the training kit and enjoy the dressing room banter was a bonus.

There had been a few changes while I had been away, including the arrival from Holland of Dutch international midfielder Johnny Metgod, Hans Segers, Gary Megson, who did not last very long, and a youngster by the name of Nigel Clough.

The times were- a-changing in the game and there was a rush to embrace Europe and bring over continental players. The age of clubs being chock full of English and Jock players was coming to an end. Segers was as strong as an ox and totally bonkers in the most endearing of ways; Johnny was a consummate professional and he put us to shame really with his attitude to the game. We used to train from 10-30 until 11-45 and that was the longest it ever was. Once the session had finished that sparked the race over Trent Bridge to see who could get into Uriah's wine bar the quickest.

While we were ordering the first of several pints in a regular two-hour session, there was never any sight of Johnny Metgod having a beer. He was still on the training ground with a bag of balls practising free-kicks from all ranges and all angles. That was unheard of at Forest. I don't think we ever practised a corner up until that point. The foreign mentality made us look like Neanderthals. They were obsessed with technique and we were obsessed with lager!

Johnny had so much quality. I was in the stand the day he scored an incredible free-kick against West Ham United. He was about 35-yards out and unleashed this phenomenal shot which followed a similar trajectory to a 747 taking off from terminal one at Heathrow. I swear that ball is still travelling now. Phil Parkes was in goal for West Ham and if he had not ducked it would have decapitated him. There was so much brute force and skill. I have never seen anyone strike a more pure shot than that. A few games later we were losing 2-0 to Manchester United and he curled in an absolute beauty as we came back to win 3-2. It was all down to practise, but it never stopped me racing to Uriah's.

Not that I could race anywhere with the state of my back though gradually I was able to do more and more and kept setting dates for a possible return. Initially it was November, but that came and went until the frustration was finally released a month later and I was selected for an A team game against Notts County which was to be played at Highfields, a training ground own by the University of Nottingham to the west of the city.

It had been almost six months since I had played my last game in Australia and I even managed to oust the gaffer's son from the team on a miserable, soaking wet Saturday morning which attracted 200 hardy souls, including BC.

'It's like running in the Grand National. The first fence is always the most difficult. If he gets over that, Beecher's Brook will come easy to him'. That was the Gaffer's simply analysis of the whole affair. It was a million miles away from the Bernabeu. It was not the Olympic Stadium in Munich, but it was bloody brilliant for me and I scored to make the comeback even more enjoyable. After all the doubts and concerns the back held up and I still had a career.

Seven months after my last competitive senior game I returned for a 0-0 draw in the FA Cup against Dave Bassett's Crazy Gang. If ever I needed a real test of the back that was the perfect one, getting smashed around by Vinnie Jones and his mad Wimbledon mates and partnering Nigel up front.

I even managed to get a few games in as a central defender that season too. We had a bit of a defensive crisis at the back and out of the blue the Gaffer asked me to play there to help the team out. I had not been in the team, I had lost my place to Nigel and Davvo, when we travelled to Blackburn where I slotted in at centre half for a game we ended up winning 3-0.

I followed that up as a central defender in two top flight games, the first was against Arsenal at the City Ground and I was up against my old mate Tony Woodcock and his partner Charlie Nicholas. We strolled into a 3-0 lead and I helped create one of the goals carrying the ball out of defence and launching a counter attack. I was libero Birtles and loving it, until I got back in the dressing room and the Gaffer collared me. "What the fuck were you doing in setting up that goal! Hey well done, but don't do it again," he said.

Football was simple to him and central defenders only had two jobs. The first was to head it and the second was to kick it. Kicking it as far as he was concerned was to pass the ball to someone who could actually play!

He hated frills and over-elaborate frippery. I can recall watching a County Cup final once and Neil Webb went through and tried to chip the goalkeeper. It was a decent effort and the ball landed just on the top of the net, which shows how close he came to getting the execution of the shot right. Within seconds BC was out of his dug-out with his hand to the side of his mouth in that trademark way and told Webby to get off the pitch. He was substituted for trying to lob the goalkeeper. It might have looked good to Webby, but for the Gaffer it was unnecessary and unwanted.

I enjoyed my short stint as a central defender. As a striker I knew what my opponents were going to do and had reacted to it, before they had even done it. My old mate Lloydy even went into print suggesting that I should be selected as a centre back for England! That might have been a bit far fetched but I certainly needed to be putting in some impressive performances towards the end of that season. I had only played for half of it and my contract was up that summer. To make matters worse, the club was in a financial mess.

Forest had an overdraft of £1million and times were hard again. So hard there was talk about either Nigel, Davvo or me being sold to help ease the pressure. I was in the frame to be moved on because I was earning close to £1,000-a-week and was comfortably the highest earner at the club. I certainly had no intentions of moving on, but it looked like the matter would be taken out of my hands. The messages that BC was sending out were pretty clear. 'I want him to stay, but I can't continue paying him at his current level. He's been a magnificent servant to the club, but he'll have to give way if we are to continue the relationship' was the way he saw it.

He made sure that he laid it on pretty thick. He was brilliant at out-flanking opponents. He launched a newspaper offensive telling everyone I was on the verge of making the biggest decision of my career since I had walked out of the City Ground for Old Trafford six years earlier. In his typically blunt fashion people were informed my career was at a 'crossroads'. The pressure was being applied in the most transparent of ways. I was plagued by fitness problems and knew the treatment room better than the physio Graham Lyas. My place had been taken by Peter Davenport and Nigel Clough and no one was knocking the door down for my services.

It was all about cash and he made it abundantly clear he could not afford to pay me anything to stay. In fact he was about to cut my wages and as far as he could see, he was doing me a favour! It was nice of him to tell everyone else what he planned to do before he had even broached the subject with me, but I should have been used to it by then. Fortunately, just like they had several years earlier, Manchester United came to the rescue. They made a £750,000 offer for Peter Davenport and he decided to leave the City Ground before the end of the season. Perhaps I could have warned him about the pitfalls of moving to Old Trafford. That said, I was so glad he took up the challenge because it enabled me to stay.

It gave me the leverage to negotiate another 12-month contract, throwing in my biggest selling point of being able to help develop some of the exciting young talent at the club, which included the Gaffer's son. I wanted to stay and help the kids and I got what I wanted. I became a 30-year-old babysitter to the likes of Nigel, Phil Starbuck, Brian Rice, Terry Wilson and Steve Chettle was my boot boy. Allied with Stuart Pearce and Des Walker, the nucleus of the second coming of the club was in place. It was a rebuilding process which enabled the club to get themselves virtually a season ticket to Wembley in the late Eighties and early Nineties.

Pearcy had arrived from Coventry as the makeweight in a deal with included centre back Ian Butterworth and one of his first experiences of the Gaffer was a surreal one after a game against Luton Town on their revolutionary plastic pitch.

That was an experiment which went totally against the beliefs of BC. Football was meant to be played on grass. Real grass. Not the synthetic stuff. So he was not in the best of moods when he had to go down there and deal with the unnatural bounce of the ball at Kenilworth Road.

His mood was even darker after the game when one particular car was blocking our team coach from beating the usual hasty retreat back to the sanctuary of Nottingham. After a short wait, to see if the owner would return, a request was aired within the club for it to be moved so Albert could manoeuvre his way out of the car park. After several more minutes of waiting and thumb twiddling, BC's patience finally snapped. He leapt out of his seat and marched off towards the main reception to sort the matter out himself.

RED LETTER DAY

Within minutes he was on his way back and instead of climbing back into his seat at the front of the coach, he just popped his head through the doors and shouted, 'Albert, follow me!' With that, he proceeded to get into the offending vehicle which was obstructing our departure. However, instead of moving it into another space, he drove it out of the main gates and onto the ring road out of Luton, until he decided he had gone more than far enough to inconvenience the owner, whoever it might be.

At that point, he pulled the car over, got out and locked it and calmly climbed back on to the team coach which Albert had dutifully pulled up to a halt behind him. The look on the faces of people like Pearcy and Butterworth was priceless. They had never seen anything like it in their lives. For the rest of us, it was bog standard normality. The coach pulled away and BC had was listening to the Ink Spots tinkling out of the CD player while Albert had been told to 'get a fag on, old man, I like the smell'.

Everyone knew he had committed a crime. All the players were in a state of amusement. The entire coaching staff fell silent and no one said a word. There was not a dissenting voice amongst us, apart from the 'old man', in between a deep pull on his cigarette. Albert, bless him, casually pointed out that what the Gaffer had just done was theft. At the very least he had taken a car without the owner's consent. The words created that kind of silence a stranger generates when he walks through the swing doors into a saloon in a wild west movies. Even the Ink Spots seemed to have stopped to listen for the reaction it caused.

'Old man, you are right. Turn the coach around and get me back to the car' came the instruction. Albert dutifully obliged and we had to follow BC back to Luton Town FC for him to re-park the car and return the keys to reception. Rumour has it that the car belonged to Nick Owen, one-time presenter of TV-am with Anne Diamond and a mad Luton Town fan. True or not, to this day I am not sure he even knows what happened to his car.

Yet if you think it was a source of amusement and bewilderment for the vast majority of the squad, especially the new boys like Pearcy, imagine what it must have been like for Nigel.

Later in life, I became a solid friend of Nigel's. He has the same take on the game as I have, as well as a startlingly similar take to that of his old man. He and his wife Margaret and Samantha, my second wife, and me regularly meet up for dinner, but as colleagues at Forest we were precisely that. I was the experienced pro and part of my bargain over the new contract was to help bring him on. That appealed to BC but Nigel did not need looking after and he handled an incredibly difficult situation, barely batting an eyelid.

If we thought we had it tough for an hour or so in our daily working routine, Nigel in the early days did not drive. So he travelled to and from training with his dad. All the attention, all the accusations of paternalism and nepotism. Every time he stepped on the pitch there were 11 players queueing up to see who could get the first Daddy's Boy jibe in. That was bad enough but can you imagine the scepticism he had to deal with from within the camp as well. If he was a Daddy's Boy to everyone on the outside, he was a potential spy to everyone on the inside. What a crap spot to be in.

The Daddy's Boy thing lingered for a while but any thoughts of him being a nark for his Old Man were dispelled in an instant. We assumed that we would have to watch what we were saying in case everything was reported back yet Nigel was brilliant. He joined in with the usual banter and when the flak was flying in the direction of his dad not a word of it ever got back. He took the jokes, he was part of the furniture from day one and the way he handled himself was incredible. To have all that pressure and attention and deal with it in the unflappable way he did, well it must have made Brian very proud.

Nige had no great pace. Everyone in the game was always telling him that and it used to infuriate the Gaffer. What he lacked for in physical speed he made up for in the ridiculous pace his brain worked.. He took pictures of the entire football field faster than any camera Canon might have produced. He was as brave as a lion, his first touch was sublime and if ever he passed you the ball it arrived carrying the kind of velocity that momentarily knocked your boot back as you cushioned it. It was pinged at you at the perfect height and demanded to be brought under control in the same effortless way he did it.

With Davvo gone, I was Nigel's new strike partner. Old Father Time and Daddy's Boy up front. Nigel never said a lot off the field. He was quiet and got on with his business. On it, he was different. He had came through all the flak, dealt with centre backs whacking seven shades out of him from behind every Saturday and his physical courage was outstanding. We hit it off as partners too and I had a real flying start to the 1985-86 season. At one stage I hit six goals in three games. One came in a 3-1 win over Southampton, two in a 6-0 win at home to Villa and three in a 6-2 win over Chelsea at Stamford Bridge.

Not bad for a striker who was prone to injury and spent all his time in the treatment room. I thought I had done pretty well then Neil Webb went one better with seven goals in that same stretch of games! It was a bright start to a season that was punctuated with niggling injuries which cost me a couple of spells on the sidelines. Still I ended up joint top scorer in the league with Nigel on 14 goals, a reasonable return. However, the injuries inspired more doubts about whether I should be given another contract that summer and my prospects of squeezing out another 12 months of my career at the City Ground were not helped by my one and only real act of defiance towards the Gaffer in eight years, at the end of that season.

Instead of a jaunt to Cala Millor for some sun, we were scheduled to go on a four-day trip to Varan in Bulgaria. It was to be a fun trip with a friendly game thrown in but Sandra was expecting our third child and she suffered a fall down the stairs in the week we were supposed to be going. She was eight-and-a-half months pregnant. Even before the fall I was hugely reluctant to go on the trip, just in case she ended going into an early labour. There was no way I wanted to be stranded in Bulgaria and miss the birth of our baby.

Her accident made me even more concerned. Anything could have happened as a result of the tumble and to make matters worse, James had contracted chicken pox and I just did not feel inclined to go. I had responsibilities at home. Surely the Gaffer would see that it was best for me to miss the trip. Not a bloody chance. I asked permission to be left out of the travelling party and was told in no uncertain terms that I was to be on that plane. But there was no way I was going to Bulgaria.

It was ridiculous. He refused to back down and insisted I was on the plane. On the day they were due to fly, I just did not turn up. I stayed at home with Sandra and helped with the application of calomine lotion. What was any self-respecting husband and father supposed to do? I felt I was fully justified in the stance I had taken and would sort out the consequences when they came back. I had barely asked for a thing in eight years at the club, the least he could do was let me stay home and look after my wife and children.

Obviously my absence was noted and I went to the ground to see him when they got back. I wanted to clear the air and more importantly we still had the business of sitting down to sort out a new contract. Fat chance. I did not want the matter to fester any longer than necessary. Especially as sometimes he could really surprise you. When you thought you were due a major bollocking, he would have had time to reflect and on the odd occasion would actually come around to your way of thinking.

I remember going into the ground thinking that after he had been given a few days to mull things over he would have come to the natural conclusion that I should have been allowed to stay home in the first place. I never got to find out if that was the way he was leaning because he avoided me that day. He knew I was on the premises but he steadfastly refused to see me and I was spitting. Not a word was exchanged between us. He had left me to stew over my actions and my contract. I was so pissed off I did an interview with Roger Duckworth from the Sun newspaper which appeared the next day. I was not one to lose my cool but the way it appeared in print made it look like I had gone mad over the situation. I accused the Gaffer of being 'petty' and banged on about never asking for a thing in eight years of service, stressing the point that my wife and child were not well.

I felt I had the right to express my disgust at the way I had been treated. It was only right to show some backbone and I sat back and waited for the repercussions. If I had not been disciplined for my absence at the airport, I would get it in the neck for this. In those days, fines were always administered by letter. They would be delivered in an official envelope bearing the Forest insignia on the front. So when a letter dropped on my doormat with the Forest tree on the front of it a few days later I was getting ready to cough up for my insubordination.

What was it to be? Any kind of misdemeanours usually carried a two week fine. That was the maximum permitted under League rules and I would have suffered the consequences and paid. Nothing, however, prepared me for the contents of that particular 'red tree' envelope. There had been no discussions between the Gaffer and me about a new contract and now I knew why. The letter was not a fine, it was a very terse communication informing me that I had been given a free transfer. After nearly ten years of service I was being told by post that my services were no longer required. There was not even a thank you for all my efforts!

I was devastated. It was a complete bolt out of the blue which I had never seen coming. That was how Forest told me I was no longer needed. With an impersonal letter signed by the club secretary. It was a bloody disgrace. I was so upset. It would have nice to have been told to my face by the Gaffer that he no longer needed me.

Instead he decided to give an interview to the Evening Post explaining what had happened. "I don't relish doing it, but I feel it is the best thing as far as the club is concerned," he said. He stressed it had nothing to do with the Bulgaria trip, although that seemed more than pure coincidence. At the same time I got the elbow so did Ian Bowyer. That was it, the final two links with the European Cup glory days had been severed with two swipes of the sword.

I deserved another 12 months. I had finished equal top scorer in the league that season with Nigel and I could have gone on for another year. Instead, on FA Cup final morning, as Coventry were preparing for their shock victory over Spurs at Wembley, I was shredding an envelope and letter that told me my life at the club I loved was over. I was distraught and took myself off to play golf. I could not stand football and did not want to watch the Cup final. I just wanted to keep out of the way. I never saw Keith Houchen's famous header or Gary Mabbutt's own goal that denied Spurs an eighth win in the final.

I was approaching my 31st birthday and I had until the end of the month until my wages ended at Forest and I would effectively be on the dole. For the first time in my career I was sitting waiting for the phone to ring. There were plenty of rumours of interest in me. Leicester apparently wanted me as a replacement for Alan Smith, who they had sold to Arsenal for £800,000. Birmingham and Dundee United were also mentioned. But the only phone call I received was from Keith Burkenshaw, who was the manager of Sporting Lisbon. He wanted me to go out there and have a crack at that. He flew me out to Lisbon, gave me a tour of a wonderful stadium that was packed with 50,000 fans for every home game and took me on a tour of the lavish facilities and board room. I was shown the house I would live in rent free that they had earmarked for me. Not to mention the tempting contract which was waiting to be signed. The figures all added up, the lifestyle seemed magnificent as we ate sardines in a fabulous restaurant. Even if I did get food poisoning.

Sometimes I look back and wonder if I missed a trick when I decided against going to Lisbon. All players should broaden their horizons and try a new culture if they get the opportunity. My logic dictated that I had young children who were starting to settle in schools and the timing of it was all wrong. So I said a polite no and returned to fretting about having no money and three mouths to feed as the clock ticked down on the remaining few days I was being paid by Forest. I thought the game was up.

That was until one evening at West Park when I was playing cricket for

Chilwell Misfits. A group of mates who would have, and regularly did, infuriate the more committed players of our summer game. One lad who opened the bowling for us often had a tomato in the pocket of his whites and let that fly at opening batsmen. To spice things up, we had an irreverent way of selecting the batting order too, which basically consisted of drawing cards. So if luck was against our best batsmen, they could be coming in nine, ten, jack.

It was the night Liverpool played Juventus in the European Cup final and the terrible tragedy of the Heysel Stadium and I was getting ready to catch an edged tomato in the slips when my dad turned up. He had pitched up not to watch, we were not worthy of supporters, but he had a message for me. Derek Pavis, one-time member of the Forest boardroom, was the new chairman of Notts County and he wanted to talk to me about the possibility of crossing the River Trent to play for them. Apart from Sporting Lisbon, that was the only concrete lead I had received in weeks.

Fortunately I had drawn well in the batting order, got in and got out and shot off to see Derek, who had been a Forest committee member until he failed to secure a place on the board, the vote apparently going against him influenced by a certain Brian Clough. He subsequently left Forest and turned up at Meadow Lane. It was an unusual switch but having sold his plumbers' merchants business for several million pounds, he wanted to put a spanner in the works of the football order in the city. County gave him that opportunity -- and perhaps a bit of payback to the man in the green tracksuit over the river.

There has never really been any unwritten rule about players not crossing the Trent from one club to another. Several others have done so. Trevor Christie left Notts and came to Forest to replace me for a while, when I was out injured following the back surgery. Justin Fashanu made the trip in the opposite direction and now it was my turn in what was essentially an amicable atmosphere in a tolerant city. It was helped by the fact that we had a good social arrangement with the County lads too. Players like Pedro Richards, Brian "Killer" Kilcline, Rachid Harkouk and Dave McVay had been far more fierce opponents in Uriah Heeps and the other drinking dens of Nottingham than they were on the field.

At the time, Notts County had recently lost their legendary manager Jimmy Sirrel, who had been replaced by John Barnwell. The same John Barnwell that wanted to give me my first leg up on the professional ladder over a decade earlier with Peterborough United. I turned him down then and never regretted it. Now he wanted me again. I knew Sporting Lisbon were in the frame. I knew First Division clubs were interested and I knew that joining Notts County would mean a fall down to the old Third Division. It was a huge drop in standard for someone who still believed he had something to offer at the highest level, especially as Forest fans would only have to look across the river to see how far down I had descended. The challenge appealed to me, however.

There was a wind of change blowing through County. They had ambition. Derek Pavis was driven by a sense of injustice over what had happened at Forest and the ingredients were there. There were no thoughts of broken allegiances as far as I was concerned. I am a Nottingham lad and in my head that entitled me to play for either of the clubs, or both. It was everyone for himself. I did not have the kind of wad of cash lying around in an offshore bank account that would have enabled me to hang my boots up.

I had three kids to feed and buy clothes for. I had a mortgage and bills to pay. I could still see the floodlights across the road and I knew that I would have to win over the die-hard Notts County fans who would naturally be sceptical. It was Derek and Barney, with their immense enthusiasm, who sold the thing to me. They had vision. They had young players like Tommy Johnson, Mark Draper and Dean Yates coming through.

Ian 'Charlie' McParland, who went on to coach at Forest and have a spell as Notts manager, was there. Gary Lund, Adrian Thorpe and Gary Mills added to the mix. Notts had gone out and recruited experienced pros like Geoff Pike, the old West Ham midfielder, and Andy Gray was even brought in for a short time on loan as he was winding down his career after scaling the heights with Aston Villa and Everton, just before he started his broadcasting career at Sky Sports. It was a great time to be part of something that was gradually being built after the incredibly successful years under Jimmy Sirrel.

I was just happy to still have a livelihood and a career. It could so easily have ended there and then. Footballers simply did not earn the kind of riches players do now. The game has advanced a long way since I walked through the Meadow Lane gates in June 1987 and I often wonder if it is for the better. Players are certainly better treated. They have the best of everything. Great facilities, scientific analysis, ProZone stats, the best food, the best re-fuelling programmes, masseurs, the best medicine, mind-boggling advancement in injury treatment, surgery and rehab. In that respect, the game is light years on from the bacon and egg and pints of lager brigade of my generation.

So are the mountains of cash they earn. The wages of an average Championship player means he could earn as much in a month as I did in the season I won the European Cup with Forest in 1979.

But I would not swap places with Wayne Rooney, Steven Gerrard or Frank Lampard for one minute. They live in a cocoon, cosseted and unaware of the real world. There are no players' lounges at clubs these days where the common fan can go and mix with their heroes. Players' lounges now are for WAGS and players' kids. They play against each other, drink with each other and then climb into the 4x4 and withdraw to the leafy suburbs and shut themselves away in their multi-million pound mansions.

Alcohol is taboo now and drinking with members of the public is part of a fantasy world in the mind of fans. As a player I lived in an era where players were part of the football community. It was us with them. Not us and them. We loved being part of it all, but that all changed. Players go out and they are a target. I genuinely don't begrudge them a penny of what they earn. Good look to them, but it is so difficult for them in the modern era. There are so many stings and honey traps now. I would not change my playing days to be part of the millions they have thrown at them. I genuinely mean that.

Players get set up. Newspapers want to expose them and there are hundreds of girls out there who just want to marry a footballer. That is their mission in life and they work on it. If it fails, they always have the kiss and tell to fall back on. Players can get set up and be shown up in disgraceful ways in newspapers. That intrusion is something that I never had to endure, thank god. You can shove your millions right where the sun don't shine, because I could not live my life in that kind of environment.

Please don't get the impression that I think they all have it tough and we should feel sorry for them. If you get caught playing with fire, you have to accept the consequences. I have no sympathy for those people who run around and play the games and get caught and nothing makes me spew more than when they get caught and try to buy silence with court injunctions. All the culture of trying to gag the media like that is unpalatable. If you are going to mess around and get caught, then take your medicine and get on with it. Don't try and use your obscene wealth to beat the system.

No one is above the law. The public are not stupid. These are grown-up people, playing grown-up games. If they transgress, don't try to hush it all up. The problem is that they earn so much money they think they are bullet proof and they can just pay their way out of a scrape. There is even a lawyer called Mr Loophole who performs mission impossible in extricating some players out of a mire of their own creation. The Royal Box at Wimbledon is full of footballers and so are film premieres. Footballers are celebrities nowadays, up there with pop and movie stars. The only gala night I went to was the PFA awards in London. That was the only time I tied one of those ludicrous velvet dickie bows and pulled on the dinner jacket.

It's hard to get star struck among all your contemporaries at events like that, but Gary McAllister, Gary Mills and myself managed it on one particular occasion.

We had decided to get down to London nice and early and start a session of liquid of refreshment before heading across to the Grosvenor Hotel. That was the afternoon we bumped into a real superstar as far as I am concerned. Not too many players got to take the legendary Leslie Phillips to the PFA awards dinner but that was our special treat.

We were in the pub when Leslie Phillips wandered in. The three of us were nudging each other, casting glances in his direction. Being a massive fan of the Carry On films, he was a real superstar in my eyes. Eventually it was left to me to go over and start a conversation and we ended up drinking for quite some time, getting steadily oiled before I blurted out an invitation to come to the PFA dinner since we had a spare ticket. We never thought for one minute he would come, but he accepted and arrangements were made to meet.

All the way to the Grosvenor we were convinced he would not turn up and just as we were about to abandon our guest and adjourn to the bar, he made a typically flamboyant entrance wearing the full dinner jacket and a great big cape. Ding Dong! There he was, Leslie Phillips in the foyer among all these footballers and he was sat on our table. We had a brilliant evening and ended up drinking champagne into the small hours. To this day I still don't believe that Leslie Phillips had the faintest idea who I was, or Gary Mills and Gary McAllister for that matter, but we knew who he was and that was all that mattered. I was star struck for days.

I had the same feeling when Forest were heading off on one of those innumerable friendly jaunts and about five of us sneaked out of hotel in central London, ahead of a flight to Abu Dhabi. We homed in on the nearest night club and ended up in the VIP area drinking with Ian Gillan, Ian Paice and the rest of Deep Purple. We had just been standing there when some random bloke wandered over and asked us if we would like to join the band. I had always wanted to be a drummer in a rock band as a kid!

They were nervous of us and we were nervous of them. They could not believe they were drinking with footballers who played for Brian Clough and we were equally gobsmacked. It just reminds me of the fact there never seemed to be an edge to anything back then. It was such a carefree time, but a lot of humility seems to have disappeared from the game and from people that play it. Utopia in football for me would be players getting correctly rewarded for success instead of being lavishly paid for mediocrity. At Forest we got £300 a point if we were in the top three. If we were fourth to sixth we got £50 a point and if you were out the top six you got fuck all. That was the way it was. Players who finished the season with Hull and got relegated in May 2010 were on £40,000-a-week. How the hell do you give those people incentives?

If they are earning £120,000 a week and lose, who cares. That is why I admire people like Paul Scholes, Gary Neville and Ryan Giggs. They have got the cars. They have got the medals. They had it all at a very young age, but it never stopped them striving for more and you never saw them in the middle of lurid newspaper stories. They were brought up correctly at a famous club, an institution really, and by its indomitable manager. The whole of football could learn an awful lot from those methods and the actions of that Manchester United trio.

They were nurtured at Old Trafford, along with David Beckham, and shown the correct values. They were not allowed to run around like maniacs. That is why Sir Alex is incredible. Look at people who have progressed to become good managers after playing under him. Mark Hughes, Steve Bruce, Steve Coppell. All top blokes, with good values. It was not all about the money back then, although I fully understand it is not the players' fault they are handed heaps of cash. The responsibility lies with the people who hand over the ridiculous contracts. For my generation, it was all about winning. Today, it is about how many cars in the garage. But do they have anywhere near as much fun as we had?

I bet none of them have contracted septicaemia from playing football either! That was another of the potentially career threatening injuries I picked up during my stint at Meadow Lane, where I alternated between central defence and my familiar striker's role. On a very muddy Bloomfield Road pitch, so no change there then, I was operating as a central defender and was having an almighty battle with a striker playing for Blackpool. At some stage during this battle I ended up with a small cut on the little finger knuckle on my left hand. It was just a scratch and I never thought anything of it during the game though in hindsight, that surface might have been sprayed with chemicals which would not have helped my predicament.

It just seemed like one of those irritating paper cuts that became progressively sorer as Saturday evening wore on. I slapped something on it to try to draw the sting and went out for the usual Saturday night ritual of a few beers and a bite to eat with Sandra. The alcohol seemed to take the edge off the problem until I woke up on Sunday morning and the pain had got worse and my little finger was the size of my thumb. The only cure was the Cadland and a cocktail of Jack Daniels and ibuprofen. The more JDs I had the less I noticed the puss coming out of the wound. I got so smashed I ended up having to sleep in the spare room.

The following morning Sandra came to check on me and I was speaking total gibberish. I spoke gibberish quite a lot when I'd had a few so she should have been able to translate although since it was not alcohol-fuelled gibberish, she could be forgiven for failing to understand me

I was in a real mess. I had a temperature of 104 degrees and I had a pink line running all the way up my body, tracing the route the poison had taken inside my body. Within minutes an ambulance had arrived to cart me off to the Queen's Medical Centre and I was hooked up to a drip for three days with blood poisoning! The actor Christopher Casanove died of septicaemia many years later so reflecting that I was pretty lucky is something of an understatement. Needless to say, I was in no fit shape for Saturday's trip to Wigan.

My 'brush with death' got the sensational treatment in the tabloids at the time as well as the phone calls from so-called team mates like Adrian Thorpe. Always a bit of livewire and dressing room jokes, he told me that the undertakers had been in to measure me while I had slept at home and that the lads had all bought new black suits for the funeral. He added that that they wanted to know if they could get a refund after I had cheated the Grim Reaper. The concern was touching. Underwhelmingly so.

There were some sensational happenings on the pitch too although John Barnwell might not have approved as we stitched together several impressive unbeaten sequences. That included victories like the 5-3 win at York City which involved six goals in the opening 45 minutes as we tried to keep pace with Sunderland at the top end of Division Three.

I scored my fair share of goals and a 5-1 win over Brighton in the inspirationally- named Sherpa Van Trophy, one of the early incarnations of the Football League Trophy for Division Three and Division Four clubs, had me thinking about another Wembley appearance. That was until we ran into a rampaging young Wolves striker by the name of Steve Bull in the Southern Area final. Wolves were running away with Division Four at the time and the 'Tipton Terror' scored in both legs as Barney's old team prevented us from reaching the final to play Burnley. Bully went on to get his hands on a winner's medal before making a name for himself at a much higher level.

Out only possible salvation was to make sure we ended up with one of the two automatic promotion places that season to get the club into the Second Division. That was the ambition that had been spelt out to me by Derek Pavis and we had spent much of the second half of the season challenging with Sunderland for the Championship, never mind runners-up spot. Promotion seemed likely and a far greater prize than a day out at the Sherpa Van. We had beaten Sunderland at Meadow Lane and it was only in the latter stages of the campaign that they pulled ahead in first place. Still second spot appeared ours for the taking.

That would have been justification for dropping down from Forest. It was the challenge I had set myself at the time, to help get the club moving back up the leagues again, but somehow we managed to self-destruct in spectacular fashion. Brighton gained full revenge for losing to us in the Sherpa Van with a league win at the old Goldstone Ground which enabled Walsall to overtake us. That was one of five defeats in our last ten games that cost us. Even with four games remaining, if we had won one more game, we would have finished runners up to Sunderland.

Instead successive defeats against rivals Walsall at Fellows Park and a miserable 2-1 defeat by Port Vale at Meadow Lane cost us the automatic place. Victory on the final day against Preston North End meant we ended up three points short of Brighton, who came from way back to overhaul us. I did not see them crying too many tears about losing out on a Sherpa Van Trophy medal and a Wembley trip. They had got what we craved and it was a sickening feeling. Even Walsall pipped us for third spot with us and Bristol City filling the remaining play-off places, to join Sheffield United who finished in the Division Two relegation play-off place.

RED LETTER DAY

I might have ended up covering several play-off campaigns for Sky TV, but at that time they were totally new to me. I had never experienced that end of season shoot-out that is supposed to be so exciting and great for football. Let me tell you, it is no fun when you are on the end of a semi-final defeat in the competition and all your aspirations of promotion, after flogging your guts out for 40-odd games, go out the window with one miserable performance. David Kelly was a young Walsall striker back then and he gave us the run-around at Meadow Lane in a 3-1 first leg defeat that effectively wrecked our hopes.

I have been bribed out of a UEFA Cup final. I have surrendered my European Cup crown in the weakest of manners against CSKA Sofia and I have been robbed of a Wembley Cup final hat-trick by a linesman who got it wrong. Nothing in my career, though, compares to how low I sunk at the end of the second leg at Walsall when we were unable to put right everything we had done wrong in the first leg. The 1-1 draw at Fellows Park was not enough and in the space of a couple of weeks, our whole season had fallen apart. It was the biggest disappointment of my career. The only thing for it was an almighty bender and I spent hours in the Meadow Club back at the ground getting totally bladdered.

Gary Mills had to carry me to his car and would not let me go home. He took me back to his place and it was not until the next day that I had any idea of what had happened. Worse still is I look back and know without a shadow of doubt it was that result that effectively cost John Barnwell his job as manager of Notts County. It should never have come down to that. We should have been preparing for the Second Division instead of Barney trying to revive his shattered players for another crack at Division Three the following season. He did not lose his job immediately but the writing was on the wall after such a failure to push home our advantage.

The club felt it was the right thing to give the manager another chance. Before too long, though, the rumblings of discontent surfaced. It is always hard to bounce back from a disappointment like that and when the early stages of the following season did not go well a boardroom coup was on the cards. It was the beginning of the end for Barney and the beginning of the end for me at Meadow Lane. It did not take a genius to work out that the manager was on borrowed time. Somehow he made it through to December, which was traditionally the time managers under pressure finally feel the axe fall on their head. After weeks of sharpening the blade, Barney was decapitated and Notts were looking for a new boss. By the time the new year had been ushered in, they had found one. Neil Warnock.

It was completely out of the blue. Warnock was not a name on many people's or even football's radar at that stage, certainly not in Nottingham. He was managing non-league Scarborough and that was his only experience. It seemed a bit of a leap to Division Three but he must have had something more to his CV than being a qualified chiropodist. Derek Pavis wanted something far more than a manager who could sort out his corns once a month and give him a pedicure. He wanted success and as far as he was concerned, Warnock was the man to deliver it.

I had certainly never come across the bloke and had no idea what to expect, but from very early on, it was abundantly clear my methods and style were not to his liking. I was an ageing professional, sitting on the bench in the twilight of my career and earning decent money. There were never any discussions between us. He never picked my brains and never wanted to know anything from me. He was his own man intent on doing things his way. He simply thought I was too old and he wanted to bring his own people in like Craig Short and his brother Chris, not to mention others like Paul Harding and Dean Thomas. So I needed to be shifted on to make room, but at least he had the good grace to wait until the end of the season, when my contract was up.

Warnock's style, which followed him throughout his career, was something a bit of a lump it merchant and the plain fact is, I was not his sort of player. I could pass the ball! He gave me stick in his autobiography about saying that at the time I was released. It was a joke on my part, but maybe it was tinged with a bit of sour grapes. I was part of the furniture at Notts. I had won over the sceptics and they could see I was fully committed to the club. Notts had just missed promotion and that irked me. I wanted to put that right, but I did not figure so much in the second half of that season after Warnock arrived.

Whenever I bumped into him later in life I always used to wind him up about him having a dig at me. Neil polarised opinions in the game. Away from the cameras and post-match interviews I always found him a charming character and he was a lot of fun with a great sense of humour. He was not what you would call everyone's cup of tea in the way he went about things, but all he ever did to me was to make a decision and back his judgment. Neil can point to the fact that his judgment was spot on. He had a fantastic time as manager of Notts County. Within a couple of years, thanks to some memorable play-off moments, he had guided Notts back to the top flight and won the Anglo Italian Cup against Brescia. It would be churlish for me to try to argue with that. I would just have loved to have been part of it, because I believed I could have contributed.

At the time I was disappointed. I was cut dead and the plain fact was he did not want me around the club. There was no room for emotion on his part. Life as a football manager means you have to be that hard and make tough decisions. If that means calling time on a player then you have to call time. We never fell out. He just did not pick me. He wanted his own people in and Notts could not afford to have me decorating the substitute's bench like an expensive ornament. My shelf life at Meadow Lane had expired and you have to swallow the bitter pill, hope that your body is still holding up and that someone else out there might still want you.

10

REUNITED WITH THE GAME I LOVE
...and the manager too

WHEN you are closing in on your 32nd birthday, the likelihood of the phone ringing starts to decrease yet remarkably I was actually left with a choice to make between joining up with my old mate Ian Bowyer, who had taken the manager's job at Hereford and wanted me to sign for him, or taking a trip to the seaside for the bracing air of Cleethorpes, after Alan Buckley came on asking me to have a chat about moving to Grimsby Town.

The trip to Hereford was an entertaining one. I went with a pal of mine who had been in the army and that led to an interesting meeting in a pub over lunch with one of his old comrades. In 1988 the SAS, who were based in Hereford, launched Operation Flavius on Gibraltar. The brief of the special forces was to arrest three IRA terrorists on suspicion of organising a bomb attack on the changing of the guard at The Convent on Gibraltar. It ended with the three suspects, Danny McCann, Sean Savage and Mairead Farrell having something in the region of 30 bullets pumped into them as the SAS used deadly force.

It led to a massive enquiry and an award winning ITV documentary Death on the Rock which questioned the methods of the SAS and whether they were right to open fire on three IRA suspects who were later found to be un-armed. I did not like to follow the ITV's line of questioning over steak and ale pie in the pub when I came face to face with one of the SAS soldiers who had fired the bullets on the Rock that day! I discovered from my mate that he died a couple of years later from an embolism shortly before he was due to be discharged from active service. After going all through all he went through with the SAS and surviving so many incredibly dangerous situations it always seemed such an unfair way to go.

Having the SAS on the doorstep and the prospect of working for Bomber at Hereford had a certain appeal, but from the moment I went to see Alan Buckley there was only one place I wanted to spend the last days of my career. I remember sitting in one of the rooms at the ground which overlooked the pitch at Blundell Park. Buckley was so enthusiastic about what he planned to do with the club and how he wanted to play a passing game. If my passing abilities were not required by Neil Warnock, Buck was happy to have them and I was more than happy enough to sign a two-year contract.

Of course there was the odd doubt in the mind. Should I have gone out after Notts and called it a day? Was I extending myself too far for what I had left? Once again, pure financial issues were the order of the day. I had to carry on because we needed the money and I made one of the best decisions I ever made in deciding to join Grimsby Town. I loved every minute of the two years I had playing there and Buck stayed true to his word. We passed it for fun. Everything we did was about five-a-sides and working with the ball. I had an absolute hoot along the way, that after we had made a less than auspicious start to the season and I had won the day with my new team mates.

Older players dropping down the leagues can only be viewed in one of two ways by younger players in the lower divisions. You are either welcomed as the ideal old lag to provide much-needed experience and to help develop young talent already at the club. Or immediately the sceptics in the dressing room make up their mind you are going to be earning way more than them and you are only there to bolster your bank balance for a couple of seasons. In other words you really couldn't give a toss about anything other than topping up your pension. In the case of the latter, you are a fucking has-been who should have given up the game and should not be embarrassing yourself any more.

I knew I had to win their trust. I was still as fit as a flea, but players are the most naturally suspicious of animals. Anyone who arrives at a club as a new signing is automatically a threat to someone else. And that someone else is likely to have several long-standing friends in the dressing room you have just infiltrated. Dressing rooms can be welcoming and emit warmth or they can be the most lonely of places in the world. There was no way that

I was going to go up there giving it the big 'I am'. That had never been my style. I did not know the meaning of the word aloof and I just wanted to get in the middle of it all and get started. I was still dressing in my daft gear, determined to have a laugh and they took the piss out of me mercilessly. They hammered me and I loved it.

It also helped that I had a fantastic ally in the camp in the form of Keith Alexander. I had known him from my days in the Young Elizabethan League and the non-league scene in Nottingham, where he had played for Arnold Town and Ilkeston Town. I had bumped into him a lot at various levels and he was the first guy who came across and straight away that helps. From the moment I walked through the doors, he made sure that the lads were onside and knew exactly what they needed to know about me. That I was a solid professional and serious about the job I had accepted. He made it clear to all of them that I was not someone along for the ride just waiting for retirement.

Keith went on to have a far greater career as a manager than he did as a player. He was a pioneer as the first full-time black professional manager in the Football League and it was a terrible tragedy that he passed away in 2010, seven years after he had life-saving surgery on a brain aneurysm. It is always very easy for people to talk in fond terms of ex-colleagues who have passed away in the game. Keith was only 53 when he died after taking charge of a Macclesfield game at Notts County.

It is easy for people to trot out all the platitudes and tell everyone what a lovely man he was and how he was an inspiration to so many. In Keith's case, every word that was spoken about him, every tribute that was made to him, was absolutely spot-on. It is hard to find the words to do justice to what a special bloke he was. He was pure quality and is sadly missed by his family, friends and the game to which he was devoted.

As a player he was like a new born foal. His legs were all over the place, seemingly out of control. They were as long as Viv Anderson's and he used to be the central figure in passages of play when he seemed to have alternately won the ball and lost the ball, in a melee of arms and legs which would go on for ages. He created havoc on the pitch for himself, his team mates and most importantly the opposition. Whenever an opponent thought he had got the better of Keith, a right leg would snake out from yards away and nick the ball back.

REUNITED WITH THE GAME I LOVE

Keith did not come into football until he was 29 and it was great to have him in my corner in the early days. I had just walked into a football outpost. Grimsby was lagging behind and did not even have its own training facilities. We had to borrow them and I was getting paid £300-a-week for the privilege. So it was hardly a king's ransom, but from the moment Keith spoke up and they saw me train, they knew I was serious about the whole thing.

I was still pretty much the same fighting weight I had been in the final days at Forest. I had kept myself in good shape and felt I still had plenty to give to a team brimming with raw talents busting their nuts for Buckley and his assistant Arthur Mann, a really top bloke in every respect. They were a throwback to the Clough and Taylor duo. They worked fantastically well together and Arthur hailed from Nottingham which was an added bonus for me. I have lost count of the number of times I travelled back home with him from matches and passed away the hours talking football. Arthur died in a terrible accident, crushed by a forklift years later. Another tragic loss to his family and the football fraternity in general.

Between them Buck and Arthur were constructing a team of great young kids. John Cockerill and Shaun Cunnington were two exceptiopnal midfielders with immense promise and a brilliant work ethic. The club was full of people like them. Mark "Plug" Lever, Andy Tilson, Gary Childs, David Gilbert and Paul Agnew. They wanted a few older heads to speed up the development which is where I came in with the likes of Paul Futcher. It was never going to be a case of hitting the ground running, but we did plenty of that in pre-season, and 'Plug' managed to cop for more than most throughout the days building up to the first season I spent there.

I still don't know how Mark Lever earned the nickname Plug but it stuck with him and he was the one Buck used to single out for the bollockings on the training ground, irrespective of whether he had done anything wrong or not. We spent several weeks in July running around this great big field which had a massive tree in one corner. Mark had the incredible ability to wind Buck up just by looking at him sometimes. Whenever any orders were given, he was the one asking questions and wanting to know why. 'Plug, round that tree. Twice' was the only thing Buck said to him for a month! Off he would run with a stupid grin on his face.

He just typified a smashing group. They had all these young lads in there, thoroughly enjoying what they were doing. The desire was incredible but it could so easily have gone wrong and we did have a little bit of a struggle in the first half of the season. After 19 games we were stuck in the middle of the table. The good thing was there had been signs of progress, the young kids were starting to believe and no one was really running away with the league. We were only nine points off the top of the table.

If the youngsters had suffered a few hammerings and ended up losing too many games that could have been terrible but there was something for them to cling on to and develop. They were enjoying what they were doing and the more games they won, the more hungry and determined they became. I have never seen midfielders cover more ground than Cunnington and Cockerill did and the way they tackled would have stopped the bus that took you from Cleethorpes into Grimsby town centre. From the midway point of the season the whole place lit up.

After we beat Carlisle United 1-0 on January 27 we only lost three games in the final 21 matches and one of those was near the end of the season when we were probably still hungover from celebrating promotion! From a team that had been drifting aimlessly the previous season we strung together an impressive run of seven straight wins, including victory over Bomber and his Hereford team. I had made the right decision to avoid having lunch with the SAS watching over me.

Grimsby was jumping and the team was flying. They had never seen anything like it and the whole thing came to a head on Friday, April 20 1990 when we went to Southend United and won 2-0. Paul Agnew scored one of the goals that made sure we could not be caught for automatic promotion. He only scored three goals for the club in his entire career at Blundell Park but he will never forget the one that night and I will never forget the look of sheer ecstasy on the faces of those kids who grew ten foot tall at Roots Hall.

Just to round matters off nicely, in our final league game I scored a hat-trick against Wrexham, the only low point of which was the fact that Wrexham's Joey Jones broke his leg in the match which we won 5-1.

That really got the promotion party started and I ended up winning man of the match and a huge ghetto blaster the size of the one Denzil used to carry about with him in Only Fools and Horses. It was my first hat trick for the club, to accompany my first promotion, and a lovely way to mark one of the most satisfying achievements of my career.

The whole of Grimsby and Cleethorpes lit up and I ended up winning the

REUNITED WITH THE GAME I LOVE

Player of the Year award and three other gongs at the club's annual awards night a few days later. I am certain there were more suitable and deserving candidates but it was an honour and a privilege to accept them.

Grimsby probably never thought anything like that would happen to them in their wildest dreams and I was delighted to have been able to help generate the wonderful feel good factor that we could sense in the town. There was only one thing to do to celebrate. Go to Cala Millor. Where else?

If it was good enough for Forest when they were celebrating, it was good enough for Grimsby. I asked Buck if we could sort it out and he agreed. It was time for the 'Old Lag' to show the young kids a few tricks or two. They were on my stomping ground now and it was time for some respect, not that I got any. The first session we resulted in us all sat in some bar after going at it for most of the day. At that stage I had turned to the Jack Daniels and was sat there minding my own business when someone aimed a full pint of beer at the head of Plug and he had the good sense and awareness to duck. Unfortunately I was directly behind him and got a lager soaking for absolutely no reason. Perhaps I was getting too old for this game. I even set off to walk back to Cala Bona, which was a short way up the coast from Cala Millor, at 3am in the morning dripping with beer. That was an early departure by my standards and for once it worked in my favour.

When I finally came round the following morning the rest of the party were hanging around the pool, apart from three notable absentees. I asked where Tony Rees, Andy Tilson and Plug were. Apparently they had got in around 5am and had not even made it to their beds when the police arrived at the hotel! Tony was on crutches with some injury but that had not stopped him joining in a game of football with the other two on the route back to the hotel. They had managed to kick and ruin virtually every newspaper that had been left outside flats, apartments and shops on their drunken stagger home.

Tony fell over the sea wall trying to escape and was soon apprehended as was Plug, but Tilson was super fit and even in his state managed to escape, running all the way back to the hotel. Sadly, the police car containing Reesy and Plug turned up to claim their third victim and whisk them all off to the local station. It transpired that they had to get Buck up at around 5am to come to the station with their passports, before they were allowed to leave. Buck was not amused.

Once I had got the low down on events from the night before, I decided to have a lie down and catch up on my sleep around the pool. I never heard any of them creeping away as they all decided to go elsewhere and leave me to fry in the sun. They left me there for hours and I was like a piece of old leather when I finally woke up. They had left the old bastard to burn in the sun and thought it was hilarious. So much for showing your elders some respect! I was in absolute agony. I had severe sun stroke and was throwing up all over the place. I could barely walk for the rest of the trip.

If that was a problem brought about by spending too much time in the sun, the troubles I suffered for the following season were the result of spending too much time on training grounds and football pitches. My body was starting to give me the tell-tale signs of giving up the ghost. Even though Grimsby managed to follow up their promotion from Division Four by finishing third in Division Three to make it successive promotions, I barely played more than 20 full games for the club in the remainder of my time there. Still it was hugely satisfying to know I made a contribution to two of the most enjoyable years of my playing career.

I knew the game was up, literally, when my body completely ground to a halt playing for Grimsby reserves. Physically I was shattered and my body was screaming for mercy. I had arthritis in my lower back as a result of the operation I underwent several years earlier. It was the time that all professionals dread, that defining moment when you know that you cannot possibly kick another ball. I did not want to be a trophy for young semi-pros getting kicked to high heaven in non-league football.

To add to the sense of personal pain at having to retire and work out what I was going to do next, my marriage to Sandra had ended a year earlier. It was completely my fault. I was no saint as a player and temptation was never far away in terms of female attention and the inevitable separation swiftly followed.

I had brought it upon myself. I am not proud to admit I had been having an affair for some time with the daughter of my old squash partner. I had known Samantha for many years, going way back to my time as a player at Forest, and eventually the whole thing came out and Sandra threw me out of the family home. I deserved it. It was the first frost of winter and I slept in my car in the car park of the Cadland. I had never intended that to happen when I entered into the marriage. As far as I was concerned it was for keeps and I never had any intention of messing her around or messing up our wedding vows. The last thing I wanted to do was ruin my children's lives.

I had three young kids and I felt that was exactly what I had done. I had destroyed their lives. I can still remember sitting on the edge of one of their beds in the bedroom in tears, apologising for what I had done. I vowed I would always be there for them. The three of them were fast asleep and did not hear a word I had said. When I thawed out from my experience in the Cadland car park I went back to the house the next day and it was over. I used the lump sum from my PFA pension to pay off a large chunk of the mortgage to make sure the kids had a roof over their heads. That left Samantha and me virtually penniless when my career ended.

We had nowhere to live and no money coming in. Samantha had to work all the hours god sends at British Telecom to keep us and I had to endure the desperate embarrassment of signing on the dole. What had remained of the pension just went on daily living costs and paying for hotels and places to stay. We even checked into a hotel near East Midlands airport at one stage. Staying in hotels and not having a home to call our own was bad enough but by the time we had rented a little place in West Hallam, visiting the post office in the village to claim my dole was the most demeaning and soul destroying thing I ever had to do.

I had always worked. From the age of 16 I had got a job laying floors until football gave me a career. I hated the idea of being without work and not knowing what to do. To suddenly have nothing and be in such a dreadful mess was difficult to cope with. At least I was exiled in West Hallam, a small hamlet to the west of Ilkeston. Sandra, understandably, had insisted that we did not live anywhere near her and the kids. Still I lived in fear of being recognised in the post office when I went to collect my money. It was bloody horrible and made me feel inadequate. It was an awful time in my life and anyone who has ever signed on the dole will tell how terrible it feels. You cannot help imagine that everyone is looking down their noses at you and has you pegged for some kind of scrounger who has no intentions of working.

Nothing could have been further from the truth. I wanted to work and even asked myself whether I wanted to go back to floor laying. My dad was still working at that time and I did the odd job with him, but my back would not have been able to cope with all that fetching and carrying and bending down for ten hours a day. I even went labouring for a couple of mates who had a block paving business, but I was still unemployed and they were low and depressing times. I lost count of the number of times each day I asked myself how it had all gone wrong.

I had been transferred for £1.25m for god's sake. Why did I not put more in pensions? That was down to me. I had lived for the moment. That was the way I was. Rainy days did not exist in my world, although I do believe I got some bad advice in terms of pensions when I was at Forest. Every player gets the PFA pension but my personal one was not a good one in comparison to some of my contemporaries at Forest and United. I remember looking in the building society book and it was scary the way the money had dripped away. It was not easy getting jobs then and I even had to get a couple of loans from the PFA. They were absolutely brilliant, because I was potless. I had nothing.

Things were so bad I even tried setting up a business with a friend I had gained during my time at Grimsby. The club might have had Harry the Haddock inflatables during the time they were all the rage, but I was shipping the real life stuff backwards and forwards from Cleethorpes to Nottingham in a white van. I was trying to sell fresh fish to top restaurants in Nottingham. I was going in there with all kinds of really fresh fish, prawns and lobster. It was brilliant gear, as fresh as could be, but I was banging my head against a brick wall. Big companies already had those contracts and one man in a van was just not going to cut it. The odd place bought fish from me, but it was never enough. In the end we probably ate most of the fish ourselves.

There must have been something about fish, me and Sam that just did not get on. We very nearly burned down Willie Young's pub in Bramcote not long after he had let us live their rent free in a little flat that was attached to the side of the premises. Willie had retired from Forest to become a landlord of the Bramcote Manor, a few miles out of Nottingham, and we had always kept in touch. He was the first to offer us a bolt hole, before we went to West Hallam.

He would not have a penny from us for the one-bedroom flat. Our bed was over the pub and the pool table was directly below. We could hear all the balls being smashed about so we very rarely got an early night. Then one day Samantha decided to cook trout and leave it in the oven as we went down to the bar for a few drinks on Sunday lunchtime. It was only when the smell of charcoaled fish and the billowing smoke from the flat grabbed the attentions of the drinkers that the fire brigade were called to stop the whole place from burning down!

Things became so bad financially that when we eventually got our own place back in Long Eaton, after Sandra relented on the exclusion zone, I had to take the drastic step of selling the 1979 European Cup winners' medal I bust my balls to win over a decade earlier. The house we bought was in a dreadful state. Every room needed sorting out and we just did not have the cash. The only option I had available was the reluctant move of placing the medal and the shirt I had worn that night in Munich up for auction.

It was a bitter pill to swallow, but it fetched something in the region of £3,000. Something that money could not buy for me had a value placed on its head and went to a gentleman named Phil Soar, who was the chief executive of Nottingham Forest during the Nigel Wray and Irving Scholar regime at the City Ground. At least it was some source of comfort to me that Phil, an ardent Forest supporter who later went on to write a history of the club, was the person who won the day at auction. It still fills me with regret that I was forced into such drastic action and I want it back. One day I would like to buy it back. I worked bloody hard for it.

Thankfully, I still have the medal from the Hamburg game a year later but I never saw the shirt I wore that night until many years later when I agreed to attend a question and answer session. It took place in Lincolnshire somewhere and before the evening got underway a chap wandered up to me and asked me to sign the shirt I had worn the night we left Kevin Keegan close to tears. He told me that he had come to own the shirt because of some connection he had with our old trainer Jimmy Gordon. Fucking cheeky sod Jimmy. He must have swiped some shirts away that night and never put them back in the skip to be washed. Those two shirts should be framed and hanging pride of place in my house. Instead one is probably locked away in a vault owned by Phil Soar and the other is in the grubby hands of some bloke I did not know from Adam.

So I hardly have anything from those wonderful years. My winner's medal from 1980 is in the knife draw in the kitchen and all I have apart from that is the Young European Player of the Year award I won and my Super Cup medal after we beat Barcelona. It really should not have happened like that, but that is how things can turn out if you fall on hard times and the only way I could think of trying to put things right and earn some cash was to somehow get involved in the game. Difficult since management was not something that appealed to me.

I always remember John Robertson holding court with a cup of coffee in one hand and a Silk Cut in the other when he was selling insurance for the Prudential, before he hooked up with Martin O'Neill on their magical ride into management that took them from places like Wycombe Wanderers, Norwich City, Leicester City, Celtic and Aston Villa. He had strong opinions that players like ourselves, with a wealth of experience, medals at the highest level and international caps accumulated in extended careers, should be welcomed into football as valuable assets to any club. The idea that we would have to sit coaching badges frustrated and angered him.

What could any coaching course teach him, or me, that working with Brian Clough for the best part of a decade had missed out? Any other industry would have fast-tracked people with so much experience at shop floor level into positions of authority, but not football. Yet looking back, so many of that European Cup winning side had a go in management and only two really made a success of it. Martin stands out obviously and the other was Frank Clark, who was very successful in stepping into the breach at Forest after the Gaffer retired in 1993.

Many years earlier BC had been swift to pin-point Frank as his successor and once again he got it spot on. Frank restored Forest to the Premier League, after they were relegated in their final season, and took them back into Europe in the UEFA Cup. Nearly everyone else, Larry, John McGovern, Kenny, Tony Woodcock, Trevor Francis, tried their hand at doing what they had watched him do with wide-eyed amazement so many years earlier. They had the best teacher in the world, but it was so hard to replicate what he did. Playing for the master is one thing, emulating him is an entirely different matter.

To even stand a chance of coming anywhere near his genius you had to get your Pro Licence and UEFA badges before you could be a manager. It was not for Robbo and it was not for me, but that did not stop me accepting the job as assistant to my mate Paul Futcher at non league Gresley Rovers. I got on well with Futch and it seemed the right thing to do. It was decent pay and I thoroughly enjoyed being back in an environment I knew. How Futch never managed to progress in the managerial sphere I will never know, he had some truly unique and pioneering ideas.

REUNITED WITH THE GAME I LOVE

In our first season we won the league by ten points but were unable to take our promotion place in the Vauxhall Conference because Gresley's ground was not good enough. It did not comply with the required standards and it just killed everyone's enthusiasm. Cheltenham, managed by Steve Cotterill, went up in our place instead. Fate works in mysterious ways.

I just could not wait to get away on holiday. I had spent weeks combining my coaching duties at Gresley doing hard labour block paving to save the cash for a three-week break for Sam and me in Spetses. We were phoning the kids every night to check they were OK and we had only been there about a week when I phoned James and he told me Futch had gone to Stockport County as manager!

I said: "You must be joking! Are you sure?" James was adamant he had seen the appointment on TV but Futch had not mentioned a word of it to me and I was straight on the phone to find out what had been going on. When I finally got hold of him, he told me he had not taken the Stockport job. He had taken the job at Southport in the Conference. He was very apologetic, explaining that he felt he was swimming against the tide at Gresley and that we could never get the ground straight for promotion because we just did not have the cash.

He could not take me with him to Southport and suggested that I cut short the holiday and got back to see the chairman at Gresley. Reluctantly, much to Sam's annoyance, we packed up and shot back to England at the first opportunity. When I rolled up at Gresley to find out what was going on, they were amazed I had cut short my holiday. 'There was no need for that. The job is yours if you want it' was the chairman's message. I had wasted all that money coming back and could have still been lying on the beach. Instead I was in a management job I never really intended to take when I retired and was training part-time players twice a week. We had a good team and we were top of the league by Christmas and managed to get ourselves into the first round proper of the FA Cup where we were beaten by an 86th minute goal from Walsall's Ian Roper at the Bescot Stadium and we were denied a stonewall penalty. But then I would say that, wouldn't I?

Earlier in the season it did not look as if we would make it to the end of September. The club was in financial trouble and the players were not being paid. I was still getting my salary yet the players were doing it for nothing but they were brilliant and they stuck with it. To such an extent I felt I had to do something to sort the whole mess out. I felt guilty getting my wages when they were sweating blood for the club for nothing.

I still knew the secretary at Manchester United and decided to chance my arm. I made a phone call and asked if there was any way of United sending a team to play Gresley as part of a fund-raising initiative to stop the club going out of existence. I thought it was a bit of a long-shot, but the secretary took the call and basically said he would see what he could do. Normally that is code for 'forget it Birtles, who do you think you are kidding, Manchester United, Sir Alex Ferguson, at Gresley Rovers, you must be mad!'

I have to admit, I did not hold out much hope myself until I was halfway down the seventh fairway at Beeston Fields Golf club a few days later and my mobile phone started to ring. I know I shouldn't have had the thing switched on, golfing code and all that chaps, but I was far enough away from the club house and out of sight. So I answered.

'Garry, how are you. It's Alex Ferguson, what can I do to help?' I dropped my golf bag in disbelief. He knew all about the dire situation at Gresley and what we needed. He told me it was not a problem and that he would send a team down. I had to leave it with him for a few days, but he would be in touch again.

Not too long after the surprise call, I received notification that United would send a team down to play us and Nigel Clough was manager at Burton Albion at that time. He agreed to loan us the ground, to accommodate more fans and to make it a little bit more comfortable for United's superstars. In the meantime I was on the phone to Bryan Robson, Viv and Neil Webb and a host of Manchester United old boys who agreed to play as part of a Gresley side for nothing. People rarely hear about gestures like that from Fergie. He is always portrayed as some kind of ogre in the press, but that was a touch of class from a class man and a top class club and all the old boys that basically clubbed together to save Gresley from going out of business.

I was delighted. I had a real sense of achievement. I had helped to save the club and made sure that the players who had been playing for nothing were being paid again. I did not want a plaque erecting in my honour at the ground. I had no designs on a bust of me in the reception area but I was not expecting the way the club thanked me for all my efforts. In their infinite wisdom they decided to sack me a couple of months later when we had a little dip in form and Sam was heavily pregnant with our first child!.

REUNITED WITH THE GAME I LOVE

She was under enough pressure as it was because she had miscarried before. If what Sir Alex Ferguson did was a fabulous touch of class what Gresley did was the lowest of the low. What a shit game I was involved in.

It was February and we had suffered an alarming drop in form. After losing an away game at Grantham, the Gresley board members asked their counterparts at Grantham if they could borrow their board room! The suits from Gresley assembled and summoned me into a meeting shortly after the game. What a touch of class. They could not even wait and do it in privacy. They took the decision to sack me in offices of another club! I was dismissed on the spot. I had ensured they still had a club to ponce around in and pretend to be big shots and they treated me like that when my wife was having a terrible time worrying about the pregnancy. I was so bitter after that.

Within days, the job as manager of Alfreton Town came up and I got a phone call saying it was mine if I wanted it. They offered me a fabulous deal to take over and I was so disillusioned with football I turned it down. It was a polite refusal, but I made it clear I was in no frame of mind after the scandalous way I had been treated at Gresley and told them I would be doing them a disservice taking the post. That finished me and any lingering desire I had to be a football manager.

Fortunately I never looked back. Gresley paid me until the end of the season and during that time I was approached by BBC Radio Nottingham to do some work with them as an analyst for their football commentaries on Forest and to take part in their Monday evening phone-in. It was perfect for me. It was a way of remaining in the game, watching the club I loved and talking football. No wonder people like Alan Hansen and Mark Lawrenson look so comfortable on the Match of the Day sofa and have no inkling to get their hands dirty in management. The game just chews people up and spits them out, while dissecting the decisions and play of other managers and players is far easier.

The intervention of the BBC opened up a whole new avenue for me, for which I will be eternally grateful, but it was not until the local independent station, Century FM, came along that my media career really began to take off/

Mind you, there was a massive fall-out along the way with Larry Lloyd, who accused me of stitching him up to take his job! He even made those allegations in a book he wrote later in life, but I would just like to put the record straight.

I was still employed by the BBC when Darren Fletcher, who went on to work for BBC Five Live, gave me a call. At the time he was the sports editor at Century and he wanted me to go around to his house for a chat. I knew Darren, I had bumped into him enough times at Forest games and I was interested to hear what he had to say. He basically told me that the powers that be at Century had decided not to renew Larry's contract for the following season and would I like the job. It was as straightforward as that.

To be honest I couldn't believe my good fortune. It was a fantastic opportunity for me. It was more money and although the BBC said they would to match it but I chose to go to Century. A few days after the chat with Darren I had to go into the Century studios which were at the bottom of Meadow Lane, near Green's Windmill in Sneinton. Larry had been informed he was not being kept on by that stage and happened to be driving past the offices and saw my car. He came in and wanted a blazing row. He thought I had gone behind his back like some snake and pinched his job.

I liked Lloydy and regularly went into his office for a cup of coffee. While summarising for Century, he was working in some kind of PR capacity at Forest too. Eventually David Platt, then the Forest manager whose team and tactics were often criticised on the Century airwaves, presented Darren and the radio station with an ultimatum. If Century continued to employ Larry, the radio station was no longer welcome at the club. That is what prompted Century to take the decision not to renew his contract. It had nothing to do with me and I have never fallen out with Larry. He fell out with me for a considerable length of time. I tried for ages to put things right. Larry and myself have a cordial relationship now, but it has never been the same as it used to be in the good old days.

I wish the circumstances surrounding my appointment at Century could have been different, but I will never regret my decision to take up Darren on his offer and jump ship across Nottingham in the same way I had done during my playing days. There was a three-man bunch there at the time, Fletch, Nick Wilson and Paul the producer. They were magnificent to work with even if they reckon that all three of their long-term relationships ended within six months of my arrival. Pure coincidence!

It was through the link-up with Fletch that I became reacquainted with the

Gaffer. Darren had a working relationship with him which stemmed back to the start of his career at Trent FM radio, when he used to spend long days waiting around outside the Jubilee Club trying to grab a couple of minutes of interview on tape with BC. Between us we hatched a plan to get him back on the airwaves now that he was kicking his heels at his family home in the village of Quarndon on the outskirts of Derby.

The Gaffer had kept his hand in to a certain extent. He still did the odd newspaper column in the Sun and had a regular article appear in Four-Four-Two magazine. He was great in print still and even though he had been away from the sharp end of the game, he never dwelt in the past. He was always up to date, berating Arsene Wenger for being French and then congratulating him on beating our 42-game unbeaten record. Naturally he qualified it with a wish that Arsene would actually manage to see when his players committed infringements in the game instead of claiming he was unsighted on almost every occasion.

To those people who argued he would not survive in an era with Arsene, Jose Mourinho and a far more advanced game where players and agents hold the seats of power, all I can say is what a load of bollocks. He would have been just as good a manager 20, 30, 40 years later. He would simply have adapted. He would have changed colour like a chameleon and blended in with any environment. People who state otherwise simply have no intimate knowledge of the man and are employing guesswork.

It was because he was still so sharp mentally that Fletch and myself decided to ask Nigel if his old man fancied doing the odd spot on our phone in which took place most nights. We proposed he could be a special guest and do a slot every now and then. It would be good to have him speaking to the people of Nottingham who still adored him and it would be great for the ratings.

Setting up the event was simple. I would call Nigel and he would sort it all out and let me know what time he would be dropping the Gaffer off. The first time he came in we decided to air the show live and it was the one and only live programme we ever did! During the course of the show the Gaffer started talking about Chris Bart-Williams, a black player who played for Forest at the time and happened to say 'if there was a floodlight failure at the City Ground, no one would ever be able to see young Bart-Williams'.

I remember taking look through the window at Paul next door and he was on a chair trying to attach his tie to a light fitting. It was a producer's nightmare having the walking opinion and irreverent motor-mouth that was the Gaffer spouting forth on any topic anyone cared to mention. If they didn't mention it, he would still start making comments. I recall one in particular when on the same show he advised Mohamed Al Fayed to 'get back to where you come from. Even the Germans can't stand you'. That was just a couple of the offerings that would have had the switchboard on any other station jammed with complaints.

Paul the producer was looking through the window and making frantic gestures, but once BC was in full flow there was no stopping him. In the end Paul was almost swinging from the lights by his tie. He was a mess and feared we would be taken off the airwaves, but Century did not receive a solitary complaint. We did however make the decision to record the shows from that point on. There was no more taking our life in his hands. It might have been great radio for the listeners, but Paul's life expectancy would have been about a year at best.

People still revered him and rang in honoured to speak to him, five years after he had left Forest. Alan Birchenall, the former Leicester player, worked on the show with us and no one ever overawed him, but even he said he felt a jabbering wreck when he discovered the Gaffer would be coming in. Birch was well past 50-years-old at that stage and all he could say was: "What do I call him?" Everyone was in awe of him, even long after he had left the game.

Away from the phone-in I was the chauffeur for games. Fletch hated driving so I would steer his company car and put him through hell. He had white knuckles at the end of each journey and he will never forget the day Marlon Harewood nearly lost his balls one afternoon playing at Deepdale. I have never seen anyone smash a free-kick so hard into a defensive wall and more precisely into Marlon's crown jewels as someone did that day. Even the subs came on with the physio to check on Marlon as he lay flat out and I could not help myself: 'Look the subs have come on to help him look for them!' Fletch melted into fits of laughter and he started me, for what seemed like five minutes we could not speak on air.

There were hundreds of fantastic mad five minutes like that, in an environment I felt comfortable with and thoroughly enjoyed and when Fletch moved on to Radio Five, myself, Alan Birchenall, Roger Davies and Kenny

REUNITED WITH THE GAME I LOVE

Burns took over the phone-in slot. Eventually, Heart Radio took over Century and even though our ratings were at an all-time high they decided to cut the show because it did not fit in with the image they wanted to promote.

While working for Century, Mick Howard, who I played with at Long Eaton Rovers, was a floor manager with Sky TV and he put in a good word for me with producer Dave Wade who looked after the Football League programme. He was happy to give me a few games as a trial period and I was happy to take the opportunity. I never believed it would result in me commentating at what was effectively Brian Clough's wake at the City Ground when Forest played West Ham United in a Sky live game in September 2004. I, like most people who played for him, thought he was indestructible and would out-live the lot of us.

Six days earlier I had received a phone call from Nigel. I knew his father had had his own problems and demons to deal with. I had a gambling issue at the time I was working for Century. For the first time in what seemed an age I had money in my pocket again and lots of free time on my hands during the day. I liked a bet, mostly on big race meetings like Cheltenham, Royal Ascot and Aintree, but that progressed into something I never saw coming. When I first started going into Ladbrokes to place a bet I used to laugh at the regulars who were in there shouting in desperation at the TV, trying to force home a winner so they could eat dinner later that evening.

I was never going to become one of those people. I was far more sensible. Within a few months, I was screaming at the TV in Ladbrokes too, ripping up losing slips in disgust and chucking away money on every race on the card, as well has having some side interest on greyhound racing in between the horses. I even got to the stage where I was betting on virtual dog racing and sneaking around to betting shops away from my regular one in Beeston so people did not get to see me going in there every day. It was ridiculous and I felt there was only one way for me to deal with it.

At the time I was still being used for a football column in the Nottingham Evening Post, but they got a column they were not bargaining for when I rang up to confess I was a gambling addict with a problem. My issues were plastered all over the front page of the newspaper for everyone to see. The Gaffer tried to confront his demons in the same manner and admitted to them much later in life. So his issues were no secret, but that did not stop me reeling from the shock when Nigel rang me in tears to inform me that his father had passed away.

Brian Howard Clough died of stomach cancer on September 20. I will remember Nigel's phone call until the day I die and his hesitant voice telling me he had some 'really bad news'."He was devastated and people who never even knew the man were in a state of shock. I was working for Sky at this point and he asked me to let them know, but asked for Sky to give the family a 'couple of hours' before they broadcast the news so they could compose themselves for what was about to unfold.

It was hardly the kind of scoop I wanted to be letting Sky know about. Sky were brilliant and waited until precisely when the family had asked for the news to come out. I phoned Century to let them know too. I was in tears myself making the calls. It was all so out-of-the-blue and sudden. He was only 69. It was like losing a member of my own family. There was such an outpouring of grief and you could barely see any of the City Ground car park because of the flowers that were laid in tribute. They were still there on September 26 for a Sunday afternoon game between Forest and West Ham, which was essentially the red half of the city's out-pouring of grief to the rest of the nation.

It was one of the hardest things I had to do that day. Trying to hold myself together in those incredible raw and emotional surroundings was a massive challenge. Most of the game I spent half choking, trying to hold back my own tears and not betray my own emotions with any wavering in my voice. To have to be so professional when you just want to join in with the mourners was hard, but even then, from his seat high up in the sky, he managed to inspire Forest to a victory with a 90th minute goal from Marlon King. The whole place erupted and you could somehow imagine him shaking his head in disapproval, wondering what all the fuss was about.

I still miss him to this day. He was such a colossal man nothing was beyond him. He would have been one of the first people I turned to for help when ridiculous red tap almost prevented my dream wedding to Samantha taking place in Spetses four years after his death. The Greek island was our first holiday destination and it was where I whisked Sam away on a surprise holiday to propose after Nina had helped me choose the ring. My good friend Kostas had sorted the restaurant. The roses and the champagne were all in place and I managed to turn up at the wrong restaurant.

REUNITED WITH THE GAME I LOVE

When I arrived at the place I thought Kostas had sorted out there was no booking in my name, but they found us a table and immediately I thought there was something wrong. I rang him in a panic and he calmly told me I was in the wrong place. When I returned to the table I had to drag Sam out of her seat and walk around the corner to where we should have been in the first place. Fortunately it did not kill all the romance and she said 'yes' when we finally got our seat with the sea either side of us and the champagne perfectly chilled. It was an idyllic setting to propose and the perfect place to get married, or so we thought.

Arranging a wedding overseas is a nightmare of bureaucracy and paperwork. The planning is never ending and the amount of forms required is the reason the Amazon rain forest is shrinking. We needed forms from Ilkeston registrar office, where we had to present our passports. We had to present birth certificates, get more forms signed off by solicitors and I had to go to the Greek Embassy in London to get everything translated into Greek for the authorities in Spetses.

We had so many documents we needed an extra suitcase. The plan was for us to spend two weeks in Spetses and guests would join us in dribs and drabs over that period for the wedding on June 24 towards the end of our second week on the island. The first thing Sam and myself had to do when we arrived was to get to the town hall and make sure everything was in order. As my Greek was not up to much, Kostas came with me to help out. My Greek was pretty much non-existent, apart from being able to order a few beers, but I did not need to understand the language to read from the look on Kostas' face that something was not right.

Apparently there was a piece of paper missing. I am English and have an English passport. Sam has a Republic of Ireland passport, but she was born in Germany on an RAF base. Ilkeston registrar office had filled in the forms stating that two British subjects wanted to get married abroad. The very first hurdle regarding our passports had been missed. We should have gone to the Irish Embassy as well before setting off to Greece. We were informed that unless we had the relevant piece of paperwork, we could not be married!

The following day we had to wake Elyshia at 5am and make a three hour taxi journey to the British Embassy in Athens. Elyshia had travel sickness and was throwing up on the journey and when I encountered the woman in the Embassy I wanted to throw up over her. She was this austere woman, sat behind bullet proof glass and virtually snatched all the paperwork from my hand while simultaneously demanding 75 euros just to handle the documents. After a brief scan she delivered her damning verdict. 'This is an illegal document. It should not have been issued in the first place and you can't get married'. At that point she just abandoned us in a state of utter shock and dismay. Elyshia was crying her eyes out, so was Sam. Sam had never been married and Elyshia was counting the days to when she could put on her bridesmaid's dress.

Out of total desperation we went to the Irish Embassy too and were invited in. Sat down in the air conditioned board room and for the sum of ten euros we had everything explained to us and what we needed to do. They could not have been more helpful and wished us a lovely wedding. We needed the relevant piece of paper if we could get it issued. It was essentially an amendment to the one we were given originally, but the British Embassy refused. Dave Wade, my producer at Sky, was even prepared to get someone to fly it out from London if we could have the document drawn up back home. I had people working for me round the clock at home and on Spetses. I even tried the office of Kenneth Clarke, MP, Forest fan and someone I thought might have some clout but we were beyond helping.

Our dream wedding looked to be in ruins until eventually the mayor of Spetses received a fax stating whether the wedding went ahead or not was at his discretion.

For the remainder of the time, the tiny Greek mayor with an incredible ego had us all dancing around like fools. One day the wedding was on, the next day he had changed his mind. There were members of the guest party who were ready to grab him by the throat and smash his face in. On the appointed day of the wedding everything looked to be on until we received a phone call at 4pm, two hours before the ceremony, to say he had changed his mind again. Sam was getting her hair done and contemplating putting on the dress!

I was ready to do a Reggie Perrin and throw myself in the sea. It was one great big bloody stressful mess until a few minutes later when Kostas rang back to say that the mayor would go ahead with the ceremony but would not sign the documents. We were getting married, but it would not be official. It was all that we could do and the 30-odd members of the party celebrated until 6am at Paradise Beach. That day will always be our wedding day as far as we are concerned, but it was not until July 10 when we were in a Derbyshire registrar office that we were officially betrothed and we went through the whole reception thing again for those who attended the wedding in Spetses and my mum and dad.

The woman at Ilkeston registrar office was so shamefaced she could not see us and the local authorities held up their hands in admission by meeting all our out-of-pocket expenses in Greece and paid for the second reception. Not that it was about the money. We did not want that. It was about the fact that the day could have been totally ruined because of their incompetence. We can look back now and laugh about it, but at the time it was one of the most stressful two weeks of my entire life and I could have done with a friend who had friends in high places. I am convinced the Gaffer would have had it sorted in a flash.

After all he did have influential people he could call upon as he reminded me one night when Derby County played Manchester United at Pride Park and Fletch asked him if he would do co-commentary with the two of us at the game. He jumped at the chance and held court in the press room before and after the game, before he decided he wanted to pop up to the boardroom for a drink. He informed Fletch and myself, as we were carrying all the equipment back to the press room, that we were popping upstairs for a drink with the chairman!

We both had jeans on and protested we would not be allowed in the boardroom, but he was having none of it. 'You are with me and you will get in. Now come on' was the curt reply. He might have been a little frail in comparison to the days when he bounced around the Baseball Ground, but he was as revered in Derby just as much. When he shuffled through the doors to the boardroom and roared 'evening Mr Chairman' the whole place fell to a deathly hush.

We were following the Pied Piper and no one said a word to us about the dress code. We helped ourselves to a glass of wine and surveyed the room for a short amount of time. Eamon Holmes was in the room and so was Labour MP Geoff Hoon, the Secretary of State for Defence, along with a number of the great and the good of the two clubs.

When the Gaffer had finished his drink, he turned to us and said: "Come on, we're off." And he turned to make his way to the door. Before he reached the exit he swivelled and shouted across the room in the direction of Geoff Hoon. "Geoffrey, you owe me son. You owe me!" he bellowed.

There was no reply from Hoon, just a quizzical look and stony, bemused silence. When he clearly could not work out the debt he owed to BC, the Gaffer was only too willing to give him a helping hand and put him out of his misery. As a staunch Labour supporter the Gaffer explained: "I got you elected son!" Upon that, he turned on his heels and shouted 'Tarra' and was gone. I often laugh out loud when I recall that comical episode in the boardroom of a club that the Gaffer helped to build all those years earlier when he was slogging his guts out at the Baseball Ground.

Geoff Hoon was not the only man in his debt. There is great long list of people who owed him considerably more than a cross on a ballot paper. I could go on at length. Somewhere on that list is the name Garry Birtles too. Brian Howard Clough and Peter Taylor saved me from a life inhaling Evo Stick and set me on a magic carpet ride to the pinnacle of club football that no amount of laying Axminster and shag pile could ever have come close to matching. I cherish every memory. And for every single second I will be eternally grateful.